Holocaust Politics

Holocaust Politics

JOHN K. ROTH

*To Steve — great friend,
dedicated educator —
with thanks for your encouragement
and support through many years.*

John K. Roth
March 21, 2002

Westminster John Knox Press
LOUISVILLE
LONDON • LEIDEN

Scripture quotations unless otherwise indicated, are from the New Revised Standard Version of the Bible are copyright © 1989 by the Division of Christian Education of the National Council of the Churches of Christ in the U.S.A. and are used by permission.

Grateful acknowledgment is made to the following authors and publishers for kind permission to reprint the following previously published material: Excerpts from *Auschwitz and After,* by Charlotte Delbo. Translated by Rosette Lamont. Copyright © 1995 by Yale University Press. Reprinted by permission of Yale University Press. "Black and Blue," by Harry Brooks, Andy Razaf, and Thomas "Fats" Waller. © 1929 EMI Music Inc. Copyright renewed and assigned to Razaf Music Co., c/o The Songwriters Guild of America, EMI Mills Music, Inc., and Chappell & Co., Inc. All rights reserved. Used by permission of Warner Bros. Publications U.S. Inc., Miami, FL 33014. Excerpts from *History, Religion, and Meaning,* ed. Julius Simon, Greenwood Press, an imprint of Greenwood Publishing Group, Inc., Westport, CT, copyright © 2000. Excerpts from *Holocaust Scholars Write to the Vatican,* ed. Harry James Cargas, Greenwood Press, an imprint of Greenwood Publishing Group, Inc., Westport, CT, copyright © 1998. "How We See," by Edward Bond, from *Poems 1978–1985.* Reprinted by permission of Methuen Publishing Limited. "I Keep Forgetting," by Lily Brett, from *After the War.* Reprinted by permission of Lily Brett. Excerpts from *Invisible Man* © 1952 by Ralph Ellison. Reprinted by permission of Random House, Inc. "The Woman Poet," by Gertrud Kolmar, from *Dark Soliloquy: The Selected Poems of Gertrud Kolmar.* Translated by Henry A. Smith. Copyright © 1975 Seabury Press. Reprinted by permission of The Continuum International Publishing Group, Inc.

Book design by Sharon Adams
Cover design by Jennifer K. Cox

First edition
Published by Westminster John Knox Press
Louisville, Kentucky

This book is printed on acid-free paper that meets the American National Standards Institute Z39.48 standard. ⊗

PRINTED IN THE UNITED STATES OF AMERCA

01 02 03 04 05 06 07 08 09 10 — 10 9 8 7 6 5 4 3 2 1

Library of Congress Cataloging-in-Publication Data

Roth, John K.
    Holocaust politics / John K. Roth.—1st ed.
      p. cm.
    Includes bibliographical references (p.) and index.
    ISBN 0-664-22173-4 (alk. free)
    1. Holocaust, Jewish (1939–1945)—Influence. 2. Holocaust, Jewish
(1939–1945)—Moral and ethical aspects. 3. Memory—Religious aspects—
Judaism. 4. Memory—Social aspects. I. Title.

D804.3.R75 2001
940.53′18—dc21   2001026109

To

Michael and Melissa Berenbaum
Sara J. Bloomfield
Elizabeth Boyd
Erik Brooks
Eva Fleischner
Irving Greenberg
Nancy Kane
Lawrence L. Langer
Miles Lerman
Elisabeth Maxwell
Carol Rittner
Don and Barbara Raymond
Richard L. and Betty Rogers Rubenstein
Paul Shapiro

A friend is always a friend.
Proverbs 17:17 (CEV)

You cannot go down into hell with impunity.
You must pay an entrance fee, and an exit fee too.
Philip Hallie,
Tales of Good and Evil, Help and Harm

Contents

Preface and Acknowledgments

It's the hurricane we're in. Don't forget it.
Philip Hallie

More than half a century after Nazi Germany's genocidal assault on the Jewish people, the Holocaust grips human attention as never before. The event's widespread power is especially significant for moral reasons because it convincingly shows that right and wrong, good and evil, justice and injustice are embedded in history. Otherwise their reality is dubious. What is sometimes undeservedly disdained as "the Americanization of the Holocaust" reflects these points. The Holocaust did not take place on American ground, but it impacts American life nonetheless. Depending on the quality of what I call Holocaust politics, the results of that Americanization can be very good, not least because the Holocaust gives anti-semitism and racism a bad name.[1] Meanwhile, the Holocaust continues to take its toll, including the shattering of optimistic cultural, religious, and meta-physical assumptions that have been long and fondly held. High school students who visit the United States Holocaust Memorial Museum, as many of them do during senior-year trips to Washington, D.C., are often upset by what they see. They also frequently stress the importance of their museum visits.

Historian Peter Novick was wrong when, in the introduction to his 1999 book *The Holocaust in American Life*, he stated that "contemplating the Holocaust is virtually cost-free: a few cheap tears."[2] Any action that can justifiably be called contemplation takes thoughtful consideration and serious meditation. In addition, no event calls for contemplation more than the Holocaust. Answering that call is unlikely to be cost-free. The philosopher Philip Hallie gave a more accurate appraisal. His Holocaust contemplation taught him that "you cannot go down into hell with impunity. You must pay an entrance fee, and an exit fee too."[3]

For three reasons, Hallie's judgment became this book's governing epigraph. First, Holocaust contemplation requires immensely difficult study. Almost without relief, that study plunges one into abysmal darkness. Disorientation, melancholy, despair, even shame—those are among the somber moods that result. Once touched by Holocaust contemplation, moreover, a person does not easily walk away. One reason is that a serious encounter with Holocaust history raises questions as disturbing as they are challenging: How must I live differently? What must communities do better? Second, as my participation in Holocaust politics provoked me to write this book, I found Hallie's statement expressing what I often felt during my writing. Third, Hallie's assessment encapsulates his larger outlook, which is very close to mine. Further explanation of these second and third points, which requires a brief account of my relationship to Hallie, can introduce what follows.

I first met Hallie on February 15, 1986. The occasion was a University of San Diego conference on ethics. *Lest Innocent Blood Be Shed*, his important book about Le Chambon, a French village that rescued Jews during the Holocaust, had appeared several years earlier. Hallie was doing follow up work on Major Julius Schmäling, the officer who led the German occupation force around Le Chambon while the rescue activities were under way. Schmäling knew what was going on and let it happen, but he was also a loyal soldier in Nazi Germany's army. Schmäling fascinated Hallie as an example of "maculate," not immaculate, goodness, the term Hallie used in the title of the paper on which I was asked to comment during a session devoted to "Virtue in Strained Circumstances."

Hallie helped me to understand better how philosophers and philosophy play vital parts in contemplation of the Holocaust. Shared elements in our life histories encouraged that understanding. We were both philosophers influenced by Albert Camus. Our professional lives had been changed by encounters with the Holocaust that made us impatient with the ahistorical tendencies of most academic philosophy. In addition, Hallie's roots, like mine, included the American Midwest. Our educational and career paths were similar too. He had gone to a liberal arts college (Grinnell) and then to a major research university (Harvard) for his graduate work before spending his teaching career as a philosophy professor at a small university (Wesleyan) in Middletown, a Connecticut village. A similar pattern had taken me from Pomona College to Yale University and then to Claremont McKenna College in Claremont, California, where I have taught for more than thirty-five years.

Our histories have differences too. Hallie was my senior by eighteen years. He grew up in Chicago; my early homes were in small-town Michigan and Indiana. Born in 1922 (he died in 1994) Hallie had seen combat in World War II, while I have scarcely any direct memories of that event. Religion was important to us both, but he was Jewish and I am Christian—a difference that put us more in agreement, I believe, than at odds. Our outlooks, then, could not be the same, and yet again and again, Hallie's resonated with mine.

"No ideas but in facts," Hallie liked to say, "no ideas but in things."[4] He called himself a skeptic. I agree with his skepticism, which had two parts: (1) a suspicion of abstraction, closure, and finality and (2) a conviction that details, particularities, and facts contain moral insights and have lessons to teach if we pay attention. "Lucidity and passion," he urged, "that's my motto." Hallie knew much about ancient philosophy. He reminded people that the early skeptics were doctors. Lucidity meant getting as clear as possible about what was happening, especially if disease was the focal point. Knowing what was going on was not enough, however, especially if disease was the focal point. Passion sharpened the focus. Hallie's skepticism entailed that one must be moved to act and, in particular, stirred to get people out of harm's way and to give them help.

Hallie's skepticism resisted moral indifference and ethical relativism. His blend of lucidity and passion, forged in the continuing collision between his wartime killing and his moral philosophy's emphasis on the preciousness of individual human life, stressed that right and wrong are matters of fact, not opinion. To say that it is wrong to be tortured or starved, or to say that the people of Le Chambon did the right thing when they welcomed Jewish refugees, should not succumb to the relativist's subverting question, "Who's to say?" When challenged to prove that more than opinion is involved in those judgments, Hallie understood that "I cannot prove this belief the way I can prove that I am alive," but, he argued, there is an expert, qualified judgment in such cases, and it belongs especially to "the drowned ones and the saved ones. . . . They know."[5]

For Hallie, knowledge could never be purely "objective," for there is no such thing as pure objectivity. Knowledge roots itself in experience; human experience, in turn, depends upon our embodied selves and the times and places of the communities in which we live and on which we depend. The fact that knowledge exists in a historical context, however, does not mean that it is reduced to opinion on the grounds that human judgments are merely "subjective." Instead, Hallie's skepticism understood that the quality of experience determines the qualifications of the knowledge claims that are made. It is not, for instance, the judgment of the perpetrators or the bystanders that counts the most, if at all, when the claim in question is that the Holocaust was wrong. As Hallie put the point, "cruelty has authority and that authority is its *victims*. The victim of cruelty has an empirical authority like the authority of a doctor who's observing a patient, or better yet, like the authority of a patient about his or her own feelings."[6]

My contemplations in *Holocaust Politics* echo Hallie's themes. They do so in one more way that needs acknowledgment. Hallie's penchant for detail and particularity made him an eloquent philosophical storyteller. One of his favorite stories centered on a hurricane.[7] This particular storm reached his Connecticut home, where he observed its havoc. But havoc was not all that Hallie saw. Even while the storm raged all around, there was space for calm and quiet within the hurricane's eye. Hallie's eye, moreover, was drawn to the pale blue sky overhead. From an ethical point of view, I believe, blue was his favorite color.

Hallie's hurricane experience contained vision that provided him with moral insight. We are in the hurricane, he stressed, and we must not forget how menacing that place will always be. Within the storm, however, there can be space like the haven provided by Le Chambon. More than that, Hallie's passion was to use his lucidity to do what he could to "expand the blue."[8]

"Some people," wrote Hallie, "make a larger space for blue, for peace, for love." This book argues that those who contemplate the Holocaust should be in that company. Making a larger space for blue, he added, "takes power as well as love. It takes force of will. It takes assertion and commitment."[9] In these pages, I have tried to give further expression to Hallie's vision and insight as they apply to my understanding of Holocaust politics.

* * *

No book can explore all the dimensions of Holocaust politics. The field is too large, complex, and varied. In what follows, I draw upon my philosophical training and my thirty years as a Holocaust scholar to define Holocaust politics and then, with primary reference to the United States, to probe selected issues about memory and memorialization, historical interpretation, and the importance of the Holocaust for American life, religion, ethics, and education. My approach stresses the decisive importance of the attitudes and dispositions, as well as the policy priorities, that we bring to the many tables of Holocaust politics. The attitudes and dispositions most needed bear a striking resemblance to Hallie's wise skepticism.

My debt to Hallie is one of the many I owe. Just as I am thankful to him for philosophical guidance, I am grateful to many other people and institutions for helping me to complete this book. Since 1969, I have published books with Westminster John Knox Press. I have benefited greatly from its encouragement, editorial guidance, and marketing expertise. On this book, the press's former director, Richard Brown, and former editor, Nick Street, have been especially helpful. The editorial assistance provided by Ella Brazley and Donald Parker-Burgard improved my work as well. A 2000–2001 sabbatical leave from Claremont McKenna College, which included time in England at the Oxford Centre for Hebrew and Jewish Studies where I was privileged to hold a 2001 Koerner Visiting Fellowship for the Study of the Holocaust, provided writing time when I needed it most. Furthermore, parts of this book were first developed for invited lectures at various universities, including Brandeis University, California State University at Long Beach, Grand Valley State University, Hebrew Union College, San Diego State University, Stanford University, University of Southern California, University of Texas at El Paso, Vanderbilt University, and Yale University; conferences, such as Remembering for the Future 2000 and the Annual Scholars' Conference on the Holocaust and the Churches; and museums, such as the Holocaust Museum Houston and the United States Holocaust Memorial Museum. For penetrating questions and constructive criticism, as well as the generous hospitality and kindness extended to me by countless people from those places and many others, I am enormously grateful.

In addition, I am indebted to numerous editors and publishers for the opportunity to draw on earlier versions of essays that I wrote for other books. These books include: Harry James Cargas, ed., *Holocaust Scholars Write to the Vatican* (Westport, Conn.: Greenwood Press, 1998), Peter Hayes, ed., *Lessons and Legacies III: Memory, Memorialization, and Denial* (Evanston, Ill.: Northwestern University Press, 1999), Carol Rittner and John K. Roth, eds., *Different Voices: Women and the Holocaust* (St. Paul: Paragon House, 1993), Carol Rittner and John K. Roth, eds., *"Good News" after Auschwitz? Christian Faith within a Post-Holocaust World* (Macon, Ga.: Mercer University Press, 2001), Alan S. Rosenbaum, ed., *Is the Holocaust Unique? Perspectives on Comparative Genocide* (Boulder, Colo.: Westview Press, 2001), John K. Roth, ed., *Ethics after the Holocaust: Perspectives, Critiques, and Responses* (St. Paul: Paragon House, 1999), John K. Roth et al., *The Holocaust Chronicle: A History in Words and Pictures* (Lincolnwood, Ill.: Publications International, 2000), John K. Roth and Elisabeth Maxwell, eds., *Remembering for the Future: The Holocaust in an Age of Genocide* (New York: Palgrave, 2001), and Julius Simon, ed., *History, Religion, and Meaning: American Reflections on the Holocaust and Israel* (Westport, Conn: Greenwood Press, 2000).

Even while the Holocaust continues to take its toll, there are many compensations along the way for those who study that event. Everyone who works in this area has met amazing people—survivors prominent among them—who have challenged and encouraged us. I am no exception to that rule. As an author, I also enjoy the privilege of dedicating my books to people who have been special in my life. When I thought about men and women who fitted those descriptions, especially during the part of Holocaust politics dubbed "the Roth affair," I knew where the dedication list should begin but not where it could end, for so many people belonged on it. I compromised by dedicating this book to seventeen people, a larger number than customary but still too small.

Readers of this book will see that I like epigraphs, those brief quotations that introduce a theme or express a mood. Epigraphs typically appear at the beginning of a book or a chapter. The quotation I have included on the dedication page does not fit the description exactly. Nevertheless, that biblical proverb—"A friend is always a friend"—expresses so well the friendship I have felt from these people and aspire to give back to them that I could not resist using it any more than I could make my dedication more concise.

Four of the men and women in my list are more than friends. Sociologist Elizabeth Boyd and artist Erik Brooks are my daughter-in-law and son-in-law. Good friends as well, these multitalented family members challenge and encourage me in the ways most needed by their Holocaust scholar father-in-law. I thank them for sharing their lives with me. My family-by-marriage also includes Don and Barbara Raymond. They warmly entered my life more than forty years ago when I fell in love with Barbara's sister, Lyn Austin. When we married in 1964, neither of us could have imagined that we would spend sabbaticals and vacations, even wedding anniversaries, at Auschwitz and other Holocaust sites. With her exceptional love, Lyn bears with me, and I cannot express gratitude enough. The same is true of the Raymonds. Blessed with a combination of down-to-earth common sense, business and legal savvy, joy in spite of difficulties, and overflowing generosity, Don and Barbara sometimes travel with Lyn and me—but so far not to Holocaust sites.

In June 1998, when Holocaust politics tracked me from one town and bed-and-breakfast to another, we explored Ireland together. As Lyn and I wrestled with difficult decisions, the Raymonds' support meant more to me than I can say. Thanks to their help, the right decisions were made. They included the determination to write this book. I hope that its Holocaust contemplation proves worthy of the supportive care that the Raymonds and so many others have graciously bestowed upon me.

Prologue

What Is Holocaust Politics?

What happened, happened. But *that* it happened cannot be so easily accepted.
Jean Améry, *At the Mind's Limits*

A Jewish survivor of the Holocaust, Nazi Germany's destruction of the European Jews and
millions of others who were caught in that genocidal
web, Jean Améry (1912–1978) was a philosopher who
thought long, hard, and well about what he had experienced in Auschwitz, the Nazi concentration camp
and killing center that has nearly become synonymous
with the Holocaust itself. Writing in Brussels during
the winter of 1976, Améry prepared a preface for the
new edition of his 1966 book, *At the Mind's Limits:
Contemplations by a Survivor on Auschwitz and Its Realities*. This book's penetrating, passionate essays
remain among the most important writings about the
Holocaust and its implications that any author has
produced.

Toward the end of his book's new preface, Améry
observed that the Holocaust had created "a moral
chasm."[1] Time would eventually close it, he thought,
but that prospect increased his anguish because the

1

price for closure was likely to be forgetting or even what Améry called "hollow, thoughtless, utterly false conciliatoriness." Where the Holocaust is concerned, Améry contended, "nothing is resolved, no conflict is settled, . . . nothing has healed." Deniers have persistently claimed that the Holocaust never took place,[2] but Améry knew that "what happened, happened." The past could not be undone. The Holocaust would not go away, "but *that* it happened," Améry went on to say, "cannot be so easily accepted." Thus, he wanted the Holocaust's chasm to "remain wide open."

No Closure

Améry got his wish. The Holocaust's chasm continues to defy closure, and that situation is not likely to change any time soon because so much was lost in that watershed event. First and foremost, millions of Jewish lives were lost, but when Améry noted how those losses are not easy to accept, he had more than sheer numbers in mind. What gnawed at him was *how* and *why* the Holocaust happened. He understood many of the answers to those questions, and historical research keeps adding to the responses. Nevertheless, the difficulties ran deeper for Améry then, and they still do for us now. One can study the history of antisemitism and racial theory, for example, or one can document how Adolf Hitler and the Nazi Party rose to power. One can track how Jews became a relatively powerless and vulnerable minority in Christian-dominated Europe. Evidence mounts, and explanatory accounts grow. Yet the more one knows, the less acceptable the Holocaust becomes.

Two factors are especially crucial in that unacceptability. First, historical analysis emphasizes that the

Holocaust resulted from human decisions, but neither historical scholarship nor any other analysis derived from human inquiry shows that those decisions and their outcomes had to be exactly what they turned out to be. Constraints, pressures, traditions, the interdependence of human life—all of those factors and more exerted their conditioning influences, but none of the Holocaust's catastrophic particularity was inevitable. At the end of the day, we are left to wonder how and why the Holocaust happened, and the fact that the Holocaust did not have to happen is a key factor in its unacceptability. I make this point not to mystify the Holocaust, not to give it some special religious or cosmic status because it eludes human understanding. For decades my own thirst has been to find out as much as possible about the Holocaust's history, which I believe to be grounded in human decisions, but the event is so vast, complicated, and fraught with telling implications that I do not believe, even in principle, that it can be completely understood by minds human or divine. We can always learn more about the Holocaust, but we will never learn everything about how and why it happened. It remains an unmastered trauma.

Here it could be objected that what I have said about the Holocaust is applicable to anything and everything in human experience. No event, one may argue, can be fully comprehended without remainder. That point is well taken, but it is not an objection to my position. When added to the second factor I want to identify early on, the point about comprehension intensifies the Holocaust's unacceptability. That unacceptability involves not only the Holocaust's eluding of human understanding when it comes to how and why it happened but also the implications of that event. As it destroyed Jewish lives, the Holocaust called into question the status of fundamental human beliefs that are at civilization's foundations. When one thinks of human rights, governmental power, justice, ethics, religion (Judaism and Christianity specifically), and God, the Holocaust's legacy continues to be one of scars and cracks in traditions that can never be the same as they were before the Holocaust's moral chasm left its shattering mark on our world. The Holocaust is unacceptable because it showed how inadequate our belief systems were to prevent or halt it, or, even worse, how deeply implicated those belief systems were in unleashing the Holocaust's devastation. In this sense, the Holocaust is also an unmastered trauma, for it is a good, but not always encouraging, question to ask whether we can mend the post-Holocaust world that is ours. Focused on some of the most important philosophical and religious issues raised by the Holocaust (no single study can deal with them all), this book addresses the challenges of that question.

What I call *Holocaust politics* helps to focus and amplify the points I have made. To clarify what I mean by that term, note that *politics*, an unavoidable and essential aspect of human existence, typically refers to at least three dimensions of human activity: believing, governing, and maneuvering. In the first instance—believing—we may speak of a person's or a group's attitudes, perspectives, values, visions, and convictions, especially insofar as those outlooks involve interpretations and commitments about action and policy. In the second case—governing—politics points toward the institutionalizing, organization, management, and implementation of beliefs and the actions and policies toward which beliefs point. In the third category—maneuvering—politics emphasizes strategies devised to advance special interests and tactics employed to serve particular constituencies. Depending on the substance and style of these three dimensions, politics is more or less contentious or congenial, more or less cutthroat or constructive. Holocaust politics, then, refers to the ways—often conflicting—in which the Holocaust informs and affects human belief, organization, and strategy, on the one hand, and in which human belief, organization, and strategy inform and affect the status and understanding of the Holocaust, on the other. Its existence unavoidable, Holocaust politics, like all politics, is not an end in itself but a means to achieve higher goods. Our attitudes and priorities determine its all-important quality.

Briefly described to illustrate the point, three examples show that Holocaust politics involves high stakes. First, the aftermath surrounding the 1993 publication of *Denying the Holocaust: The Growing Assault of Truth and Memory*, Deborah Lipstadt's unmasking of Holocaust deniers, showed that more than reputations and careers were at stake. Truth itself can be on the line. Lipstadt's book led to a crucial moment in Holocaust politics, which focused on the British libel suit brought by David Irving against Lipstadt and Penguin Books, the publisher of her book in the United Kingdom. Irving claimed that Lipstadt had falsely accused him of Holocaust denial with the result that his reputation as a historian had been discredited. Irving's lawsuit contained huge implications. If his maneuvering prevailed, the cause of Holocaust denial would be advanced; Lipstadt, a respected scholar, and her publisher would suffer; and the integrity of history as a scholarly discipline, to say nothing of the credibility of Holocaust survivor testimony, would be impugned.

British libel law put the burden of proof on the defendants, which in this case meant that Lipstadt and Penguin Books, never backing away from identifying Irving as a denier, had to show that he was indeed a Holocaust denier. The case went to trial in the High Court in London on January 11, 2000. Closing speeches took place two months later on March 15. Mr. Justice Gray, the judge who heard the case, rendered his decision in favor of the defendants on April 11. As his lengthy and detailed decision reported, the defendants did show that Irving persistently distorted historical evidence in writings and speeches that denied the Holocaust. Significantly, leading Holocaust historians—Christopher R. Browning, Richard J. Evans, and Robert Jan van Pelt—gave decisive testimony, driving home the point that Irving's use of historical evidence in the service of Holocaust denial definitely undercut his credibility as a historian.[3]

While the Irving-Lipstadt trial ensued, the media contained almost daily reports about another aspect of Holocaust politics that had been in the international spotlight since the mid-1990s. These stories showed that Holocaust politics involved not only immense amounts of wealth but also the status of justice in a post-Holocaust world. In the news were Swiss banks, German industries, Austrian insurance companies, American firms such as International Business Machines (IBM), and attempts on the part of Jewish Holocaust survivors and their families to recover deposits for pre-Holocaust accounts, to obtain restitution for slave labor, or to receive payment on life insurance policies that belonged to Jewish relatives who had been murdered in the Holocaust.[4] Other news stories concentrated on efforts to catalog and return to their rightful owners the tens of thousands of Nazi-confiscated art treasures that had been stolen from Jewish homes and businesses. The highly valued artworks constituted only a small fraction of the vast amounts of Jewish property seized by the Nazis—furniture, furs, family heirlooms—that are "too small" to be considered by the Holocaust-era assets negotiations that have continued into the twenty-first century.

Plenty of maneuvering took place on all sides as government officials, lawyers, Jewish groups, and other interested parties negotiated and bargained in deliberations that strained civility as the restitution amounts soared into billion dollar territory. Few speak of it openly, but the resentment in the boardrooms of German industries, to cite but one example, must parallel the renewed Jewish outrage that sometimes accompanied the difficult negotiations. Meanwhile, how much of the restitution of funds and property will actually find their way to Jewish individuals, or to Jewish organizations, or to lawyers remains contentious. Coming so late in the day and with so much controversy (unless one is naive, neither reality is all that surprising) the politics of Holocaust restitution has done very little to close the moral chasm that Améry identified. The Holocaust continues to defeat justice. At the most, restitution provides scant restoration of property or financial compensation, but there is no recompense for the Holocaust. On all sides, that raw recognition keeps nerves on edge, frustration levels high, and anger seething even if repressed. Far from putting Holocaust politics to rest, that environment intensifies it.

A third example from the year 2000 indicates that Holocaust politics involves more than disagreements about history. It also includes international relations, global instability, and violence. Late that summer, with the American president Bill Clinton brokering a deal at Camp David, it appeared that Israeli prime minister Ehud Barak and Palestinian leader Yasser Arafat might be very close to a lasting peace agreement. However, Israel's offer of Palestinian statehood, control over part of Jerusalem and more than 90 percent of the West Bank plus the Gaza Strip, did not fully meet Palestinian demands, especially those concerning the right of millions of refugees and their descendants to return to Israel, a condition unacceptable to the Israelis. The outcome was that the Camp David talks proved to be the lull before an autumn storm in which violence swept through Jerusalem, the West Bank, and the Gaza Strip, igniting Intifada II, as some have called the spiraling bloodshed. Undermined all around—by the alleged desecration of holy places, Palestinian "days of rage," terrorist attacks and mortar barrages, Israeli rockets and gunfire from tanks and battle-armed helicopters, bulldozed properties and Israeli incursions in Gaza, escalating numbers of dead and wounded on both sides, and charges and countercharges about where blame and responsibility belong—realistic hopes for a just and lasting peace all but collapsed. The Palestinian economy is in shambles; Israeli hopes for safety and security are tenuous. In the foreseeable future, a sustained cease-fire will be no small accomplishment.

Scholars argue about the origins of the modern State of Israel, which declared its independence in 1948. Some say that its existence, far from being dependent on the Holocaust, would have come earlier had it not been held back by World War II and the Holocaust. Others emphasize that the Holocaust was decisive in Israel's emergence. Holocaust politics of a scholarly kind infuses those debates, but the fact remains that the Holocaust continues to play a large part in Middle Eastern affairs, and the problematic effects of instability in that region—owing partly to the oil reserves found there—ripple throughout the world.

Even if Holocaust survivors and their families did not number into the hundreds of thousands in the Israeli population, how could the State of Israel fail to be immersed in memory of the Holocaust? Awareness of that history is seminal in Israeli consciousness, and thus the Holocaust affects Israeli policy, which deep down intends that "Never again!" will Jews—at least in Israel—submit to defenseless vulnerability that potentially targets them for destruction. Those intentions are tied to land and secure borders and to control of Arab and especially Palestinian forces that would compromise them. As events in the autumn of 2000 made clear, the Palestinians tend to view Israeli power as an unjust occupying force that thwarts their hopes for an independent nation in the West Bank and Gaza. Far from sharing Israeli memories of the Holocaust, Palestinian perspectives are not without their own versions of Holocaust denial and antisemitism. Meanwhile, within Israel itself, differences of opinion can be found about the Holocaust's implications for Israeli politics. To a considerable extent, Middle Eastern politics and Israeli politics in particular are intertwined with Holocaust politics. There is no certainty about where those troubled interconnections will lead.

Jean Améry got his wish. The Holocaust's moral chasm, reflected in Holocaust politics, as yet admits no closure, for the Holocaust's trauma defies mastery. Nevertheless, a question remains: Should the fulfillment of Améry's wish be the end of the matter? Even if the Holocaust eludes closure, such an outcome is not the end but a point of departure. What will we do with the lack of closure? How should we respond to, participate in, and craft Holocaust politics? How might we turn memory of the Holocaust to ends that divide people less and bring them together more—not by forgetting and certainly not by what Améry called false conciliatoriness but by turning contemplation of the Holocaust in directions that can increase respect and compassion, the very ingredients whose absence did so much to unleash the Holocaust's fury? Holocaust politics invites reflection on these themes. Governing all the reflections that follow, they can be amplified further by narrating some of my personal experience with Holocaust politics and then, before this prologue ends, by considering how philosophy— the discipline I bring to Holocaust studies—might help to make good responses to the questions that Holocaust politics raises.

Wonderful Opportunities

My definition of Holocaust politics includes the establishment, maintenance, and governance of institutions whose missions emphasize remembrance of the Holocaust and attention to the implications of that disaster. Holocaust institutions take varied forms. Consider, for example, conferences about the Holocaust. In 2000 alone, there were more than forty major meetings of that kind. No significant decline in their number seems likely in the immediate future. Founded by Franklin H. Littell and Hubert G. Locke in 1970, the Annual Scholars' Conference on the Holocaust and the Churches, which held its thirtieth meeting in 2000, is among those with the greatest longevity. It regularly attracts hundreds of scholars for deliberations that are interfaith, interdisciplinary, and international. Inspired by Elisabeth Maxwell and following its earlier versions in Oxford, England (1988), and Berlin, Germany (1994), Remembering for the Future 2000 brought more than six hundred scholars from some thirty-five countries to Oxford for a week-long conference on "The Holocaust in an Age of Genocide." Six months earlier, in late January 2000 and with extensive security measures in place, the Stockholm International Forum on the Holocaust, a conference on education, remembrance, and research, included delegations from forty-eight countries and international organizations. Conceived and convened by Prime Minister Göran Persson of Sweden, the Forum provided an unprecedented occasion for high-ranking politicians—some twenty heads of state attended, including Federal Chancellor Gerhardt Schroeder of Germany and Prime Minister Ehud Barak of Israel—as well as civic and religious leaders, Holocaust survivors, historians, and educators to discuss, plan, and express commitment to an immense expansion of Holocaust education. Who organizes and sets the agenda for these conferences? What purposes do they serve, and how well do they serve them? What follows from these meetings, and how should the significance of those results be appraised? Political issues, large and small, weave in and out of such questions.

Conferences, of course, provide only one example of Holocaust-related institutions, whose number and visibility lead to another dimension of Holocaust politics—namely, the criticism that there is a "Holocaust industry," which uses and abuses the Holocaust for problematic ends ranging from personal advancement to political advantage.[5] Later there will be more to say about these allegations, but the point to make now is that, as the twenty-first century unfolds, there are hundreds if not thousands of education and research centers, endowed professorships in universities and colleges, and museums and memorials dedicated to Holocaust remembrance. They can be found in Israel, Europe, North America, Africa, Australia, and Asia. Many of the former concentration and death camp sites are integral parts of this still-expanding network.

As illustrated by ongoing debates about the Auschwitz site (should religious symbols be permitted there, for example, or what about the discotheque that opened in a former tannery where slave laborers worked and died during World War II?) or by the controversy surrounding the German Memorial to the Murdered Jews of Europe that will stand in the heart of Berlin, it is rarely simple or easy to settle what the style and substance, the contours and contents of Holocaust institutions will be.[6] How should Holocaust sites be preserved and protected? What narrative will a museum emphasize? What topics will get priority in Holocaust research centers? Where should a memorial be situated, what design should it have, what messages ought it express? Who should have the authority to answer such questions? Strong differences of opinion make Holocaust politics swirl around issues such as these.

Among the earliest and most prominent Holocaust institutions is Yad Vashem, the national Holocaust memorial of the Jewish people in Jerusalem. Reflecting additional dimensions of Holocaust politics, its full and official name—Yad Vashem Martyrs' and Heroes' Remembrance Authority—was not chosen casually, for it bears special meanings that involve religion, national identity, and even the future destiny of Israel and the Jewish people. First, the Hebrew words *Yad Vashem* mean, literally, a monument and a name and, figuratively, a monument and a memorial. Their source is biblical, specifically a verse from the prophet Isaiah (56:5) that reports God's intention to remember those who keep his covenant: "I will give, in my house and within my walls, a monument and a name better than sons and daughters; I will give them an everlasting name that shall not be cut off." Second, the emphasis on martyrs and heroes both ennobles the immense loss that the Jewish people suffered in the Holocaust and pays special tribute to the Jewish resistance against the onslaught. Combining its memorial functions with those of a museum devoted to narrating the history of the Holocaust, Yad Vashem also promotes important research, oral history, and educational projects. Its impact, symbolic and substantive, is felt worldwide.

The Holocaust took place in Europe. As Yad Vashem indicates, however, the event's impact reaches far beyond European boundaries. From Houston and Minneapolis to Miami and Seattle, in places large and small, hundreds of American institutions with diverse functions, styles, and constituencies recall the Holocaust. Some of these institutions are memorials in public spaces that feature outdoor monuments or works of art, such as sculptor George Segal's *Holocaust* in San Francisco. These sites are often used on Yom Hashoah. Israel's parliament established that Holocaust remembrance day in 1951, and it has been widely observed in the United States, especially since Jimmy Carter's 1978 Executive Order established the President's Commission on the Holocaust, whose duties included recommending appropriate ways to remember the Holocaust's victims.[7]

Many other American Holocaust institutions take the form of museums, research centers, professorships,

foundations, councils, and commissions that emphasize education, oral histories from survivors and liber-
ators, and publications. Several of these institutions
enjoy special prominence, but at times stormy conflict
clouds their high visibility. These conflicts often reveal
that, to some extent, all politics—Holocaust politics
included—is local. The Holocaust is not institutionalized in general. The institutionalizing process always
involves a specific context that reflects the interests,
concerns, and perspectives of particular constituencies.
One result is that there has been an Americanization
of the Holocaust. What this process of Americanization involves, and whether it should occasion
applause, abhorrence, or ambivalence is itself an item
on the agendas of Holocaust politics, but, in general,
suffice it to say that the Americanization of the Holocaust refers to the ways in which the Holocaust is
interpreted and institutionalized by and for Americans—Jews and non-Jews alike.[8] More specifically, it
involves interpretations and forms of institutionalizing
that reflect and support interests, outlooks, and values
that resonate with American history, identity, and
hopes for the future. The Americanization of the
Holocaust has much to do with the significant Jewish
population in the United States, but by no means do
Jews alone influence that process. In fact, the Americanization of the Holocaust cannot be adequately
understood apart from the many non-Jewish Americans who are seriously interested in and deeply moved
by the Holocaust's history.

Pervading the Americanization of the Holocaust,
debate and often disagreement have centered around
questions such as the following: How is the Holocaust
best remembered? Where should Holocaust museums be built, if they should be built at all? What

design should they have, what should their exhibits contain, and how should they interpret the Holocaust's history? What should be emphasized in school curricula and postsecondary teaching about the Holocaust? What research is most important? How should these Holocaust-related projects be funded? Are the funds well spent? Who should answer these questions and, specifically, what influence should Holocaust survivors and scholars have in such deliberations? Some times these questions are laid to rest. Some times they erupt again or anew. Rarely do they disappear completely.

Issues of this kind arose in the United States as early as 1947, when planning began for a Holocaust memorial in New York City.[9] Politics and power struggles within local government as well as within the organized Jewish community stalled the project. Fifty years later, the Museum of Jewish Heritage, which calls itself a Living Memorial to the Holocaust, opened to the public. Situated at the Battery Park waterfront in Manhattan (the location offers views of Ellis Island, a key immigration center in American history, and the Statue of Liberty), the museum's exhibit describes, first, the pre-Holocaust vitality of European Jewish life. Then, after documenting the Nazi destruction, it focuses on post-Holocaust Jewish renewal.

Like the Los Angeles–based Simon Wiesenthal Center, whose contributing membership has grown to several hundred thousand since its founding in 1977, the Museum of Jewish Heritage receives a steady stream of visitors, non-Jews as well as Jews. No American Holocaust museum, however, attracts more people than the United States Holocaust Memorial Museum (USHMM) in Washington, D.C. By 2001, even before the eighth anniversary of its opening in April 1993, USHMM's visitor total topped fifteen million, which included 11.4 million non-Jews, 4.8 million children, and more than 50 percent of the American Jewish community.

Chaired by Elie Wiesel, President Carter's Commission on the Holocaust initially recommended the development of USHMM in 1979. Soon chartered by a unanimous Act of Congress in 1980, the museum represents a distinctive federal-private partnership. Constructed and equipped through private initiatives that raised the necessary $194 million, USHMM's award-winning building, designed by architect James Ingo Freed, stands four hundred yards from the Washington Monument on federally donated land adjacent to the National Mall. Legislation passed in 2000 by the United States Congress granted the museum permanent authorization for federal appropriations. Continuing to be funded by private funds as well (the museum's operating budget for fiscal year 2001 was $55.7 million [$34.4 federal, $21.3 private]), USHMM conducts extensive educational outreach programs and houses more than thirty-five thousand artifacts, thirteen million archival document pages, and more than sixty-five thousand photographic images, as well as films and books, a solemn Hall of Remembrance, research and learning centers, a web site that averages about two hundred thousand user sessions per month, and a registry of Holocaust survivors. Covering three floors, USHMM's permanent exhibition features a historical narrative that includes an emphasis on the roles played by American institutions and individuals in that dark chapter of human history.[10]

With its dual function as America's hub for "the documentation, study, and interpretation of Holocaust history" and as the nation's official memorial to "the millions of people murdered during the Holocaust,"[11] USHMM could scarcely escape Holocaust politics. Of necessity, every artifact it exhibits, conference it holds, question it raises, or decision it makes deals with a history so grimly awesome and charged with emotion that passionate beliefs and heartfelt convictions—to say nothing of the strong personalities that embody them—are bound to clash and collide. When applied to the Holocaust, the meaning of words such as *interpretation* and *memorial* is neither as straightforward as might be assumed nor as agreed upon as might be desired. Magnificent as it is, USHMM finds itself at the center of unfortunate and acrimonious disputes. As is the case with nearly all Holocaust politics, these disputes do not take place in a vacuum, nor is their character abstract. They take place in specific contexts, and they involve particular people. As I know firsthand, the impact—for good or ill—that those disputes have on individual persons can be profound.

In 1994, President Bill Clinton appointed me to the United States Holocaust Memorial Council, which serves as the museum's board of trustees. Miles Lerman was the council's chairman. Having escaped from a Nazi camp in 1942, he led Jewish resistance against the Germans in southeastern Poland, lived for eight months with his wife, Rosalie (Chris) Cherman (a survivor of Auschwitz-Birkenau) in a postwar displaced persons camp, and then immigrated to the United States where he became a successful New Jersey businessman and a tireless supporter of the museum. He retired as chairman in 2000. Shortly after my appointment to the council, Jeshajahu "Shaike" Weinberg stepped down as USHMM's founding director, and Lerman convened a committee to search for Weinberg's successor. That process tapped Steven T. Katz, a notable Jewish philosopher, theologian, and Holocaust scholar who was a Cornell University professor at the time. In Holocaust studies, Katz has been known best as a staunch defender of the Holocaust's uniqueness, a position that he is still developing in a multivolume work called *The Holocaust in Historical Context*. Katz's arrival at the director's office was abruptly halted, however, when allegations that he had misrepresented his scholarly achievements at Cornell led to a parting of the ways before his Washington appointment had really begun. Katz returned to academic life at Boston University, where he continues a distinguished, if bruised, career.

Much sooner than he had hoped, Lerman launched another director's search. This time the committee turned to Walter Reich. A psychiatrist and scholar, a teacher and a writer, Reich is a child survivor of the Holocaust who held appointments at the National Institute of Mental Health and the Woodrow Wilson Center for Scholars in Washington, D.C. By the end of 1997, I had become fairly well acquainted with Reich because he had consulted me about museum restructuring that included development of a Center for Advanced Holocaust Studies (CAHS). This center would replace what had formerly been known as the United States Holocaust Research Institute. The scholarly division of the museum, the Research Institute had been headed by my close friend, Michael Berenbaum, since the museum's opening in 1993. Berenbaum had competed unsuccessfully for the USHMM directorship when Weinberg vacated the position. Not seeing eye-to-eye with Reich, particularly with regard to the future of the Research Institute, Berenbaum left the museum to become the chief executive officer of the Survivors of the Shoah Visual History Foundation, which Steven Spielberg established in Los Angeles in 1994. Under Berenbaum's directorship, the foundation completed the videotaping of more than 50,000 interviews. Conducted in thirty-two different languages, the interviews were given by survivors from fifty-seven countries. A falling out between Berenbaum and the foundation's administration, however, resulted in his departure in 1999, but he thrives as a writer and much sought after speaker, teacher, and consultant.

Meanwhile, my love for USHMM, along with encouragement by friends such as Berenbaum and interest in the plans that I had discussed with Reich, led me to the realization that full-time work at the museum, specifically as director of the newly forming CAHS, was increasingly attractive to me. So I pursued that wonderful opportunity on September 22, 1997, by mailing my application for the center's directorship. Recusing myself from activity on the Holocaust Memorial Council, I was subsequently invited to meet with the CAHS search committee, and on January 21, 1998, I traveled to Washington for my interview, which took place the next day.

On January 22, 1998, USHMM was truly embroiled in Holocaust politics. At the time, that fact had little to do with the search for the CAHS director, although the results of that search would also exacerbate the museum's political situation. Instead, the immediate eruption centered around the news reported that morning in Marc Fisher's *Washington Post* story, which was headlined "Holocaust Museum to Welcome Arafat."

Earlier that January, Miles Lerman had learned that State Department officials—in particular Dennis Ross and Aaron Miller, specialists on the Middle East who were also members of the museum's council—thought it opportune to include the museum in the schedule for Yasser Arafat's upcoming visit to Washington for talks with President Clinton, which were scheduled to begin on January 22. The head of the Palestine Liberation Organization would be the first major Arab leader to visit USHMM. If all went well, he would acknowledge the full reality of the Holocaust and its singular importance for the Jewish people.

As events unfolded in this case, nothing went well. At first, museum chairman Miles Lerman embraced the State Department initiative, but museum director Walter Reich did not. He and his allies contended that an Arafat visit, especially if the Palestinian leader received VIP treatment, would be highly offensive to Jews who held Arafat responsible for anti-Israeli terrorism and implicated in the antisemitism that could be found in the Palestinian press. Momentarily, Reich's view—Arafat's museum visit would be too divisive; it should not go forward—prevailed, and the press quoted Lerman as saying, "We believe the museum should not get involved in a political dispute where half of the people are for something and half are against it."[12] Holocaust politics, however, does not permit the luxury of such uninvolvement for an institution such as USHMM. Not only was the Clinton administration displeased, but also public opinion supported Arafat's tour of the museum. So the visit was "on" again. This time, quoting Lerman as saying that the visit is "good for Arafat and it's good for the peace process," the *Washington Post* indicated that Arafat's museum tour would take place on January

23.[13] It did not. Under the circumstances, Arafat declined the snubbing "invitation." He is not likely to visit USHMM any time soon.

The museum's bungling gave Arafat an "out" that he could play to good advantage. The same could not be said for either Lerman or Reich. Acknowledging that it had been improper to put off the Arafat invitation, Lerman contended that Reich had given him bad advice. Sticking fast, Reich refused to greet Arafat even after members of the executive committee of USHMM's governing council argued that his duties as an officer of the museum required him to do so. Prior to the Arafat episode, Reich's tenure as museum director had been less than smooth. Now increasingly rocky, it soon ended. As an unnamed senior museum official was quoted as saying, "the minute Reich refused to greet Arafat, he was finished."[14] After a carefully brokered departure scenario was in place, the museum announced on February 18 that Reich had "decided not to pursue renewal of his contract when it expires this June." Another casualty of Holocaust politics, Reich nicely landed on his feet as a senior scholar at the Woodrow Wilson Center and as the first holder of the Yitzhak Rabin Memorial Chair at George Washington University, where he teaches in the Elliott School of International Affairs, with secondary appointments in medicine and health sciences and in Judaic studies.

Reich's settlement with the museum brought his official duties to an end on March 31, 1998. This timing meant that, with direction from the search committee, Reich would appoint the director for the CAHS. Back on that stormy January 22, when the Arafat episode was exploding, he was closeted in his office where intense negotiations with the museum's leadership were taking place just a few doors away

from the room in which interviews for the directorship of the CAHS were under way. I did not see Reich,
but by midafternoon when I arrived for my interview
with the search committee (I was the last of several
candidates), it was clear that this had been a tense day
for the USHMM. Some members of the search committee were unable to meet with all the candidates
because they were preoccupied with the Arafat deba-
cle and Reich's involvement in it. Nevertheless, an
impressive committee met with me. Chaired by Alfred
Gottschalk, then chancellor of Hebrew Union College in Cincinnati, that group included Thomas Buer-
genthal, an eminent scholar from the George
Washington University Law Center; Randolph Bra-
ham, the primary authority on the fate of Hungarian
Jewry during the Holocaust; Deborah Lipstadt, the
Emory University historian who would be a key
defendant in David Irving's Holocaust denial trial two
years later; and Irving "Yitz" Greenberg, a leading
Jewish scholar and an Orthodox rabbi who succeeded
Miles Lerman as chairman of the United States Holocaust Memorial Council in 2000.[15]

I was not Reich's choice. The CAHS directorship
was offered first to Alvin H. Rosenfeld, a specialist in
Holocaust literature, who for many years has led the
superb Jewish studies program at Indiana University.
Apparently unsure that Rosenfeld would accept the
position—he did decline it—some museum officials
kept in touch with me to inquire about my continuing
availability. The directorship, I assured them, still
interested me very much. Several weeks passed. I
spent much of March 29 with my friend Elie Wiesel.
Before I introduced him to a large Claremont audience that afternoon, we talked about the prospects at
the center. Two days later, Walter Reich's tenure at the

museum came to an end. No director for CAHS had been appointed.

A few days later, I received a telephone call from Sara J. Bloomfield. At the time, she was the museum's acting director. Bloomfield's long service at USHMM and her success as acting director soon led her to become the museum's chief executive, a position she fills with wisdom, high energy, and dignity. She invited me to come to Washington for further talks about the CAHS directorship. I gladly accepted this invitation, and on April 12, Easter Sunday, I flew east. That Monday and Tuesday I went from one meeting to another. One of them even took place at Washington's Union Station, where Bloomfield and I spoke with Ruth B. Mandel, the U.S. Holocaust Memorial Council's vice-chairperson, who was rushing to catch a train to her New Jersey home. At that meeting, Bloomfield asked whether, to the best of my knowledge, I had ever done anything that might cause problems for the museum. No, I answered without hesitation, my closet contained no skeletons. In ways that I scarcely could have imagined at the time, however, Holocaust politics would intrude to contest that judgment. Meanwhile, I returned to California during the night of April 14. The next day Bloomfield called again. If I wanted it, she said, the CAHS directorship was mine.

So it was that after thirty-two years on the faculty of Claremont McKenna College (CMC), I seized a wonderful opportunity. Beginning that August, I would direct the Center for Advanced Holocaust Studies at the United States Holocaust Memorial Museum. That felt and sounded good. My commitment to study the Holocaust and also an equally long-standing scholarly interest in American culture and history (for many years I have taught a course called

"Perspectives on the American Dream") meant that this notable position would probably cap my career. As a 58-year-old scholar, that was my American Dream, and it was not diminished by the fact that best wishes from Washington and Claremont were accompanied by realistic advice. Use an academic perk, it urged. Request a leave of absence from CMC. If things go wrong, your Claremont life can continue.

CMC's board of trustees held its June 4 meeting on campus. A small item in its big agenda was my request for a two-year leave from the college, which the board generously granted. As the board's meeting concluded, I waited for a fax in an office nearby. Board chairman Robert J. Lowe saw me and extended congratulations. As we parted, he remarked that perhaps I would return to CMC in the not-too-distant future and use the Washington experience to enrich my teaching. Neither of us knew how quickly his remark would come true, but my leave of absence—probably the shortest in CMC's history—scarcely began before I brought it to an end.

Two days before my conversation with Bob Lowe, a stranger interrupted my plans. Although we have never met, Morton Klein, who heads the Zionist Organization of America, has been part of my life ever since. Dredging up fragments from an op-ed piece I wrote for the *Los Angeles Times* in November 1988 and then spinning those ten-year-old sentences to suit his purposes, Klein claimed that I had "publicly compared Israel to Nazi Germany and compared the Palestinian Arabs to the Jewish victims of the Nazis."[16]

Further alleging that I had "blackened Israel's name and desecrated the memory of the Six Million," Klein spearheaded an unrelenting campaign—aided and abetted by the *Forward*, the Jewish weekly in New

York, and by that paper's zealous Ira Stoll in particular—that became increasingly malicious despite my public apology, which appeared in the *Forward* on June 12.[17] While clarifying that I had been falsely accused of making comparisons that were historically inaccurate, morally outrageous, and a contradiction of my own studies and life experiences, which included living in Israel, I nevertheless regretted the *Los Angeles Times* essay because it had made, for some readers, an impression I never intended to create.

Holocaust politics can escalate hostility. Nothing, I now see, could have placated my right-wing critics—pundit George Will and two Republican congressmen were among the small but vocal minority—whose attack also assailed much Holocaust scholarship and teaching, as well as the U.S. Holocaust Memorial Museum, for what they regarded as failure to memorialize the Holocaust properly. There is even good reason to see some of the criticism leveled at me as part of the "payback time" directed by some of Walter Reich's supporters who felt that USHMM had savaged him. Meanwhile, especially within the scholarly community and the museum, strong support for my appointment resounded. Action taken by the museum's governing board on June 17 summed it up. Staunchly reaffirming my appointment, the museum's resolutions also repudiated and condemned "the character assassination being waged against John Roth."

As those turbulent June days unfolded, responsibilities at a Holocaust conference took me and my wife, Lyn, to England. We also traveled in Ireland, deciding what to do while the controversy tracked us and we sized up our "homelessness." (We had sold our thirty-year Claremont home in preparation for moving east.) When debate about my Washington appointment had not abated upon our return to Claremont at the end of June, I knew that I did not wish to begin important work in Washington with controversy as its prelude. The choice was mine: I stayed at CMC for a thirty-third year and more.

As a philosopher, questions are especially important to me because we can learn so much by pursuing them. Thus, I have often thought about a good question that friends asked me during the summer of 1998: Have I been angry about the Holocaust politics that snared me? My response, now as well as then, is that anger defers to sadness. Sadness, in turn, is displaced by an intensified desire to inquire, write, and teach. Opportunity to inquire, write, and teach fills me with gratitude.

What some have called "the Roth affair" is not an experience I would have chosen. Klein and his allies created a poisonous atmosphere; it provoked unwarranted suspicion and divisiveness. They cloaked their attack in claims that they were protecting memory of the Holocaust. Ironically, their behavior undermined the very goal that they so self-righteously professed to serve. That outcome does arouse my anger, but more than that, it saddens me and many others because good opportunities were missed all around—for the museum, for Holocaust research, and for me.

* * *

Given that "the Roth affair" exists (it seems destined to be at least a footnote in USHMM's history), I would not have missed it for anything. For me, the affair raises so many significant questions that have been put in perspective anew by the controversy. So in these pages of a book that I would otherwise not have written, I want to reflect on those questions, which include: Who "owns" the Holocaust? How is that unprecedented event best remembered? What lessons does it teach? CMC's board chairman, Bob Lowe, was right. My Washington experiences have enriched my thinking and, I hope, my writing—not only sooner but perhaps more thoroughly than he or I could have guessed in June 1998.

Everyone needs reminders not to take good things for granted. That summer I was reminded that I already had a position as good and meaningful as any this world offers, namely, to be a professor of philosophy in a small liberal arts college and at CMC in particular. Perhaps I should even thank Morton Klein for inflaming "the Roth affair," for it led me to think more deeply about the contributions that philosophy itself might bring to Holocaust studies and how those contributions might help to make Holocaust politics less poisonous and more promising. The Holocaust is never separable from politics. Emerging from Nazi Germany's toxic atmosphere and the political contexts that preceded it, which prominently included religion, its legacy is charged with divisive dilemmas. Philosophy can provide some constructive help in that context, but this depends on how philosophy responds to the Holocaust, an issue that has political ramifications of its own. So I want to end this prologue by turning to philosophy, the discipline that informs my thinking, and by considering how philosophy might position itself for constructive contributions to Holocaust politics.

Philosophy's Part in Holocaust Politics

On October 2, 1938, less than a year before Nazi Germany's invasion of Poland would begin World War II, British philosopher R. G. Collingwood put

the finishing touches on his autobiography. Its observations underscored his belief that "the chief business
of twentieth-century philosophy is to reckon with
twentieth-century history."[18] Collingwood's primary
intention was to urge philosophers to pay more attention to the discipline of history—its methods, consciousness of context, and attention to detail—so that
philosophy might be less abstract and more aware of
its own historical heritage, while also inquiring about
problems raised by historical thinking (for example,
how is historical knowledge possible?). At least by
implication, this call for an up-to-date philosophy of
history meant that philosophy's responsibilities
included paying close attention to twentieth-century
events as well.

Unfortunately, twentieth-century philosophy did
relatively little to meet Collingwood's expectations.
Whether philosophy will do better in the twenty-first
century remains to be seen. Illustrative evidence for
those latter judgments can be found by noting that the
late December 1985 meeting of the American Philosophical Association's Eastern Division featured a symposium on the Holocaust. An article in the prestigious
Journal of Philosophy provided a prelude for that event.
Authored by Emil Fackenheim (with a brief commentary by Berel Lang), the article was entitled "The Holocaust and Philosophy." As if echoing Collingwood in a
minor key, it began with a lament that still stands as an
indictment: "Philosophers," wrote Fackenheim, "have
all but ignored the Holocaust."[19]

Jean Améry probably would not have disagreed with
either Collingwood or Fackenheim, a distinguished
Jewish philosopher and theologian who narrowly
escaped the Holocaust when he fled his native Germany
after the November pogroms of 1938 (euphemistically

called *Kristallnacht*) and his release from the Nazi concentration camp at Sachsenhausen.[20] In phrasing akin to Améry's calling the Holocaust a moral chasm, Fackenheim went on to observe that the Holocaust was "devastatingly negative."[21] He wondered if the "power and respectability" of the Nazi worldview that led to the Holocaust's uniqueness could have been maintained "without the prestige of philosophers like Martin Heidegger."[22] The historian's task is to explain the Holocaust, Fackenheim insisted, and "the philosopher must reflect on the historian's work."[23]

About five years later, Robert Nozick, a leading American philosopher, published a book called *The Examined Life*. "I want to think about living," he began, "and what is important in life, to clarify my thinking—and also my life."[24] Two hundred pages later, the author included a brief, seven-page chapter called "The Holocaust." The Holocaust's "significance and implications," Nozick stated, dwarf our understanding, for this event "distorts everything around it."[25] Nevertheless, he insisted, "the Holocaust is something we have to respond to in some significant way."[26]

Amplifying that understatement, Nozick made a stunning assertion. The Holocaust, he said, reveals nothing less than the fact that "humanity has lost its claim to continue."[27] After Auschwitz, he explained, there would be no "*special* tragedy" if humankind destroyed itself or if it were annihilated by some other means. He did not mean either that humanity deserved such a fate or that the tragedy of individual suffering and loss of life in such a case would be anything less than "wrong or monstrous," nor did he want to engage in invidious comparisons of cruelty and disaster. Nevertheless, the Holocaust "*sealed* the situation, and made it patently clear" that humankind had so shamed itself—in Nozick's words, the Holocaust so "ruined the reputation of the human family"—that the following sentence must be pronounced: Humanity "no longer deserves *not* to be [destroyed]."[28] Is Nozick right about that? What if he is, and what if he is not? Philosophy thrives on such questions, or at least it should.

Life goes on after the Holocaust. Fackenheim, Lang, Nozick, and some other philosophers have reflected deeply about the Holocaust, but I remain concerned about philosophy's tendency to be silent about that catastrophe.[29] I wonder how philosophy might be different—less abstract and technical, for example, and more focused on ethics and politics—if Holocaust studies governed its work more decisively. I do not mean that the remedy for that silence is for philosophers to abandon their traditional work and to become Holocaust scholars instead. Nevertheless, I would like to see more philosophers joining, or at least taking more seriously, the rather small number who have tried to pursue versions of what Fackenheim recommended when he urged philosophers to reflect on the Holocaust historians' work. Doing so would open up a vast variety of questions—historiographical, epistemological, metaphysical, and ethical—that would take philosophers more deeply into the historical particularity of the Holocaust, including the particularity of Jewish life. Such Holocaust-related reflection, I believe, would change some features of philosophical work and Holocaust politics in ways that help people to follow better Robert Nozick's urging to "think about living and what is important in life."

Philosophers and philosophy have avoided the Holocaust and Holocaust studies primarily because so much history is involved. To encounter the Holocaust philosophically, one must study what happened, to whom, where, when, and how. Reckoning with detail and particularity of that kind is not what philosophers are trained or naturally inclined to do. So it is likely that only a few philosophers—probably some of those who have grown impatient with the abstraction and distance from history that most contemporary philosophy reflects—will immerse themselves in this field of study. Once there, however, they are unlikely to want to be anywhere else, for the work to do is so intense and important.

Think of the questions that now and forever will need to be explored and that must be handled with great care: How did the Holocaust happen? Who is responsible for it? How can we best remember this history? What can words say? What about God and religion after Auschwitz? What about human rights and morality in a post-Holocaust world? What can I know, what should I do, for what may I hope in the shadow of Birkenau? How do such questions reflect and touch off Holocaust politics? How can Holocaust politics be more constructive than it has often been?

The primary task of philosophy that takes the Holocaust seriously (by extension I would say of Holocaust studies in general and also of Holocaust politics at its best) is an ethical one. We do not and should not study the Holocaust as if the study of history is an end in itself, for it is not. Contrary to the havoc and waste that often flow from them, the struggles of Holocaust politics are worth pursuing just to the extent that they increase respect for human life and mend the world. If Holocaust politics does anything less, it only opens wider the Holocaust's moral chasm. As Emil Fackenheim pointed out in 1985, what happened in the Holocaust has changed "the ancient wonder" with which philosophers greeted the question "What is Man?" That wonder, said Fackenheim, "is now mingled with a new horror."[30] To confront that horror makes—or should make—unavoidable the questions that Robert Nozick raises when he asks: "Is there anything we can do by our behavior over time, so that once again it would be a special and further tragedy if our species were to end or be destroyed? Can we redeem ourselves?"[31]

Nozick's challenges have much to do with Holocaust politics because the success or failure we will have in redeeming ourselves is connected with the ways in which we respond to the Holocaust. For good or ill, those responses and the quality of Holocaust politics are intertwined and interdependent. If humanity's reputation is to be redeemed, there needs to be a stronger link between ethics and Holocaust politics. How to forge that link is a question that may have no final closure, for the inquiry will need to continue with changing times and circumstances. By attending to the Holocaust and its aftermath, philosophers can help to keep that inquiry going. If their efforts are sound, they will not make the Holocaust acceptable, but they can help to make Holocaust politics an asset and not a liability.

Chapter One

Who Owns the Holocaust?

Unresolved issues—historical, political, moral and theological—still swirl around the Holocaust, and studying them remains a task of great importance.

Gabriel Schoenfeld,
"The 'Cutting Edge' of Holocaust Studies"

Gabriel Schoenfeld, senior editor at *Commentary*, the influential monthly published by the American Jewish Committee, contributes regularly to Holocaust politics. In September 2000, for example, his article on Holocaust reparations and restitution spoke of "a growing scandal," which, in Schoenfeld's judgment, has tainted the turn-of-the-century effort to obtain compensation for Jewish losses and to return stolen Jewish property to its rightful owners.[1] Schoenfeld's article concluded by quoting both columnist Charles Krauthammer, who said that the pursuit of billions in Holocaust reparations "has gone from the unseemly to the disgraceful," and the Anti-Defamation League head Abraham Foxman, who observed that the emphasis on financial reparations has become a "desecration" and "too high a price to pay for a justice we will never receive." Endorsing their views, Schoenfeld added that "it is past time to reconsider."[2] Taking the challenge, many of his readers replied, and *Commentary*'s January 2001 issue featured a "Controversy" article based on some of the responses.

In the September article, Schoenfeld noted how the reparations efforts have fueled canards from the anti-semitic far Right, which slurs Jews by picturing them as greedy money grabbers. He was more concerned, however, about the reparations efforts' effects on Europe's political center. Schoenfeld assessed Jewish litigation about and reaction to reparations matters ranging from Switzerland's laundering of "Nazi gold" to its mishandling of bank accounts established by Jews in the 1920s and 1930s. He explored claims against European insurance companies that issued policies paid for and held by Jewish families. He probed the pressure for multibillion dollar slave labor compensation, which was brought to bear on German industry by Jewish and governmental agencies. These inquiries led Schoenfeld to question some of the claims' legitimacy and, even if the claims were legitimate, to doubt whether they were properly pursued. In many instances, he contended, the facts were unclear, the judgments unreasonable, the attorneys greedy, and the Jewish community had allowed its needy survivors to languish even as millions were spent on prosecuting the cases. Jewish moralizing to the contrary notwithstanding, Schoenfeld implied, the scandal remained that the renewed push for Holocaust reparations has been about money more than ethical principle. At the end of the day, he feared, "moral and political capital has been heedlessly squandered."[3]

About two years earlier, Schoenfeld ignited another *Commentary* "Controversy" when he published "Auschwitz and the Professors." A briefer advance version of the same article—entitled "The 'Cutting Edge' of Holocaust Studies"—appeared in the *Wall Street Journal*.[4] These essays expressed Schoenfeld's worry that academic study of the Holocaust frequently disrespects that watershed event—not least, in his words, by spreading "jargon, ideology, and distortions both monstrous and trivial."[5] In particular, what he called "feminist scholarship on the Holocaust" made him shudder.[6] Responding to Schoenfeld, I underscored that the Holocaust should provoke fear and worry and that its awesome magnitude ought to make us shudder. But I also found that his intention to spread anxiety was misguided because his analysis of Holocaust studies was ill-informed and unfair. To be sure, some pedagogy and scholarship on the Holocaust are better than others, but Schoenfeld's attack made the field of Holocaust studies, where I have worked for thirty years, scarcely recognizable to me.[7] It did so by casting unwarranted suspicion on scholars, teachers, and institutions whose work solidly supports sound understanding of Holocaust history as well as appreciation of that event's implications. That work, which becomes ever more important as the survivors' numbers dwindle, is the best long-term insurance that this history, its particularity and its lessons, will not be forgotten, trivialized, distorted, or denied.[8]

Before this chapter ends, it will return to Schoenfeld's disdain for gender analysis in Holocaust studies. At the outset, however, I introduce Schoenfeld not so much to debate our specific differences of opinion as to suggest that the controversies he helps to spark contain an issue of even more fundamental importance: Whose Holocaust is it? As this chapter's title indicates, I put that issue in the form of a related question: Who owns the Holocaust?[9] When Schoenfeld, or anyone for that matter, argues about how to interpret the Holocaust and its implications, debates how the Holocaust is properly remembered, or contends that its history has been distorted or abused, those concerns involve power. Typically, positions on such issues reflect special interests, deep-seated differences about right and wrong, disputes about truth, and struggles over who will occupy the institutional leadership positions that set agendas of one kind or another. These struggles regularly arouse intense emotion and sharp division. Owing to the Holocaust's horror and devastation, how could they not?

Out of those differences good can come, but that depends on how they are handled. Schoenfeld once stated that "unresolved issues—historical, political, moral and theological—still swirl around the Holocaust, and studying them remains a task of great importance." That statement is exactly right. Studying those questions well, I believe, entails reflection on the question to which this chapter is devoted.

The Holocaust's Burdens

To take up that deliberation, consider an aspect of the Holocaust's particularity: At frequent intervals, especially after a severe typhus epidemic broke out at Auschwitz-Birkenau during the summer of 1942, an Auschwitz truck went to Dessau, Germany. It returned with large quantities of 200-gram, hermetically sealed tin canisters. They contained Zyklon-Blausäure, or Zyklon B, whose trade name—meaning "cyclone"—also referred to prussic acid, which in German is called *Blausäure* because it produces deep blue stains. In the gas chambers at Auschwitz-Birkenau,

Zyklon B crystals would asphyxiate more than a million Jews.[10]

A powerful pesticide developed during World War I, Zyklon B was used to combat contagious disease by fumigating lice-infested buildings. First used at Auschwitz in July 1940, it initially served those purposes in that vast camp complex, where overcrowded barracks, malnutrition, and poor sanitation made dysentery, typhoid fever, and especially typhus constant threats. By the late summer of 1941, however, much more destructive uses for Zyklon B were found. Experiments on Soviet POWs confirmed that Zyklon B's vaporizing pellets offered a particularly reliable and efficient way to advance the Final Solution.

Two German companies—Degesch, or the Deutsche Gesellschaft für Schädlingsbekämpfung mbH ("the German Vermin-combating Corporation," a subsidiary of I. G. Farben) and Tesch and Stabenow Verlag—profited immensely by supplying Zyklon B to the SS. They even modified it for Auschwitz by removing the special odor that ordinarily warned people about their product's deadly presence. Especially in 1942 and 1943, Auschwitz used tons of Zyklon B. Most of it went to conventional fumigation, but there was plenty left to pour into gas chambers packed with Jews. Once exposed to properly heated air—bodies tightly packed in the gas chambers helped to ensure that the temperature was right—the crystals produced lethal gas. Minutes later its human victims were dead.

Particularities about Auschwitz and Zyklon B are a significant part of the burdens of history created by the Holocaust, an event that shows how murderously destructive human ingenuity, technology, and organization can be. A phrase such as the latter, however, must be qualified—made more personal and less abstract—because ingenuity, technology, and organization exist in particular persons and specific social relationships, or they do not exist at all. When it comes to Auschwitz and Zyklon B, the same is true about memory of their reality, study of their significance, our responsibility for both, and the politics that those tasks entail. The Holocaust—its reality, history, and politics—creates burdens. Those burdens are not abstract, nor are they impersonal. As the term itself suggests, burdens are carried by something and typically by somebody. Usually a burden is something difficult, even impossible, to bear physically or emotionally. Often burdens confer responsibilities and duties. The question burdens often raise is how, or even if, those responsibilities and duties can be met.

The Holocaust's burdens pivot around the question "Who owns the Holocaust?" which I saw in print, probably not for the first time but definitely in a way that riveted my attention, on June 21, 1998. Jane Eisner, an editorialist for the *Philadelphia Inquirer*, raised that question in an opinion piece that she wrote as controversy swirled around my appointment to head the Center for Advanced Holocaust Studies.[11] I have thought about her question ever since, because how people respond to it goes far toward determining whether post-Holocaust debate is fruitful or whether it breaks down. That line of inquiry can be advanced by thinking in two ways about Eisner's question.

First, one could take the question uncritically. Who might own the burdens of Holocaust history? Obviously, one cluster of responses should focus on Jews. It could become more specific by concentrating on Holocaust survivors and perhaps on their children, the "second generation," as they are increasingly known. The immediacy of their involvement argues that Jews of one kind or another, in one way or another, have a privileged position as far as "owner-ship" of the Holocaust is concerned. To a considerable extent, its history is their history.

Nevertheless, at least two problems emerge if this path is taken. First, if Holocaust history and its bur-dens are particularly Jewish concerns, and surely they are, responses to those concerns can still be con-tentious and divisive. Do some Jews, for example, own this history more than others? If so, where does that question lead? What if there are even disagreements and quarrels—and there are—about who counts as a Jewish Holocaust survivor? Who gets to say what's what with the Holocaust in these circumstances? How will such issues be decided?

A second problem is that the Holocaust could not be "owned" by Jews alone, for the burdens of Holo-caust history spread too far and wide for that. Not only are there the so-called other victims—Roma and Sinti (Gypsies) and the mentally and physically dis-abled, to name only two groups who were Holocaust-related targets of the Nazis—but without perpetrators and bystanders, the Shoah would not have taken place. In their own ways, they are candidates for Holocaust ownership too.

The burdens of Holocaust history are immense because the Holocaust itself was immense. It was so vast, it involved so many people, professions, institu-tions, and governments that no candidate group for ownership can qualify for that distinction, at least not by themselves. Even if they tried to do so, Nazis or, even more broadly, Germans could not "own" the Holocaust, although it would not have happened without them. Even if they tried to do so, Christians could not "own" the Holocaust either, although it would not have happened without them as well. In intellectual ways, scholars may claim prerogatives and privileges regarding interpretation of the Holocaust. Nevertheless, when it comes to saying definitively what the event was and what really happened in it, scholars cannot "own" the Holocaust. In part, scholars cannot do so because increasingly most of us were not there, but also because the event eludes all of our efforts to comprehend it completely, for those efforts are always finite and fallible and developed from perspectives that are less than omniscient.

Far from ending the inquiry about Holocaust ownership, these outcomes point to three further possibilities. One is that *nobody* owns the Holocaust. This option has the virtue of denying that some particular group or faction does own this history, but its liabilities outweigh the advantages. If the burdens of Holocaust history belong to nobody, to no one in particular, then the burdens dissolve, the history is likely to be forgotten, and that outcome is as perilous as it is irresponsible. A second option, and it might be invoked to reclaim responsibility and to check the perils of indifference and forgetfulness, is to say that *everybody* owns the Holocaust. This option has the virtue of underscoring that the Holocaust's realities and implications can and even do affect all of humankind, but its liabilities also outweigh the advantages. If the burdens of Holocaust history belong to everybody, the resulting universalization of the Holocaust too easily leads to the banalizing blur found in clichés about "man's inhumanity to man." Such banality overlooks differences that make all the difference in the world. A third possibility is that there is *joint ownership* of the burdens of Holocaust history. This option has the virtue of keeping particularities and differences center stage; it might properly distinguish different forms and domains of ownership. Nevertheless, this option's liabilities also outweigh its advantages. If the burdens of Holocaust history call for joint ownership, there is no neat division of labor that follows. Instead, constituencies and factions are likely to form. Who decides, and at what price, how the Holocaust shall be memorialized, which historical interpretations shall prevail, what shall be said and done at the Holocaust's historical sites, or who shall have influence in and control over the world's growing number of Holocaust-related institutions (museums, research centers, professorial chairs, for example)? In principle, joint ownership might work smoothly; in practice, it has produced more than a fair share of factionalism, infighting, and outrage as perceived prerogatives clash and conflicting interpretations collide.

The line of inquiry taken thus far seems to lead to a dead end. Who owns the Holocaust? There does not seem to be an adequate response to that question. So what next? Sometimes if a question does not have an adequate answer, we might conclude that something is wrong with the question. Perhaps it is poorly worded. Maybe it should not be asked at all. Such an outlook, however, does not elude difficulties, for even if a question cannot be answered well, it does not follow that the question should or will go away. At least for many people, the burdens of Holocaust history keep weighing us down. Whose those burdens are and should be still forms a very important agenda, especially when we think about how those burdens ought to be carried and shared. Still, it may be true that there is something wrong about the question. Some further stocktaking remains in order.

Our first approach was to take the question "Who

owns the Holocaust?" more or less uncritically, an approach that led to unsatisfactory attempts to answer it. Now let us consider a second approach that might build on what was seen at first. Instead of plunging ahead more or less uncritically, this second approach pauses with the question itself, and it does so particularly with respect to what it might mean to *own* that event and its burdens.

To own something can mean at least three things, the most obvious of which is to possess it and thereby to have the authority to control or the power to determine what happens with respect to it. Such an understanding of owning works well enough if we are thinking about a house, car, or business. We may feel obliged, or we may just try, to own a historical event in that way too, but it is dubious whether history, especially the burdens of Holocaust history, can be owned in that way. Human beings make history. Nevertheless, in the sense of possessing history like we possess a house or car, we do not and cannot own history—not even the history that we, in particular, help to make. We cannot do so because history is not property. It is more like the air we breathe, the climate we experience, the culture we share, the family we inherit. They are ours even before we may realize it, not because we own them but because to a large degree they make us what we are and will become. The burdens of Holocaust history are not exceptions to these realities.

There are, however, two other meanings of *own*. Although less well known, they deserve attention, for they may infuse our question with meaning and self-criticism that we can scarcely afford to be without if our post-Holocaust dialogues are going to be at their best. In different but complementary ways, the two meanings do not emphasize our possessing history. Instead these two meanings stress our *belonging to* history so that we not only admit history's grip upon us but also recognize the claims and responsibilities that its grip confers. Here is what I have in mind: To own something can mean not to possess it but to acknowledge or admit a reality for what it was and is. One can own a mistake, to offer a very simple example, by admitting it. Or one can own a fault in the sense of acknowledging it. In related but far more profound senses, the Holocaust and its burdens could be owned in these ways. They could be owned by Jews, Germans, Christians, scholars, and others, not identically but in ways that might be related and, at times, complementary. That is, the reality of the Holocaust and its burdens could be acknowledged. They could be admitted in the sense that the Holocaust scholar Lawrence L. Langer may have had in mind when he began his 1995 book *Admitting the Holocaust* by saying that "if the Holocaust has taught us anything, it is that we were other than we believed, masters of neither time nor space."[12]

When owning involves Holocaust-related acknowledging or admitting, those acts, as Langer aptly suggests, result in "stunned minds staring blankly at alien modes of living and dying in the monstrous milieu of ghettos and camps."[13] But that is not the end of the matter, because there is another sense of owning, one that goes beyond acknowledging and admitting to recognition of the claims that history, in this case the burdens of Holocaust history, place upon us. Thus, we may own the Holocaust in this sense: when we might say, "I (or we) own the Holocaust to make a claim on my life (or ours)." To own the Holocaust in this sense is to live so that the Holocaust enjoins us to remember, study, teach, give, or work not to possess the Holocaust but to be moved by it in a particular way that the Holocaust survivor Elie Wiesel has articulated well.

When I begin teaching my annual course on the Holocaust, I usually show the students a film in which Wiesel responds to the question, "Why should anyone study the Holocaust?" His answer is as disarming as it is simple, as challenging as it is brief, as critical and self-critical as it is succinct: We should study the Holocaust to make ourselves more sensitive, more sensitive to one another, and more sensitive about ourselves. Wiesel's meaning includes being more aware of our blind spots, our self-serving tendencies, our often undeserved self-assurance, especially when it comes to thinking that we can or should *own* the Holocaust in the sense of possessing it. Wiesel's answer is not all that needs to be said about the question of why we should study the Holocaust, but that answer is definitely on the mark where Holocaust politics is concerned.

In the same film, Wiesel adds his belief that study of the Holocaust should bring people together. Concern about the Holocaust has done that, but only up to a point. Concern about the Holocaust has also divided people; often it has done so needlessly and at great personal and communal cost. This is not to say that honest differences can always be smoothed over and eliminated, but the Holocaust's tragedy is compounded when differences about its history and that history's burdens escalate into fractures and factions that do more harm than good. When such a result takes place, and too often it does, that result should sadden and sober us.

When factionalism and rancor govern Holocaust politics, my suspicion is that this unfortunate outcome often hinges, at least in part, on a version of the question, "Who owns the Holocaust?" (the question itself is rarely spoken but nonetheless implied), that inappropriately takes *own* to mean *possess*. Where Holocaust politics is not sour but fruitful, we are likely to find neither that the question "Who owns the Holocaust?" has been dismissed as the wrong question nor that it has gone away for some other reason. Instead, I think we will find that a different sense of ownership, one that is not possessive, comes into play. In that perspective, one owns the Holocaust, first, by acknowledging and admitting its burdens of history. Then we also belong to the Holocaust in the sense that we own its burdens to require us to become more sensitive. That means, in turn, to remember and honor those whose lives were taken in the Holocaust by working to bring the living closer together in understanding and respect.

Equality, Neutrality, Particularity

One of the particular burdens of the Holocaust is that the Zyklon B trucked from Dessau to Auschwitz-Birkenau was used to murder hundreds of thousands of Jewish women. That number soars into the millions when the death toll includes the Jewish women who were killed at the Holocaust's other major death camps—Chelmno, Belzec, Sobibor, Treblinka, and Majdanek—as well as in the Third Reich's concentration camps and ghettos. In the most basic way, of course, the Holocaust's killing drew no distinctions among Jews: Hitler and his followers intended oblivion for them all—every man, woman, and child. That fact incited Gabriel Schoenfeld's blast against what he called "the voguish hybrid known as gender studies," whose practitioners, he argued, were committing "the worst excess of all on today's campuses" when it came to what he labeled "witless and malicious theorizing" about the Holocaust.[14]

Numerous Holocaust scholars—men and women alike—took vigorous exception to Schoenfeld's position.[15] I argued that sound Holocaust teaching and research must concentrate on the particularity of the Holocaust, for the evil—and the good—exists in the details. Therefore, study about what happened to women is legitimate and necessary in Holocaust studies. Some years ago, the students in my own Holocaust courses drove home this point for me by asking questions about women during the Holocaust years. I will return to these points in more detail, but one result was *Different Voices: Women and the Holocaust*, a volume I edited with Carol Rittner. Although Schoenfeld mentioned this book, there was no evidence at the time that he had studied it with much care.

Drawing on survivor testimony and the insightful, at times controversial, work of pioneering scholars, *Different Voices* takes a position that is representative of most teaching and scholarship about women in the Holocaust. Supporting the pioneering efforts by significant scholars such as Joan Ringelheim, Myrna Goldenberg, Dalia Ofer, Lenore Weitzman, and others, its position is that the hell was the same for Jewish women and men during the Holocaust, but the horrors were frequently different.[16] Attention and respect need to be paid to testimony, teaching, and scholarship that reflect those differences. One can share Schoenfeld's concern that study about women in the Holocaust must meet the highest standards, but his Holocaust politics led to nearly wholesale, and therefore unwarranted, condemnation of scholars who are doing key work in an area of Holocaust studies that is basic, serious, and still lacking the regard it deserves.

To follow up on those claims, consider further some points about equality, neutrality, and particularity that bear on the theme "Who owns the Holocaust?" On July 30, 1997, I received a fax from Laureen Enright, an editor at Paragon House, the publisher of *Different Voices*. Enright's message indicated that Judy Cohen, a Holocaust survivor, wanted permission to include portions of the book on the web site that she was constructing. This site would deal specifically with the experiences of women in the Holocaust. Copyright restrictions limited the fulfillment of Cohen's requests, but as the twenty-first century unfolds, her web site, "Women and the Holocaust: A Cyberspace of Their Own," makes important contributions. It opens with a dedication that reveals some of the wide and varied scope of women's experiences, and Jewish women's experiences in particular, during the Holocaust.[17] The web site, she indicates, is

> dedicated to all those women who were murdered while pregnant. Holding little hands of children or carrying infants in their arms on the way to be gassed. In hiding. To the mothers who gave their children to be hidden, many never to find them again. Or as fighters in the resistance: in ghettos, forests, partisan units. And to the lives of those few who survived and bravely carried on.

In addition to an extensive and often updated bibliography, which includes hundreds of entries, Cohen's web site includes a preface by Holocaust scholar Joan Ringelheim, who has long been a leader in urging that attention ought to be paid specifically to the experiences of women during the Holocaust years.

Those experiences were many and varied. While German women, for example, were expected to bear children for the Third Reich (and they were decorated for doing so abundantly), Jewish women had to be prevented from becoming mothers. The Nazis invested considerable time and energy to find the most effective ways to sterilize them, but the "final solution" for this "problem" was death. Of course, if they were healthy and neither too old nor too young, Jewish women could be used before they were used up or killed. At Auschwitz, for example, some were "selected" for slave labor; others became objects for the "scientific" experiments that were intended to advance Nazi programs of racial hygiene and purity.

Women could be found among other victim groups during the Holocaust—Roma and Sinti, political prisoners, Jehovah's Witnesses, and the so-called "asocials" to name a few. In addition, women were among the neighbors who stood by while Jews were rounded up and deported all over Europe. They were among those who rescued Jews as well. Women could be found in virtually every intersection and intricacy of the Holocaust's web.

Some of the victims trapped in the Holocaust's web were non-Jewish German women, but German women, in particular, had other parts to play in the Final Solution as well. Organized by figures such as Heinrich Himmler, Reinhard Heydrich, and Adolf Eichmann, the Final Solution was instigated and dominated by men. The same can be said of virtually all modern genocides. In the case of Nazi Germany, however, some women held positions of responsibility in the Third Reich's concentration camps and killing centers. Others were officials in the Nazi Party. Still others aided and abetted the destruction process as medical personnel, civil servants, secretaries, and members of other sectors of the home front's man-power-depleted workforce. Some German women stood trial and were convicted by postwar tribunals that judged war crimes and crimes against humanity.[18] Nevertheless, German women were not the primary perpetrators of the Holocaust. In general, their role was different: They worked in the German economy, and they were the sympathetic mothers, sisters, and daughters, the reassuring wives, friends, and lovers, of the German men who were usually more directly implicated in that disaster.

In general, one could scarcely say that German women were defenders of Jews or protesters against the Nazi regime, although significant exceptions to that rule could be found. Depending on the extent of their knowledge about the destruction of the Euro-pean Jews, awareness that could have been greater or smaller depending on individual circumstances, many German women occupied for the most part a position between that of *perpetrator* and *bystander*—two of the categories that are often used to classify the various parts that people played during the Holocaust. We might speak of them as *partners*, for in multiple ways that is what they were in relationship to the German men who launched and carried out the Holocaust.

As Judy Cohen's web site illustrates, times are changing as far as serious study about women and the Holocaust is concerned.[19] It remains true, however, that issues in this area have not received the attention they deserve. Three areas of research that need fur-ther attention are the following: (1) As the particular-ity of women's Holocaust experience is identified and documented, what conclusions, if any, are to be drawn from that particularity? Is it enough to clarify and report what happened, or is more than that at stake? (2) What will happen when, not if, the theories of gender analysis are brought fully to bear on the Holocaust? What are the promises and pitfalls of such work? (3) Is there more to be learned about Nazi policy where women, especially Jewish women, were concerned? As Dalia Ofer has argued, for example, Nazi policy increasingly dictated the unlimited intervention that brutalized Jewish family life.[20] No doubt race relations had priority over gender relations in Nazi ideology,[21] but did the Nazi destruction process still take more cognizance of the differences between Jewish men and Jewish women than previous research has emphasized? Study about women in the Holocaust is still too much in its early stages to answer such questions definitively, but Schoenfeld's wishes to the contrary notwithstanding, there will be more Holocaust scholarship about women. Overall, acknowledging and admitting the history that informs it, as well as taking responsibility for the implications of that research, will be a desirable outcome of Holocaust politics.

In such considerations, the concept of *equality* has a place. The Holocaust was Nazi Germany's planned total destruction of the Jewish people and the actual murder of nearly six million of them. Millions of other people were also destroyed in the Holocaust's complex web, but the primary targets were Jews. As far as the Jews were concerned, the Nazis were equal opportunity killers. The Nazis' intentionality, if not all of their actions, made clear that all Jews—young or old, male or female, it made no difference—ought to disappear. I believe that it is with this perspective in mind that one should read the opening line of Joan Ringelheim's contribution to Judy Cohen's web site. "Every

Jew, regardless of gender," writes Ringelheim, "was equally a victim in the Holocaust."

During the Final Solution, Jews were destroyed because they were Jews. In the Holocaust, no bottom line was more basic, undeniable, or deadly than that. That fact accounts for the gender neutrality that most Holocaust scholarship has typically displayed. Although many Holocaust memoirs written by women have existed for a long time, questions specifically about women, or about gender differences in any respect, got relatively little attention in Holocaust scholarship until the 1990s were well along. The scholarship had proceeded as if neither the writers, nor their texts, nor their readers were gendered. Victims and witnesses, for instance, were mentioned often, but it was as if they were genderless. In fact, of course, this was not the case at all. It could even be argued that the gender "neutrality" was not quite what it appeared because most of the Holocaust scholarship was being written by men, and it is probably not accidental that the canon of Holocaust literature—its chief authors include Elie Wiesel, Primo Levi, and Jean Améry, to mention only a few—was implicitly, if not explicitly, influenced by gendered perspectives.

My own example illustrates this analysis. It was almost twenty years after beginning my study, teaching, and writing about the Holocaust that I was nudged to think more explicitly about what happened to women as women, and to men as men, during the Holocaust. My students at Claremont McKenna College did much of that nudging. Commonly, women are a majority of the students who take my courses on the Holocaust. As they kept asking questions about what happened to women, I had to study more and learn more. I found my understanding challenged, expanded, and revised by extensive listening to women, especially to survivors and the relatively small but increasing number of scholars who have focused attention on the particularity of women's Holocaust experiences.

As my work advanced, I discovered something more. While attention has been paid to the fate of Jewish children during the Holocaust, until recently studies about the particular roles played by fathers and mothers, brothers and sisters, husbands and wives, men and women have not only been neutralized, but to some extent they have also been resisted. The fundamental reasons for that resistance have been four in number. Each plays its part in Holocaust politics. The first argument, voiced mainly—but fortunately not too often—by men has been that such approaches were either not interesting or unimportant. It took time, but now it goes without saying that those points were not convincing. More specifically, it has been argued that bringing gender perspectives to bear on the Holocaust might (1) detract from the fact that Jews as Jews were its victims, (2) lead to a hijacking of the Holocaust by gender studies advocates, or (3) wrongly privilege the suffering, survival skills, cooperation, and caring of Jewish women and girls over that of Jewish men and boys, an outcome that Lawrence Langer regards as reflecting "only our own need to plant a life-sustaining seed in the barren soil that conceals the remnants of two- thirds of European Jewry. The sooner we abandon this design, the quicker we will learn to face such chaos with unshielded eyes."[22]

Some of these claims have more merit than others, but neither individually nor collectively do they warrant setting aside an emphasis on women in the Holocaust. Nazi antisemitism meant that race—specifically the "purity" of German blood and culture—counted for everything. Nothing could be tolerated that might pollute the racial strength on which the Third Reich depended. According to Nazi theory, Jewish life posed this threat to a degree that surpassed every other. Germans could not afford to let Jews remain in their midst.

As the history of Nazi Germany so emphatically shows, racism's "logic" ultimately entails genocide, for if you take seriously the idea that one race endangers the well-being of another, the only way to remove that menace completely is to do away, once and for all, with everyone and everything that embodies it. The racism of Nazi ideology ultimately implied that the existence of Jewish families, and especially the Jewish women who mothered them, constituted a deadly obstacle to the racial purity and cultural superiority that Germany "deserved." Jewish women constituted that threat fundamentally because they could bear children.

Precisely because the Nazis targeted Jews and others in racial terms, they had to see those victims in their male and female particularity. To destroy Jews in general—and to destroy them forever—they had to override any protection that cultural convention afforded even Jewish women and girls and decimate in particular those potential mothers who might bear the next Jewish generation. Heinrich Himmler, head of the SS, clearly understood this point. "We had to answer the question: What about the women and children?" Himmler remembered in one of his speeches. "Here, too, I had made up my mind. . . . I did not feel that I had the right to exterminate the men," he went on to say, "and then allow their children to grow into avengers, threatening our sons and grandchildren. A fateful decision had to be made: This people had to vanish from the earth."[23] It took the targeting of Jewish women as women to implement that decision. Far from reducing the Holocaust to an example of sexism, let alone making the Holocaust prone to some alleged hijacking by gender studies, an emphasis on what happened to women during the Holocaust reveals what otherwise would remain hidden: a fuller picture of the unprecedented and unrelenting killing that was the Final Solution.

As for the protest that such an emphasis will somehow privilege the suffering or the endurance and survival skills of Jewish women and girls over against that of Jewish men and boys, Holocaust scholar Raul Hilberg makes a persuasive point: "The Final Solution was intended by its creators to ensure the annihilation of all Jews. . . . Yet the road to annihilation was marked by events that specifically affected men as men and women as women."[24] Similar experiences are not identical. In the Holocaust, differences between men and women made a vital difference. The goal should not be to argue that what happened to women during the Holocaust was worse than what happened to men, that one gender's endurance and survival skills were necessarily superior to the other's, or that one gender's reflections and memories are clearer, more truthful, or more important than the other's. Nevertheless, it is a legitimate and important aspect of Holocaust politics to advance the growing realization that the history of the Holocaust is incomplete without responses to questions that focus explicitly on what women did and on what happened to them during those dark years.

Testimony and scholarship that reflect gender differences deserve more attention and respect. Holocaust history, however, grants no comfort, and therefore differentiating does not entail privileging. Done well, differentiating leads to increased insight and greater depth of understanding. As we learn more about what women and girls did and what happened to them during the Holocaust, we should and will learn more about what men and boys did and what happened to them during the Holocaust. The words *women* and *gender*, after all, are neither identical nor synonymous. *Gender* involves both women and men, and we cannot learn well about either without getting specific about the other. As the title of one of Raul Hilberg's books suggests, such learning would involve perpetrators, victims, bystanders—all sorts of people, men and women, who were within the Holocaust's web.

Fortunately, wisdom on these matters prevails in Holocaust studies more than it used to. In the early 1990s, for example, it would have been unusual for a Holocaust conference to feature topics about women in the Holocaust. Now it would be unusual if such topics did not appear. More and more publication in the field of women and the Holocaust is taking place too. How did women respond to their circumstances during the Holocaust? What was most important to women who had to live under conditions of deprivation, humiliation, terror, and death? Were there gender-related resources that women drew upon to sustain hope as well as life in the ghettos and camps? What vulnerabilities exposed them to particular kinds of suffering and death? What parts did women play or not play in partisan groups and other resistance efforts during the Holocaust? Does the study of women and the Holocaust highlight new or at least different questions that we should be asking, not just about women but about every human being who had to endure the

Holocaust's darkness? As scholars not only raise these previously unasked questions but also present and debate their responses to them, we will learn more of what we need to know about the Holocaust.

Particularity helps point out what we need to know. Having taught about the Holocaust for many years, I have discovered that the best learning strategies often involve concentrating on small details, on events that are utterly particular but charged with intensity. As one explores how those details developed, how those events took place, they lead outward in spiraling concentric circles to wider historical perspectives.

In my college's library a few years ago, I was looking for some lines and themes that could become part of *Different Voices*, which Carol Rittner and I were then preparing for publication. I discovered what I needed in a poem called "The Woman Poet," which includes these lines: " . . . You do not think / A person lives within the page you thumb. / To you this book is paper, cloth, and ink, / Some binding thread and glue, and thus is dumb, / And cannot touch you . . . / [But] you hold me now completely in your hands. . . . / So then, to tell my story, here I stand. . . . / You hear me speak. But do you hear me feel?"[25] As I read those lines and felt tears well up in my eyes, I knew that I had found the right words for *Different Voice*'s governing epigraph.

This poem was written by Gertrud Kolmar (1894–1943). She was one of the most promising writers of her generation. Like so many in her time and place, however, her talent and her life were taken from her by antisemitism, racism, and genocide. Gertrud Kolmar was a German, but she was also a Jew and a woman. She managed to survive in Berlin until the winter of 1943. In February of that year, the Germans made a special drive to deport the last Jews from that

city, even those who worked in war-essential industries. The last writing we have from Gertrud Kolmar
is a letter dated February 20–21, 1943. She was most
likely caught in the roundup of Jewish workers that
took place a few days later.

Camp records indicate that from late February
until mid-March 1943, numerous transports brought
several thousand Jews from Berlin to Auschwitz-
Birkenau. Most of the women and children were
gassed on arrival. The circumstances of Gertrud Kolmar's death are uncertain, but she was probably
among those who were immediately killed by Zyklon
B. Berlin was declared *judenfrei* in June. The liquidation of German Jewry was officially completed in July.
"You hear me speak. But do you hear me feel?"
Gertrud Kolmar wrote those words some time before
she entered Auschwitz, but especially after Auschwitz
her words speak even more poignantly, tragically, and
urgently than before.

Much of the detail we possess about transports to
Auschwitz comes from the careful work done by
Danuta Czech, a woman who painstakingly collated
the data that forms the *Auschwitz Chronicle*, a day-by-
day, night-by-night record of what transpired there.
Drawing on documents that the Germans left behind
or that the camp resistance kept, she lists how transport after transport arrived, and she indicates how
many men and women were selected for immediate
death or for slave labor. Gertrud Kolmar's name does
not appear in that more than 800-page book, but again
and again its entries remind us that Jewish women
were targeted for destruction. Where women in the
Holocaust are concerned, one event in Czech's book
is particularly poignant. It happened on June 25, 1944.
In a two-sentence paragraph, awesome not only for

what it says but also for the questions its silence contains, Czech describes it this way: "Empty children's strollers are taken away from the storerooms of the personal effects camp, known as 'Canada,' which is located behind Camp B-IIf between Crematoriums III and IV. The strollers are pushed in rows of five along the path from the crematoriums to the train station; the removal takes an hour."[26]

Although Czech states the facts without embellishment or commentary, one may surmise what went on. Probably some of those baby carriages had arrived with Hungarian Jewish mothers. Perhaps they had been permitted to bring that equipment along—all the way to the gas chambers—to prolong the deception that made murder simpler. True, sometimes children were born in Auschwitz-Birkenau; some even lived long enough to have numbers tattooed on their frail bodies. But most mothers and children, especially Jewish ones, could not keep their lives, let alone their strollers, in that place. Having no utility, mothers and children usually disappeared in fire and smoke. German efficiency, however, could not let their empty prams be wasted. They had value. So off the carriages went, first to "Canada" and then to the train station in the camp's official five-row formation. Probably they were headed to Germany, where there still were mothers, raising children for the Reich, who could use them.

Czech says simply that the strollers were pushed to the train station. The removal, she adds, took about an hour. Testimony from an Italian Jewish woman named Giuliana Tedeschi brings the stark brevity of Czech's account to life. Part of a transport of 935 Italian Jews who reached Auschwitz-Birkenau on April 10, 1944, she was one of the 80 women and 154 men who did not go directly to the gas.[27] Those women were tattooed with numbers ranging from 76776 to 76855. Tedeschi's was 76847.

Tedeschi was the wife of an architect and the mother of two children, but as a woman in Birkenau, she was alone, at least until she made friends with some of the other prisoners. Her moving memoir, *There Is a Place on Earth: A Woman in Birkenau*, not only recalls and records the horrors that surrounded her, but also repeatedly draws attention to those human relationships that helped her to survive. With a remarkably sensitive and insightful feminine touch she describes, for example, how much it meant to discover "Zilly's hand, a small, warm hand, modest and patient, which held mine in the evening, which pulled up the blankets around my shoulders, while a calm motherly voice whispered in my ear, 'Good night, dear—I have a daughter your age!'"[28]

A feeling and a need for connectedness, for relationships with others, for sisterhood, permeates Tedeschi's book.[29] Zilly comforted her when she was overcome by a wild desperation. Also there was Olga, the woman who became her soulmate:

> I came across Olga one day and we hid ourselves away together in a corner of the hut. I suddenly felt I would be able to speak to her and she would understand. . . . The huts disappeared, we forgot the barbed wire, and an unbounded liberty of spirit intoxicated us beyond any limit imposed by human bestiality. We decided to be friends.[30]

There were moments of reprieve, but in Birkenau friendship meant sharing and resisting the limits that were imposed by human bestiality. As Tedeschi would learn, that bestiality involved children's strollers.

There had been times in the camp when, at least comparatively speaking, Sundays were days of rest. During Tedeschi's time, however, that tradition had been abolished and special Sunday tasks were assigned. Sometimes she had to work along the railroad tracks that brought the Hungarian Jews to Birkenau during those late spring and summer days of 1944 when the Third Reich was collapsing but the gas chambers were operating at full and frenzied capacity. Close up, she saw the transports unload. She knew what the new arrivals did not, that death was imminent for all but a few. She also associates those Sundays with a smell:

> The whole camp was gradually pervaded by a smell that only we old hands could recognize, the smell that haunted our nostrils, that impregnated our clothing, a smell we tried in vain to escape by hiding away inside our bunks, that destroyed any hope of return, of seeing our countries and children again—the smell of burning human flesh.[31]

Sundays could make Tedeschi feel "morally destroyed, physically exhausted; the awareness of our impotence humiliated us, the instinct to rebel choked us."[32]

June 25, 1944, was a Sunday. That day Tedeschi was one of fifty women who turned right when she went through the gate from her part of the camp. Ordinarily her work column went left, toward Birkenau's main gate and the road that led beyond. But on this particular Sunday, the route was different. It led in the direction that most of the Hungarian Jews took only once. Up ahead, at the end of the rail spur, were Crematoriums II and III. It might be their turn, some of the women thought, but they were directed on, turned right again, and followed a path through the birch trees from which Birkenau takes its name.

The path led to another crematorium. "The women went in through the big door," Tedeschi recalls, "and stood in the hall."[33] There death met them—not directly but in the form of fifty empty baby carriages. The Germans ordered them to push these strollers to safekeeping. Tedeschi says the distance was two miles; Czech says the removal took about an hour. That was neither far nor long—even to push a child's stroller—on any normal Sunday, but for Giuliana Tedeschi, June 25, 1944, was a Sunday she would never forget, nor in all likelihood could any woman who experienced it as Tedeschi did.

Fear for their own lives "drained away," Tedeschi writes, "yet each face was stamped with a grimace of pain." And here is how her description of "this place on earth" continues:

> The strange procession moved forward: the mothers who had left children behind rested their hands on the push bars, instinctively feeling for the most natural position, promptly lifting the front wheels whenever they came to a bump. They saw gardens, avenues, rosy infants asleep in their carriages under vaporous pink and pale blue covers. The women who had lost children in the crematorium felt a physical longing to have a child at their breast, while seeing nothing but a long plume of smoke that drifted away to infinity. Those who hadn't had children pushed their carriages along clumsily and thought they would never have any, and thanked God. And all the empty baby carriages screeched, bounced, and banged into each other with the tired and desolate air of persecuted exiles.[34]

The accounts of Danuta Czech and Giuliana Tedeschi are close but not identical. Czech does not say who pushed the children's strollers. Tedeschi says that women were assigned the task and that her company's strollers came directly from a crematorium. Neither report mentions that men got stroller duty, but perhaps they did, for the fifty carriages mentioned in Tedeschi's report were by no means the only ones that reached Birkenau. More of them can be seen in Lili Meier's photographic *Auschwitz Album*, and there is at least one woman survivor whose testimony at the Nuremberg Trials said sometimes there were hundreds of children's carriages that arrived during a day's work in Birkenau.[35] If men got such assignments, their feelings would be no less important than those of Tedeschi and the other women she describes. But Tedeschi's report, a woman's testimony, is certainly one that needs to be heard and felt.

Was it an accident that women in Birkenau were assigned to move those baby carriages, a journey whose yearning and pain, grief and hopelessness, so far exceeded the hour and two miles that it took? It is hard to think so. Far more likely, the mentality that created Birkenau would have reasoned precisely: Who better than women—Jewish especially, mothers even—to move empty baby carriages from a crematorium to safekeeping for the Reich? That possibility was a real limit imposed on Tedeschi and her sisters by human bestiality.

The Holocaust leaves behind heartbreaking memories and images—so many they cannot be counted. But none symbolizes more poignantly the plight of women during the Holocaust than the one offered by Giuliana Tedeschi: a Jewish woman prisoner pushing an empty baby carriage in Birkenau. In that vision, the unrelentingly cruel calculation of the Final Solution's impact on women—theft, enslavement, and murder—is reflected in ways that no words can express, let alone forgive and redeem.

"There is a place on earth," Tedeschi's memoir begins, "a desolate heath, where the shadows of the dead are multitudes, where the living are dead, where there is only death, hate, and pain."[36] Birkenau stood in the very heart of Western civilization, within easy reach of the great universities, cathedrals, and institutions of European culture. In that "place on earth," so many of Western culture's humanizing promises failed. "Birkenau," says Tedeschi, "existed to suffocate hope and annihilate logic, to provoke madness and death."[37]

To remember that "there is a place on earth," to excavate the scraps of time that remain in the ruins of memory, even to feel what we hear from the particular voices of women in the Holocaust—none of this can restore what was lost. Yet Gertrud Kolmar's question remains: "You hear me speak. But do you hear me feel?" If we hear that question well, it should beckon us to be suspicious of generalities that equalize experience too much. It should make us aware that neutralizing differences can obscure too much. Hearing Gertrud Kolmar's question well should lead to our keeping attention focused on the Holocaust's particularity, which entails never overlooking or underestimating the importance of the fact that the Holocaust's history—and its legacies and lessons, whatever they may be—are unavoidably about men and women, boys and girls, who were not so different from us.

Gabriel Schoenfeld was right when he wrote that "unresolved issues—historical, political, moral and theological—still swirl around the Holocaust, and studying them remains a task of great importance." How that work is done determines the quality of owning the Holocaust, and the quality of Holocaust politics hangs in the balance.

Chapter Two

What Can and Cannot Be Said about the Holocaust?

> The debate is blurred by the vagueness of the idea of an episode being unique. Every event is in some ways unique and in other ways not.
>
> Jonathan Glover,
> *Humanity: A Moral History*
> *of the Twentieth Century*

Is the Holocaust unique? Can it be compared to other events? Is it possible to comprehend the Holocaust? Few disputes in Holocaust politics are separable from those questions. One reason is that words such as *uniqueness*, *comparison*, and *comprehension* are not free of ambiguity.

Why should the Holocaust receive special attention? Or, to pose another question, why should the United States have a federally funded Holocaust museum? The answers depend on what people think about the Holocaust's uniqueness and the possibility of comparing other events with the Holocaust. Should education about the Holocaust be mandated in schools? What interpretation of the Holocaust should a school's curriculum emphasize? The responses will reflect views about our ability to comprehend the event itself. Who gets to decide such matters, including the appointment of personnel to administer the policies that emerge? Typically, the replies pivot around power equations whose factors include positions that people take on the Holocaust's uniqueness, its comparability to other events, and our ability to comprehend Holocaust history.

Often these debates take place in scholarly settings, but by no means are the disputes merely academic. They affect the allocation of funds, how institutional policies are established and governed, and who makes decisions. The effects are felt locally, nationally, and even internationally. Therefore, the goal of this chapter is to consider what can and cannot be said about the Holocaust by focusing on issues about uniqueness, comparability, and comprehension. The purpose is not to argue for one perspective that everyone ought to accept. That aim would be unrealistic, even undesirable, for there is much that remains contentious and needs to be discussed in these areas. Instead, the objective is to mark some boundaries for the debates that should be part of a worthwhile Holocaust politics. Primarily, these boundaries are ethical. They involve attitudes about inquiry, dispositions about dialogue, that emphasize the importance of deepened sensitivity as people—Jews and non-Jews alike—contend with the Holocaust's particularity and its universal significance as well.

Comparability and Singularity

Some philosophical groundwork is important for this chapter. First, historical events depend on human existence, action, and awareness. In addition, historical events are singular; two can never be the same. It is also true that historical events exist neither in isolation nor in a vacuum. The existence of a historical event requires a focusing of attention so that particular features in the flow of human experience stand out against a background of other happenings. The Holocaust is no exception. It took place within human history; it emerged from a social, historical context. Its implications may be metaphysical and thus not entirely confined to history because they are ethical, theological, and cosmological, but those implications are rooted in the soil of history nonetheless.

Although every historical event is singular, all of them have features in common. Otherwise no historical event could be distinguished from any other, and history as we know it would not exist. Human history's existence depends on the ability of consciousness to compare. Absent comparison, moreover, our human form of consciousness would scarcely be conceivable, for our experiences of perception, judgment, knowledge, truth, and falsity all depend on discrimination that is able to say *this* is different from *that* and *now* is not the same as *then*. Difference, however, is not sheer difference. Difference depends on relationships. Without relationships there can be no singularity, at least none that is discernible.

The existence of any historical event depends on the existence of others. As a result, any historical event can be compared to any other, but the verb *compare* deserves close attention. It has two meanings that are crucial in Holocaust politics. On the one hand, to compare means to examine two things or more. This examining focuses on similarities and differences. With historical events, the goal of comparison includes comprehending as best one can what happened here or there, what took place now or then. A second meaning of *compare*, however, points in a related but not identical direction. Already assuming that two things or more can be examined for similarity and difference, this second meaning *likens* two things or more. This meaning of comparison tends to emphasize similarity more than difference, at least with respect to the features that are most of interest when a comparison is made. Comparison may be weaker or stronger as far as *liken* is concerned, but taken as far as *liken* can go, comparing two things or more could suggest equating them, taking them—at least in some crucial ways—to be equivalent.

Even in the case of the Holocaust, the first meaning of *compare*—examining two things or more for similarity and difference—would seem to be as unobjectionable as it is inescapable One cannot say anything about the Holocaust without implying that this event is different from other events, which is to say that it also bears some similarity to other events or else it could not be an event at all. If there are writers who utterly deny that the Holocaust is in any way comparable to other events, that judgment can make sense only as rhetoric that in the strongest way possible resists comparison in the form of likening.

From time to time, Holocaust survivor Elie Wiesel stresses that the Holocaust "can be compared to no other event," or that the Holocaust goes beyond or transcends history.[1] Wiesel's critics attack him for removing the Holocaust from history and for mystifying it because, in his judgment, the event ultimately eludes final human comprehension. I do not share these critics' reading of Wiesel. I interpret him to mean that the Holocaust is so different from other events that it cannot be *likened* to—and definitely not equated with—them without distortion, trivialization, or falsification. If my reading of Wiesel is correct, his position may still be arguable, but it does not make his view nonsensical.

As for Wiesel's belief that the Holocaust goes beyond or transcends history, which entails that this event ultimately eludes final human comprehension and thus reduces us to silence, that position is far from nonsensical too. It need not be read as denying either that the Holocaust is thoroughly a historical event or that we can comprehend a great deal about the Holocaust. Nevertheless, Wiesel may be correct that our comprehension of the Holocaust has serious limits, partly because of our finite and fallible human capacities and partly because the event raises questions and possesses implications that are more than history can contain. To the latter points I will soon return, but for now the point to stress is that Holocaust politics heats up just to the degree that comparison involves likening and especially the extreme move of equating the Holocaust with other events or vice versa.[2]

To liken the Holocaust to other events, or other events to it, is to enter a minefield because the moral, political, rhetorical, emotional, and even financial stakes can be very high. A focus on the United States, to cite only one area, produces instructive examples of provocative questions that are loaded with implications of that kind. Why, some critics ask, has the United States government provided a site and funding to memorialize the Holocaust when no similar initiative has occurred to deal with the American history of slavery and racism? Of course, people typically reserve memorialization for the triumphs they achieve, not for the atrocities they inflict, but that reasoning does more to intensify the question than to put it to rest. Why, other critics wonder, has the United

States taken so many steps to recognize the Holocaust, but nothing comparable has transpired with regard to the Armenian genocide, let alone with regard to the genocidal (some would say) treatment of Native Americans in centuries past?[3] Still other skeptics inquire, If United States government officials have taken leading roles to ensure that Holocaust survivors and their families receive reparations and restitution from institutions and governments that bear responsibility for their abuse and their relatives' deaths, then what about situations closer to home and in our own history that may place similar debts on the doorsteps of institutions that exploited blacks and indigenous people on American ground?[4] Versions of these questions linger in the United States. At the end of the day, cannot other events be compared with—likened to—the Holocaust? What is so singular, so special, about it?

Those criticisms draw responses that join key issues in Holocaust politics. Basically, the responses affirm that the Holocaust *is* special. It deserves recognition accordingly, not to the exclusion of other concerns necessarily but distinctive acknowledgment nonetheless. One intriguing factor is that the credibility of these replies to criticism depends on careful comparison. Singularity in the sense of uniqueness that calls out for special attention is not self-evident where historical events are concerned, nor can that status be conferred legitimately by pronouncement or fiat. The sifting of evidence, the careful examining of similarity and difference, the deliberate forming of considered judgment—these are the ingredients that set forth the case for documenting the Holocaust's claim to uniqueness and for evaluating the implications that follow if the case is sound or falls short.

The Ethics of Uniqueness

No issue has dominated Holocaust politics more than the debate about the Holocaust's uniqueness. Reasons for the persistence of that issue include the point that Jonathan Glover underscores in this chapter's epigraph.[5] As Glover implies, there is unlikely to be universal agreement about how events are or are not "unique." That fact suggests that the concept of uniqueness is too fuzzy to carry the weight of the Holocaust that is often put upon it. Be that as it may, closure on the question of the Holocaust's uniqueness—no matter how extensive the scholarship, to say nothing of what future events might produce—should not be expected. Thus, it is important to consider Gavriel D. Rosenfeld's observation that the Holocaust uniqueness debate raises "important questions concerning the utility of the uniqueness concept."[6] Rosenfeld's observation appears at the end of his descriptive overview of the uniqueness debate. He approaches but does not enlarge what I shall call the ethics of uniqueness, which is a topic that deserves consideration if Holocaust politics is to be more constructive and less contentious in controversy that eludes closure.

As I understand the Holocaust, it was the systematic, state-organized persecution and murder of nearly six million Jews by Nazi Germany and its collaborators.[7] They slaughtered two-thirds of Europe's Jews and one-third of the world's Jewish population. In addition, Nazi Germany's genocidal policies destroyed millions of other defenseless people, including Roma and Sinti (Gypsies), Polish citizens and Soviet prisoners of war, as well as homosexuals, the handicapped, Jehovah's Witnesses, and other political and religious dissidents within Germany itself.

At least four terms name this immense tragedy. Masters of euphemistic language, the Nazis spoke of *die Endlösung*, "the Final Solution" of their so-called Jewish question. In the early 1940s, Eastern European Jews turned to Jewish scripture and used a Yiddish word, *Churb'n*, which means "destruction," or the Hebrew term *Shoah*, which means "catastrophe," to name the disaster confronting their people.

Although *Shoah* is used widely in Israel and the official remembrance day for the Holocaust is called *Yom Hashoah*, *Holocaust*, a term that began to achieve prominence in the 1950s, still remains the most common name. Its diverse sources include derivation from the Septuagint, an ancient Greek translation of the Hebrew Bible, which employs *holokauston* for the Hebrew *olah*. Those biblical words refer to a completely consumed burnt offering. While the destruction perpetrated by Nazi Germany must be named lest it be forgotten, the problematic religious connotations surrounding the term *Holocaust* suggest that no name can do it justice.[8]

Genocide swirls through the Holocaust uniqueness debate. As I understand genocide, it involves state-organized destruction of a people because of what the political scientist R. J. Rummel calls "their indelible group membership (race, ethnicity, religion, language)."[9] Nazi Germany's destruction of European Jewry was genocide or nothing could be. But what of the Holocaust's uniqueness?

Arguments for the Holocaust's uniqueness do not depend primarily on the number of Jewish victims or the way in which they were killed. Rather, as Steven

T. Katz maintains, the uniqueness claim rests on "the fact that never before has a state set out, as a matter of intentional principle and actualized policy, to annihilate physically every man, woman, and child belonging to a specific people. . . . Only in the case of Jewry under the Third Reich was such all-inclusive, non-compromising, unmitigated murder intended."[10]

The Nazis intended to destroy all Jews. That aim was neither restricted to specific territory nor based primarily on what Jews had done. Instead, the Nazis' apocalyptic ideology defined Jews to be so threatening, so racially inferior and yet so globally conspiratorial, that their existence had to be eliminated root and branch. Simply to be born a Jew sufficed to give one a Nazi death sentence, and in unprecedented ways killing centers at places such as Treblinka and Auschwitz-Birkenau were established to carry it out. While I find this analysis persuasive, and thus am a defender of what Glover calls the "distinctive darkness" of the Holocaust or what historian Yehuda Bauer calls its "unprecedentedness," I do not devote my life to study of the Holocaust primarily because of its purported uniqueness.[11] One of a kind or not, the Holocaust remains immensely important, so much so that the reasons for studying it ought not to hinge on something as ambiguous as its uniqueness. Moreover, there is no doubt about it: The uniqueness debate does leave us in ambiguous territory.

Some scholars contend, for example, that Nazi Germany's targeting of the Sinti and Roma did not differ substantially from the fate intended for the Jews. Others fear that the uniqueness claim banishes other genocides to undeserved second-class status. How those disagreements will continue to unfold remains to be seen, but I believe that the debate ought to be contextualized by ethical considerations more than it has been to date. We need to ask, What is the most important issue at stake in our consideration of the Holocaust and genocide? Surely it cannot simply be uniqueness issues or even exact historical accuracy, crucial though such accuracy is, for historical understanding is scarcely an end in itself. Historical study presupposes values that are not contained in historical study alone. Intentionally or unintentionally, it functions in ways that affect the present and the future. As Elie Wiesel so often suggests, we remember not only for the dead but perhaps even more for the living. To remember *for* implies "on behalf of" and "for the sake of." Such remembering serves goals and perceived goods that go beyond the remembering itself.

Any debate about the Holocaust's uniqueness or about the relation of the Holocaust to other genocides is worthwhile just to the extent that it underscores *ethical reasons* as the most important ones for studying these dark chapters in human history. Historian Yehuda Bauer, a defender of the Holocaust's uniqueness, offers a proper qualifying reminder along these lines: "Events happen because they are possible. If they were possible once, they are possible again. In that sense, the Holocaust is not unique, but a warning for the future."[12]

To elaborate the key point—the most important reasons for studying the Holocaust and genocide are ethical—I want to step back from encountering the uniqueness debate directly and consider instead what education about the Holocaust and genocide involves. Doing so will then help to focus further the ethics of uniqueness.

A Box of Memories

Charlotte Delbo was not Jewish, but her arrest for resisting the Nazi occupation of her native France made her experience the Holocaust when she was deported to Auschwitz in January 1943. Delbo survived the Nazi onslaught. In 1946, she began to write the trilogy that came to be called *Auschwitz and After*. Her work's anguished visual descriptions, profound reflections on memory, and diverse writing styles make it an unrivaled Holocaust testimony. As the trilogy draws to a close, Delbo writes, "I do not know / if you can still / make something of me / If you have the courage to try . . ."[13] She contextualizes those words in two ways that have special significance as we consider education about the Holocaust and genocide—including issues about the ethics of uniqueness—in the twenty-first century. First, Delbo stresses that her experience in Auschwitz and then in the Nazi concentration camp at Ravensbrück gave her what she called "useless knowledge," a concept to which I shall return later in this chapter. Second, just before the lines I have quoted from *Auschwitz and After*, Delbo remembers Françoise, one of the French women who survived Auschwitz with her. Memory made Françoise mourn. When she thought of the waste and devastation she had experienced and could not forget, the permanently scarring "useless knowledge" it involved, Françoise insisted that the advice one often hears (start over, begin again, put the past behind you) rings hollow as it mocks what cannot be forgotten. "Make one's life over," Françoise protested, "what an expression . . ."[14]

Françoise was not the only survivor on Delbo's mind in *Auschwitz and After*. She had not forgotten Poupette, Marie-Louis, Ida, and many others who were with her in the camps. She could also not forget how Auschwitz forever divided, besieged, and diminished her own life. Thus, as though she were speaking for her survivor friends, as well as for herself, Delbo wondered "if you can still / make something of me."

To the best of my knowledge, Delbo did not participate in debates about the Holocaust's uniqueness. I expect she would have found them quite beside the point. Yet issues about the ethics of uniqueness are not far removed from her reflection, because the uniqueness debate needs to confront a challenge that Delbo poses: What can and cannot be done with the Holocaust? What must and must not be made of that catastrophe? If we have the courage to study, research, and teach about the Holocaust and other genocides, even to try to learn from them, what awareness should that courage embody, what questions must it raise, what pitfalls does it need to avoid?

Toward the end of a recent Holocaust course, my students and I studied Delbo's trilogy. They also wrote papers about that book. The one submitted by an art major named Sarah Yates was distinctive. Inspired by Delbo's reflection that she has two faces (one ruined, another full of light), Sarah's "paper" consisted of a handsome oak box, dark-stained and lacquered. The accompanying written text noted that the box could be "something one might set on a coffee table next to a plate of cookies or a vase of tulips." Like the appearance of Delbo's post-Holocaust life, it could seem to be normal and even decorative. However, Sarah went on to say, "when opened, the box reveals its other 'face,'" an interior of memory fragments, which are not "normal," let alone decorative.

Inside Sarah's "Box of Memories," as she called her project, there were carefully crafted wooden puzzle pieces. Some fit together; others did not. Each piece was delicately inscribed on both sides. The inscriptions were words not only from Charlotte Delbo but also from Primo Levi, Gerda Weissmann Klein, Dr. Elchanan Elkes, Raul Hilberg, and other Holocaust-related writers we had read. Their words did not fit together easily, anymore than the puzzle pieces themselves, but Sarah's advice was to "dump the pieces out onto your floor or your desk, and then try making and 'reading' different arrangements." Each time the configuration, the narratives, meanings, and comparisons between them would change, and yet they would not be entirely different. The fragments were real. Many things could be done with them, but not anything or everything, at least not if one respected the memories the box contained.

Doing as Sarah instructed, I observed—but not closely enough—that the "Box of Memories" was layered. Deep down, covering what turned out to be a face painted at the bottom of the box, there were levels where the puzzle pieces did fit together in a recognizable way that just matched the box's interior. Before I knew it, the fragments were out of the box, and I was arranging them to see what the combinations could be. But when the time came to put the pieces back in the box, I discovered that I could not make them fit.

Without replacing the bottom layers as Sarah had originally arranged them, the pieces would not go back into the box in a way that permitted its lid to be closed. Sarah had color-coded the edges of the bottom layers so she could remember how they went together, but even then, she confessed, closing the "Box of Memories" was hard to do. Later, when Sarah shared the project with her classmates during a period at the end of the semester when the students reported about work they had been doing, a few of the carefully carved memory fragments disappeared. Regretting their loss, Sarah made others, not to replace the irreplaceable but to fill the "Box of Memories" again so that it could not easily be closed.

Experience with Delbo's writing and Sarah's reflection on it makes two clusters of suggestions about the overall direction of Holocaust and genocide studies and, in particular, the ethics of uniqueness in the twenty-first century. First, just as is true of the magnitude of these events themselves, study and research about the Holocaust and genocide are increasingly overwhelming tasks. They will be no less so in the future because the aspects we have to study are not color-coded and they do not and will not all fit neatly into boxes of memory, let alone into the departments and compartments of scholarship—including definitions and debates about uniqueness.

It is not just that whole fields of scholarly inquiry scarcely imagined twenty, ten, or even five years ago have emerged and loom large. Where the Holocaust alone is involved one thinks of restitution issues, new archival materials, concerns about women, and renewed controversy about the Vatican and Pope Pius XII, to name just a few.[15] Each genocide will entail its own expanded fields of inquiry as study proceeds. In addition, the issue also involves different ways in which scholarly investigation is carried on. It takes place not just in archives and libraries, not just in the conventional forms of lecturing, writing, and publishing, but also electronically through e-mail networks and the Internet, as well as through oral history and the breaking of daily news. Given the magnitude of the events under study, the fact that no one can keep up with all that is going on in Holocaust and genocide studies is fitting, but the realization is disorienting nonetheless and especially as we think of Delbo's challenge: "I do not know / if you can still / make something of me / If you have the courage to try . . ."

Second, because Holocaust and genocide studies will overwhelm anyone who pursues that inquiry, it will take courage to direct these studies well. Certainly it is important to defend the Holocaust's particularity—the same is true of every genocide—so that these disasters are not universalized to the point of abstraction and banality. The ethics of uniqueness requires us never to forget that it is always particular people who are targeted and that they are targeted by specific people and powers. The ethics of uniqueness also requires us to remember that particularity is no guarantee against becoming a victim or a perpetrator, a point that has led Yehuda Bauer to make three additions to the biblical Ten Commandments: Thou shalt not be a perpetrator. Thou shalt not be a victim. Thou shalt not be a bystander.[16] But given these insights, how important is it to continue the debate about the Holocaust's uniqueness?

Placing the Holocaust in History

With that question in mind, I asked Sarah Yates and her classmates what they thought about six topics: (1) Why should the Holocaust be studied? (2) How should the Holocaust be investigated or taught? (3) What goals should be emphasized in teaching and learning about the Holocaust? (4) What criteria should be used to judge whether study and teaching about the Holocaust are successful? (5) What question(s) about the Holocaust remain most on your mind as our study draws to a close? (6) How do you think study about and research on the Holocaust might change, or should change, in the future? What do we need to know about the Holocaust that we seem not to know?

Here are some of the things that my students said. I share them not because the students are experts in the field but because they are thoughtful amateurs whose intuitions, fallible though they are, contain valuable reminders. The students' intuitions do so, I believe, because of the ways in which they avoid the uniqueness debate while still keeping attention focused on the particularity of the Holocaust and genocide.

The question "Why should the Holocaust be studied?" elicited responses that overlapped with "What goals should be emphasized in teaching and learning about the Holocaust?" With respect to the former, the responses included: We should study to understand, to learn, to prevent, for the sake of the future, to remember and honor those who were victimized. Other responses said that we should study the Holocaust because this event is a defining moment, because of the extreme evil it involved, and "because it happened." The students were clearly concerned about the Holocaust's particularity. They also understood something about the uniqueness debate, but this debate rarely, if ever, became their central concern because they were overwhelmingly preoccupied with the implications of the Holocaust for their own lives.

As for the goals that should be emphasized, there were two that came out repeatedly. One goal in teaching and learning about the Holocaust should be *understanding* how and why it happened. The other goal should be *prevention*. When it came to the question about how the Holocaust should be studied, the following themes were most pronounced: There should be historical objectivity, but facts alone are not enough; "all sides" should be explored, and multiple approaches are required; the importance of firsthand reports (especially from survivors) is crucial. When the students emphasized that "all sides" should be studied, they were neither relativizing nor universalizing the Holocaust. At least after a few weeks of study, they were gripped by the particularity and specificity of the Holocaust's history. That focus was what underwrote their insistence that the actions of perpetrators, victims, bystanders, neighbors, rescuers, and people active in resistance all had to be taken into account. The reasons for taking all of them into account was partly because the history could only be adequately encountered by doing so, but also because such an accounting was essential for the students' reflection about how their own lives ought to be lived.

The responses to the question about criteria for successful teaching about the Holocaust were the most tentative. Several said they were not sure there could be criteria. Others stressed greater understanding of the history. Still others said that measures of success might include never forgetting the Holocaust, the elimination of Holocaust denial, greater tolerance, and prevention of related disasters. One of the most focused and succinct responses said success would depend on answers to three questions: Has one learned about what happened? Has one been affected (emotionally, spiritually) by the teaching? Has one wrestled deeply with and been disturbed by the content of the study?

There were variations on the theme concerning lingering questions, but one student spoke for several others by saying that the key question was "how to place the Holocaust in history." That comment suggested not only the importance of continued searching for detail and the relation of one event to another, including how to place the Holocaust in relation to other genocides, but also larger issues that are not matters of history alone, a factor that one student underscored by asking, "What now? What about outside the classroom? What should I do with what I learned?" These questions were not a naive request for "lessons of the Holocaust," for these students were acquainted with what Charlotte Delbo meant when she spoke of "useless knowledge." The student's questions remain, and they are questions that ask why, at the end of the day, one should care so much that the history of the Holocaust and genocide is studied, researched, and taught. Why, in particular, should non-Jews (most of my Holocaust students are not Jewish) as well as Jews care that memory of the Holocaust is institutionalized and preserved?

Even when, indeed especially when, differences of opinion exist about such issues, clarity about them seems important because without such clarity it is not likely that very many people will continue serious study of the Holocaust. Some clarity about those issues may be found by noting what some of these "informed amateurs" had to say when the question was "How do you think study about and research on the Holocaust might change, or should change, in the future? What do we need to know about the Holocaust that we seem not to know?"

First, there was widespread concern that study and research will change because, as one student put it, "all the survivors will soon be dead and so will most others who have a vivid memory of that time." In a similar vein, another student was not entirely off the mark when she said, "soon all we will have left are books about the Holocaust." And, she might have added, quite a few of those books will contain lots of arguments about the Holocaust's uniqueness. If I read accurately between the lines, these student concerns imply worry that, as the Holocaust and perhaps other twentieth-century instances of genocide recede further into the past, they will become more and more a matter of purely historical interest and investigation. Continued debate about the Holocaust's uniqueness, ironically, could contribute to that result. It could become a largely scholastic argument that keeps swirling around itself. Such an outcome could make Holocaust and genocide studies less and less significant for the present and the future unless the historical investigation is carried on in tandem with an ongoing emphasis and evaluation of the political, ethical, and religious implications of the Holocaust and genocide.

Sarah Yates had something like this in mind, I believe, when she wrote, "I think as the last living survivors pass away, it will become important to 'let the Holocaust in.' If it is taught and [researched] with more detachment, as is the tendency with receding history, a crucial element will be lost. People must honestly, carefully, and humbly pick up the fragile pieces. They must never be scattered." Too much debate by proponents and opponents of the thesis that the Holocaust is unique fails to pick up the fragile pieces humbly. Instead, the desire is to win an argument. True, the arguments are important because they involve historical accuracy and the integrity of the particularity of events. But what can be lost—the scattering of the pieces that Sarah deplored—is an emphasis on why the historical accuracy and the integrity of the particularity are so crucial: They help us to discern what we ought to do in the present and the future, which means that the "winning" of arguments about uniqueness takes a distant second place to the task of trying to forestall further genocidal wasting of human life in years to come.

Whatever the virtues that study of the Holocaust and genocide involve and produce, such study is not an end in itself. Even more so that principle applies to uniqueness debates. Those debates may not be incompatible with an intensification of moral concern, but their content and impact do not seem to move primarily in that direction. Thus, they bear watching and need evaluating from a moral perspective that asks, How do these debates contribute to practically visible moral sensitivity? To the extent that these debates do not make such a contribution, it would be well to call them off.

"I do not know," wrote Charlotte Delbo, "if you can still make something of me / If you have the courage to try . . ." As the twenty-first century develops, the challenge we face in thinking about uniqueness debates in particular and the direction of Holocaust and genocide studies in general is the following: *We should avoid the ultimate irony that would result if Holocaust and genocide studies—including debates about uniqueness—become a kind of useless knowledge.* That fate is likely to be avoided only if the direction of Holocaust and genocide studies in the twenty-first century is oriented by increasingly articulated ethical responses to the question: Why do research, study, and teach about the Holocaust and genocide? Or, in words that Charlotte Delbo wrote in *Auschwitz and After*, words that epitomize the ethics of uniqueness, words that every participant in Holocaust politics would do well to inscribe where they can be seen each day one works: "I beg you / do something / learn a dance step / something to justify your existence / something that gives you the right / to be dressed in your skin in your body hair / learn to walk and to laugh / because it would be too senseless / after all / for so many to have died / while you live / doing nothing with your life."[17]

A Man to Remember

We should study the Holocaust, one of my students said, because it happened. What did happen during that event? Many volumes exist to answer that question, but they are not entirely successful, either individually or collectively, for finding out what happened turns out to be an inquiry without end. The inquiry has that quality because the detail of the Holocaust's history is so vast and also because the questions raised by that detail—especially questions that ask how and why did this happen and not that—go on and on in ways that history alone cannot resolve. One result is that Holocaust politics often pivots around competing and conflicting historical interpretations, which include differences about the degree of explanation and comprehension our accounts of the Holocaust can have. Nothing in Holocaust history better illustrates the problems that attend comprehending the Holocaust than the case of Adolf Hitler himself, the individual who stood at the center of the Holocaust's distinctive destruction. If Hitler cannot be comprehended, what about the Holocaust?

On Saturday morning, June 26, 1999, the *New York Times*, the *Washington Post*, and the *Los Angeles Times* made a startling announcement: The Huntington Library in San Marino, California, had long possessed but not publicized historic documents stored there since General George S. Patton donated them in 1945.[18] Those documents included the original manuscripts of the antisemitic Nuremberg Laws. Enacted by Nazi Germany on September 15, 1935, they defined conditions for citizenship, announced rules to protect "German blood and honor," and established race as the nation's fundamental legal principle. They were essential preludes for the Holocaust.

What made the Huntington's Nuremberg documents "original" was not so much the German typewriting or their red swastika seals but the signatures from Nazi officials. First and foremost, Adolf Hitler's made those ordinary-looking typescripts lethal during the Nazi period and then, nearly sixty-five years later, hurled the documents and their Huntington guardians into news headlines.

Tremors caused by Parkinson's disease eventually turned Adolf Hitler's handwriting into a scribble but arguably not before the twentieth century was marked by his "signature" more than any other. Thus, it is worth noting that, even as news broke about the Huntington's Nuremberg documents, *Time* magazine conducted a year-long Internet poll to register public opinion about the Person of the Century. Since the 1930s, *Time* has named a Person of the Year, but this time the stakes were higher. The Person of the Century, *Time* explained, would be the one "who, for better or worse, most influenced the course of history over the past 100 years."

Time's editors reserved the right to make the final decision. After considering the public's vote, they announced their choice in December 1999. It was the brilliant scientist Albert Einstein, a Jewish refugee from Hitler's Germany, whose theoretical work changed the ways we think and immensely expanded the horizons of human action.[19] One of Einstein's main competitors for *Time's* Person of the Century title (the field included nominees such as V. I. Lenin, Winston Churchill, David Ben-Gurion, Martin Luther King, Jr., and Pope John Paul II) was Hitler, whose political work also changed—in a very different way—the ways we think and act. Beyond calling him "the century's greatest threat to democracy," the capsule description that headed *Time's* nominations asserted that Hitler "redefined the meaning of evil forever."

The *Time* web site's information about Hitler included the cover story from its issue of January 2, 1939, which hailed him as the Man of 1938. *Time* gave Hitler credit for lifting Germany to unanticipated power in less than six years. "His was no ordinary dictatorship," the cover story said, "but rather one of great energy and magnificent planning." On the whole, however, *Time's* story was ominous. Anticipating its web site's 1999 commentary, *Time* found that the most significant fact about Hitler in 1938 was his becoming "the greatest threatening force that the democratic, free-dom-loving world faces today." The 1939 cover story said nothing explicitly about the November 1938 pogrom (*Kristallnacht*) that savaged Jews in Germany and Austria, but, noting Hitler's racist antisemitism, it did state that Germany's Jews "have been tortured physically, robbed of homes and properties, denied a chance to earn a living, chased off the streets." *Time*'s understated conclusion added that "the Man of 1938 may make 1939 a year to be remembered."

Hitler did indeed make 1939 a year to be remembered. One result is that few people continue to command historians' attention more than the Nazi dictator. Biographers, in particular, keep Hitler in view, a fact illustrated at the turn of a new century in major studies produced by Ron Rosenbaum, Fritz Redlich, Brigitte Hamann, and Ian Kershaw. Like *Time*'s web site, their books about Hitler include photographs. When it comes to comprehending the Holocaust, none of those photos is more puzzling than one that was taken when Hitler was probably less than two years old. It appears, for example, on the title page of Rosenbaum's *Explaining Hitler*, a popular assessment of the main scholarly attempts to fathom how Hitler became *Hitler*. Unavoidably drawn to the child's eyes—the title page centers them—Rosenbaum's readers also see the words *Explaining Hitler* and the book's subtitle, *The Search for the Origins of His Evil*. Rosenbaum's title and Hitler's picture collide. Somehow the normal-looking infant in the photo became the one who signed the Nuremberg Laws, the *Führer* who launched World War II and the Holocaust, and the man who, in *Time*'s estimate, redefined forever what evil means.

Milton Himmelfarb plays an important cameo role in Rosenbaum's fascinating book. In March 1984, Himmelfarb published "No Hitler, No Holocaust," an essay in which he contended that the decision to annihilate European Jewry was Adolf Hitler's alone, a view that has not been shared by every Holocaust scholar. Far from being impelled by historical, political, or cultural forces to murder the European Jews, Himmelfarb wrote, Hitler wanted and chose to annihilate them. More than anything else, links between Hitler and the Holocaust explain why, as Rosenbaum says, "an enormous amount has been written" about him "but little has been *settled*."[20] Persuaded by much of Himmelfarb's position, Rosenbaum keeps returning to it but also understands that, while Himmelfarb's position may explain a good deal about the Holocaust, it does not explain Hitler, at least not completely. How badly did Hitler want to destroy the Jews? When did he decide to do so? Even more basically, what made Hitler *Hitler?* Scholars have answered such questions differently, which makes the *real* Hitler elusive and the puzzles about him persistent. To a considerable degree, comprehension of the Holocaust hangs in the balance.

Hitler's baby picture raises a thousand questions that words must try to answer but perhaps never can. Starting his book with that tension-filled juxtaposition, Rosenbaum ends on a related point more than four hundred pages later. His concluding acknowledgments express special gratitude to the scholars and writers who granted him interviews. Rosenbaum honors their courageous and dedicated pursuit of what he knowingly calls "the impossible challenge of explaining Hitler."[21] A seasoned scholar-journalist, Rosenbaum showed his own courage and dedication in writing this book, which was more than ten years in the making. He tracked down people who knew Hitler and got that dwindling number to share what they remembered. He traveled to obscure archives and located long-forgotten files that shed new light on Hitler research. He journeyed to remote Austrian sites in search of details about Hitler's ancestry and

youth. All the while he read voraciously and inter-
viewed dozens of the most influential biographers,
historians, philosophers, and theologians who have
faced the challenge of bridging the abyss between
baby Adolf and Auschwitz Hitler.

Rosenbaum reports the findings of those interpreters, but how he does so makes his book much more
than a summary of other people's views. Rosenbaum's
meetings with the Hitler scholars are charged with his
penetrating questions, his insightful observations that
complicate matters for all the writers he encounters,
and his skeptical refusal to be overly impressed by the
authority of any of the experts he meets. More specifically, Rosenbaum became intrigued by what he identifies as the "wishes and longings, the subtexts and
agendas of Hitler explanations."[22]

When it comes to explaining Hitler, Rosenbaum
asks, what do people want and why? How are the
sometimes radical differences in interpretation best
understood? What would it mean if Hitler could be
explained definitively, or if he cannot? Such questions
concentrated Rosenbaum's attention as he met the
major Hitler interpreters and then as he reflected
deeply about what his investigations revealed. Thus,
as the reader travels with him, Rosenbaum shows the
strengths and weaknesses in the various Hitler "explanations." He finds the right questions to ask each text
he studies, every scholar he meets, and even any
insight that more or less persuades him. While learning much about Hitler and the scholarship about him,
one becomes a partner in Rosenbaum's inquiry, which
entails coming to see that the challenge of "explaining" Hitler may be impossible. Even that conclusion,
however, is driven home in Rosenbaum's distinctively
inquisitive way. His reasons for thinking that it may be

impossible to explain Hitler—and the implications that follow—are among his most important findings.

At the outset, Rosenbaum pays tribute to largely forgotten German journalists who reported and opposed Hitler's rise to power. These anti-Hitler journalists—one named Fritz Gerlich gets Rosenbaum's special admiration—wrote for the *Munich Post* and *Der Gerade Weg* (The right way or straight path). Before the Nazis brutally shut them down (Gerlich was sent to Dachau and then murdered in June 1934) these courageous writers sensed Hitler's evil qualities and did their best, even after Hitler took power on January 30, 1933, to expose the blackmail and murder perpetrated by Hitler and the Nazis. The German journalists planted seeds of suspicion about Hitler's sexual inclinations to subvert the deceptive wholesomeness of the images that Nazi propaganda purveyed. They cast doubt on Hitler's ethnic origins and even his physical appearance to expose the irrationality of his racism and antisemitism. As soon as he could, Hitler ruthlessly crushed their dissent.

These anti-Hitler journalists wanted to stop Hitler more than explain him, but Rosenbaum suggests that they set the stage for post-Holocaust explanations. Probing Hitler's background, they laid the groundwork for a key question in Hitler scholarship: Do Hitler's origins—psychological, familial, sociopolitical—explain him? Disclosing his corrupt and murderous deeds, they began to focus on whether Hitler was a cynical political opportunist or an "idealist" who thought that his policies, however deadly, were justified by the "right" and "good" ends they supposedly served. Emphasizing the virulence of his racism and antisemitism, the German journalists paved the way for explorations of Hitler's intentionality toward the

Jews and, in particular, whether his intentions were genocidal before he came to power or only afterward. The early anti-Hitler journalists had little doubt that Hitler did evil deeds and even that he was an evil man. Thus, they initiated inquiry about how Hitler's evil ought to be understood: Should Hitler be counted as an "ordinary man" or as an exception, an embodiment of demonically destructive power?

Rosenbaum shows that advocates for all of these positions—and many more—can be found among the leading scholars who have tried to explain Hitler. Biographer Hugh Trevor-Roper, for example, thinks that Hitler, thoroughly misguided though he was, sincerely believed in his antisemitism and thought that the destruction of the Jews was the right thing to do. Alan Bullock, another biographer, and philosopher Emil Fackenheim disagree with Trevor-Roper, finding Hitler to be a cynical political opportunist who used antisemitism for his own advancement. The philosopher Berel Lang thinks that neither of those views does justice to the magnitude of Hitler's evil. Lang believes that Hitler was aware of his criminality and even reveled in it. Rosenbaum, who sees Hitler as "a vicious, cold-blooded hater," finds Lang's analysis impressive, if not conclusive. The scope, planning, and sheer brutality of the Holocaust suggest to Lang that Hitler's evil involved what Rosenbaum calls an "art of evil," which required intention, invention, and imagining that relished suffering and destruction.[23] Nevertheless, Rosenbaum stops short of saying that Lang is absolutely right. To say that about any explanation of Hitler would go further than the available evidence permits, for too much time may have passed for anyone to find the key that can unlock the door to Hitler's identity once and for all.

Rosenbaum's conviction is that the yearning to explain Hitler often divulges a need that should be resisted, namely, the desire for closure, comfort, and consolation. Wanting an account that explains everything, we seem to await discovery of what Rosenbaum calls "a long-neglected safe-deposit box" that will grant final, irrefutable answers to the disturbing questions that Hitler raises.[24] Rosenbaum doubts the existence of such a definitive source. His investigations of Hitler explanations—Robert Waite's psychohistorical account, Rudolph Binion's speculation about the importance of the Jewish doctor who treated Hitler's mother unsuccessfully, or Daniel Goldhagen's emphasis on Hitler's use of a pervasive German "eliminationist antisemitism," to name just a few—always leave him skeptical that final and complete answers will be ours. This outcome, however, does not mean that Rosenbaum accepts the view of Claude Lanzmann, the filmmaker who produced *Shoah*, an epic Holocaust documentary. Rosenbaum finds Lanzmann asserting that it is wrong to seek explanation for Hitler and the Holocaust, because answers lead to understanding, understanding leads to legitimation, and legitimation leads to exoneration. According to Lanzmann, one can confront the raw events of the Holocaust, but to "explain" how and why Hitler's power led to Auschwitz would be tantamount to forgiving the unforgivable, an outcome more obscene than rational.

While recognizing that some explanations reduce Hitler's responsibility by making him the pawn of social, political, or psychological determinants—a view that *Explaining Hitler* rejects—Rosenbaum disagrees with Lanzmann's extreme position and concurs with the Holocaust historian Yehuda Bauer instead. Holding that in principle Hitler can be explained,

Bauer does not think it follows that Hitler has been or ever will be explained.[25] Nevertheless, ongoing effort to explain him remains important. To stop trying would mean that, in principle, Hitler is beyond explanation, an outcome that takes him out of history and thereby promotes problematic mystification.

Rosenbaum thinks that Hitler was certainly human but not ordinary, for ordinary people do not do what Hitler did. Hitler was human, but he was also exceptional in the sense that he can rightly be called an evil man, even an evil genius. Rosenbaum's conclusions on these points—he says he holds them by "default" more than out of "a metaphysical conviction"—are influenced by Lucy Dawidowicz, author of *The War against the Jews* (1975), who defended the thesis that as early as November 1918 Hitler formed his intention to destroy European Jewry.[26] Coolly obsessed by that goal, Dawidowicz contended, Hitler orchestrated his opportunities until he could do what he wanted. Twenty-five years after Dawidowicz published her views, they are less accepted by scholars than those of Christopher Browning and others who place Hitler's decision to launch the Final Solution in the late summer or early autumn of 1941. Rosenbaum urges that Dawidowicz's position deserves renewed attention. Further inquiry will determine the scholarly status enjoyed by Dawidowicz and every other interpreter of Hitler, including Rosenbaum and also Fritz Redlich, Brigitte Hamann, and Ian Kershaw, whose work deserves attention next.

Into the Abyss

Although it appeared in 1998, Ron Rosenbaum's study appeared too soon to take full account of Fritz

Redlich's *Hitler: Diagnosis of a Destructive Prophet*, Brigitte Hamann's *Hitler's Vienna: A Dictator's Apprenticeship*, and Ian Kershaw's two-volume study, *Hitler 1889–1936: Hubris* and *Hitler 1936–1945: Nemesis*, which are among the most recent attempts to explain Hitler. The fundamental dilemma these authors confront is illustrated well by the photographs their books contain. Redlich, for example, reprints the compelling photo of baby Adolf that Rosenbaum used on his title page. Solving the Hitler puzzle challenges Redlich and the others to show how baby Adolf became the *Führer*, but to what extent can this puzzle be solved? As they address that question, the biographies by Redlich, Hamann, and Kershaw become puzzle pieces themselves in three instructive ways. First, by increasing knowledge about Hitler, each writer's methodology and original research provide key pieces that help to work the Hitler puzzle. Second, the biographies themselves remain pieces of that puzzle because they cover only parts of a story whose incompleteness persists. Third, Redlich, Hamann, and Kershaw have also written puzzle pieces in the sense that their biographies provoke, but do not resolve, two basic issues: What must be known to solve the Hitler puzzle? Where might the missing pieces be discovered, if they can be found at all?

To explore these three dimensions further, note that Redlich fled Nazism in the late 1930s, immigrated to the United States, and became an eminent physician and psychiatrist who has taught at UCLA and Yale University, where he chaired the psychiatry department and served as dean of the medical school. In *Hitler: Diagnosis of a Destructive Prophet*, he seeks explanation by analyzing Hitler's medical history and mental health. This approach puts him in the tradition of biographers who have sought the missing pieces of the Hitler puzzle in the particularities, if not the peculiarities or abnormalities, of Hitler's physical and psychological individuality. Earlier proponents of this personalistic method include Walter C. Langer, the American psychologist who tried from afar to psychoanalyze Hitler for the Office of Strategic Services in 1943 (his classified report was not published until 1972), and Robert G. L. Waite, whose psychoanalytic biography, *The Psychopathic God: Adolf Hitler*, attracted considerable attention when it appeared in 1977. Redlich's book is better researched and more insightful than its predecessors in this genre. Partly for that reason, it helps to show why these individualistic approaches are insufficient to explain Hitler.

Redlich's *Hitler* has two major parts. The first reviews Hitler's life historically; the second—supplemented by appendices documenting his adult medical treatment—concentrates on Hitler's medical history and psychopathological profile. If the first half of the book is less than groundbreaking, the second half's detail could scarcely be rivaled. A photographic section, which begins with baby Adolf, divides these parts. Redlich's caption comments that "most babies, unless seriously ill, look like little angels." The early Hitler photo may support that judgment, but Redlich diagnoses Hitler as a sick man nonetheless. Hitler's sickness, however, was not primarily physical. Redlich's detailed medical profile makes clear that Hitler's bodily ailments—among them hypertension, gastrointestinal spasms, and insomnia as well as Parkinson's disease—were of "moderate severity." Physical illness did not cause his "crimes and errors."[27] Nor was Hitler insane, Redlich asserts. He underscores that Hitler knew what he wanted, understood what he was doing, and took responsibility for it all.

Hitler's signature on Nazi Germany's antisemitic Nuremberg Laws illustrates these aspects of his personality. It also points toward the key element spotlighted in Redlich's book: Hitler's psychopathology was marked most by paranoid delusions. Redlich surmises that the origins of Hitler's suspiciousness are to be found in his infancy and childhood, perhaps in "ambivalent relations with both parents."[28] Redlich's judgment is much less tentative, however, when he asserts specifically that "a paranoid belief in a Jewish world conspiracy against Germany" gripped Hitler and produced a prophetic destructiveness so great that it "made him one of the world's greatest criminals."[29] According to Redlich, the decisive turning point in Hitler's life took place in the summer and fall of 1919, when public speaking opportunities in the defeated Germany army and then in the tiny German Workers Party created synergy between his antisemitic feelings and the recognition that he possessed charisma with powerful political potential. As even Redlich senses, however, his biography's individualistic approach—steeped in conjecture and speculation as it must be in spite of the data he musters—cannot fully bear the weight that the challenge of explaining Hitler puts upon it. Redlich's wife, Herta, gets the last word about Hitler in Redlich's book. "*Er war ein schlechter Mensch*," she says after hearing a summary of her husband's analysis.[30]

Hitler, says Herta Redlich, was an evil person. Surely he was or nobody could be, but a medical and psychopathological approach alone—no matter how detailed—cannot explain Hitler, at least not completely, because the Hitler who became *Hitler* was not simply an individual. The Hitler who became *Hitler* was profoundly influenced by his sociohistorical context. More than that, he was even created in part by the followers who did his bidding and sustained by the bystanders who let him have his way. These aspects are central to Hamann's *Hitler's Vienna* and Kershaw's two volumes. Like Redlich's, these books are fine additions to Hitler scholarship, but it should not be surprising that they too fall short in meeting the challenge of explaining Hitler.

A Viennese historian whose nineteenth- and twentieth-century scholarship emphasizes Austria, Hamann also illustrates her book with photographs. Her initial picture is not of baby Adolf but of an enfeebled Hitler in his Berlin bunker shortly before he committed suicide on April 30, 1945. Engulfed by destruction of his own making, Hitler gazes at an architectural model of Linz, the Austrian hometown that he hoped to make the Third Reich's cultural capital. A few pages later, the reader sees a blurred photo from 1899. Cropped from a print of his school class, it depicts Hitler as a youngster. The full class picture shows Hitler standing in the center of the top row with his arms folded across his chest and his black hair parted on the right, but none of those factors forecasts *Hitler*. Hamann combs Vienna in search of the missing puzzle pieces that would explain how such an obscure boy became the dictator whose signature, spoken word, or nod "wreaked havoc on the world."[31]

No credible biography of Hitler can ignore his early years in Vienna. From Alan Bullock to Joachim Fest and John Toland, the standard scholarly and popular biographers explore that terrain. Yet none matches Hamann's depth as she immerses her readers in the Vienna that impressed Hitler from 1906 until he left for Munich in 1913 at the age of twenty-four. Hitler's determination to control information about his past makes her appraisal as complicated as it is necessary. Insisting that his own *Mein Kampf* was to be the sole authoritative biographical source for his early life and work, Hitler contended that Vienna fueled and focused his antisemitic vision. *Mein Kampf*, however, was written more than a decade after Hitler's departure from the city. Much had happened—especially World War I—during the intervening years. Hamann's detective work advances Hitler scholarship by providing a rich history that revises Hitler's account of Vienna's influence upon him.

Hamann emphasizes that Hitler knew best the Vienna that mirrored him. Its culture was that of the "little," even disadvantaged, people whose socioeconomic situation left them estranged from "Viennese modernity" and susceptible to forms of nationalism that attracted followers among those who felt that the city's multinational character wrongly eclipsed German preeminence. As Hitler moved in the vagabond circles of frustrated ambitions, men's hostels, and offbeat journalistic opinions about politics and race, antisemitism was never far to find, but Hamann underscores that the young Hitler's relationships with Jews were "multifaceted." Inspired by antisemitic political players such as the Viennese mayor Karl Lueger, Hitler learned the city's antisemitic vocabulary but rarely used it. To the contrary, Hamann cites eyewitnesses who noted Hitler's cordial relationships with Viennese Jews such as Josef Neumann and Siegfried Löffner, his men's hostel companions; Jakob Wasserberg, owner of a small shop where Hitler sometimes had breakfast; or Samuel Morgenstern, whom Hamann identifies as "the most loyal buyer of Hitler's paintings."[32] Only when he became a politician in Germany after World War I, Hamann indicates, did Hitler's antisemitism erupt.

Although Vienna affected Hitler powerfully, it does not explain him. The people, places, circumstances, and theories he encountered there (the latter included a scheme to tattoo identification numbers on the arms of Gypsies) contributed to his German nationalism and contempt for democracy as well as to his racism and antisemitism. Yet *Hitler's Vienna* still leaves Hitler more enigmatic than explained, for Hamann concludes that he took from Vienna "a grab-bag that was preserved inside an excellent memory."[33] No Viennese pieces in the puzzle suggest that Hitler would become *Hitler*. Jews, for example, were not among the faculty who denied Hitler admission to Vienna's Academy of Visual Arts in 1907. Nevertheless, the grab bag and memory were his. Later circumstances in Germany enabled him to put the pieces together in ways that the wildest speculations—Hitler's included—could not have imagined in 1913.

Extending the challenge of explaining Hitler, intriguing photographic juxtapositions continue in the two volumes by British historian Ian Kershaw, a veteran interpreter of Nazi Germany whose study of Hitler is, arguably, the most ambitious, accurate, and successful attempt of its kind. In *Hitler 1889–1936*, the first volume, Kershaw starts his photographic sequence with the same schoolboy picture that Hamann reprinted. A few pages beyond, the reader glimpses Hitler's face in a crowd. It is August 2, 1914. The throng in Munich's Odeonplatz listens to the proclamation of war. Soon Hitler will volunteer enthusiastically for the German army and spend the next four years on the First World War's western front, serving in France and Belgium as a dispatch runner, an often dangerous duty that entailed carrying orders on foot or by bicycle from regimental commanders to officers at the front.

Kershaw indicates that World War I was more decisive for Hitler than anything he experienced earlier. Hitler had gone off to war elated, but Germany's defeat convinced him that the German cause had been betrayed. In his mind, Jews became the chief culprits. At the war's end, however, Hitler still had few prospects, certainly none that anticipated his signing of the Nuremberg Laws in September 1935 or his orders for the German army to remilitarize the Rhineland in March 1936, two events that Kershaw punctuates at the end of his first volume.

Kershaw tracks Hitler's rise from postwar disillusionment to what he identifies as "hubris—that overweening arrogance which courts disaster," and then "into the abyss" that still leaves the world reeling.[34] The most up-to-date and comprehensive account of Hitler available at the beginning of the twenty-first century, Kershaw's astute analysis nevertheless displays how elusive success can be when the challenge is to explain Hitler, whose name, says Kershaw, "justifiably stands for all time as that of the chief instigator of the most profound collapse of civilization in modern times. . . . Never in history has such ruination—physical and moral—been associated with the name of one man."[35]

Kershaw argues that Hitler and his German followers willingly courted the self-destruction that was the inherent risk in the Nazis' arrogant attempt to dominate Europe. If not through the intervention of the Greek goddess Nemesis or any other divinity, that hubris brought retribution, but not before utter destruction took its toll. Repeatedly, Kershaw contends that Nazi hubris came from interaction between Hitler and the German people. To explain Hitler requires explaining them. The difficulty of doing so is summed up at the end of Kershaw's second volume when he acknowledges both the limits of "generalizations about the mentalities and behaviour of millions of Germans in the Nazi era" and the significance of "strong elements of pseudo-religious belief" and "quasi-religious associations" that "enabled Hitler's power to shake off all constraints and become absolute."[36] Such qualifications and descriptions, necessary and ambiguous as they are, leave one to ask how much has been explained.

Biographical inquiry is inherently paradoxical. Beyond describing the persons they study, biographies normally attempt to explain how and why individuals acted the way they did and became the persons they were. In addition, biographies are usually written because the person in question exerted substantial influence far beyond that individual's life alone. Therefore, a full explanation of the person requires coming to terms with historical and social forces that are vast in scope but not only in terms of the individual's leverage on them. The relation works the other way as well: Historical and social forces must be taken into account to explain how and why the person in question became the individual who motivates biographical investigation. Concentrating on individuals as they must, biographies are bound to be self-defeating; their forms of inquiry cannot by themselves fully comprehend the persons they seek to understand. Specifically in the case of Hitler, then, the paradox that clings to biographies, Kershaw's included, is that the Hitler who became *Hitler* was not simply an individual who can be contained in the confines of biographical investigation.

To his credit, Kershaw understands this difficulty and its implications for the immensity of his scholarly project. He emphasizes that the Hitler who became *Hitler* was profoundly influenced by sociohistorical contexts. Thus, Kershaw identifies a puzzle piece that is needed for completeness. In this case, the problem is not so much that the piece is missing but that it is too huge to permit full comprehension. Kershaw puts the dilemma as follows: Answers to "the question of how Hitler was possible . . . must be sought chiefly in German society—in the social and political motivations which went into the making of Hitler."[37] Its sheer scope makes Kershaw's task so daunting that it is bound to be uncompleted.

Biographical work can describe Hitler and tell us much about him, but no matter how many volumes it contains, biography cannot explain Hitler—at least not completely—because it took so much more than Hitler to make *Hitler*. To explain Hitler conclusively would require knowing everything, not just about him as an individual but also about the times and places that were essential to produce what he became. An omniscient, God's-eye view might permit a full explanation of Hitler, but human minds never possess it. Where Hitler is concerned, missing puzzle pieces will remain a fact of life for every biographer. The prefaces that Kershaw wrote for his two volumes reflect his wise awareness of this dilemma. Underscoring "the continuing duty to seek understanding of how Hitler was possible," Kershaw concludes that he will be "well satisfied" if his study of Hitler "contributes a little to deepen understanding."[38]

Kershaw has done much to deepen understanding, not least because his sense of scholarly duty urges continued acceptance of the challenge that attracts and resists all of Hitler's biographers and their readers. In spite of the fact that even the most accomplished biographers may never find all the pieces of the Hitler puzzle, there are two main reasons for the significance of their efforts. On the one hand, unless inquiry about Hitler continues, we will understand less than we can and should. Hitler will be placed too far beyond explanation, an outcome that promotes mystification by taking him out of history and turning him into more than the man he was. On the other hand, to think that inquiry about Hitler is ever complete would amount to costly arrogance. If Hitler ever were fully explained, his singularity would be crystal clear, his time and place lucidly unique. With all the questions answered and no more missing puzzle pieces, a Hitler wrapped up and put to rest would be someone we might foolishly think we could afford to forget.

It is another matter if Hitler, and therefore the Holocaust as well, remains explained only in part. A Hitler puzzle still unsolved strengthens the needed warning to take nothing good for granted because our undoing can emerge from sources as unexpected as they are obscure. When high quality studies such as those by Rosenbaum, Redlich, Hamann, and Kershaw remain puzzle pieces, that outcome is not a weakness but a strength.

Like Rosenbaum, Redlich, Hamann, and Kershaw, Holocaust survivor Elie Wiesel would have been saddened but perhaps not surprised if *Time* had named Hitler its Person of the Century, for when the twentieth century is remembered, Wiesel observed in the essay he wrote about Hitler for *Time*'s Person of the

Century poll, Hitler's will be "among the first names that will surge to mind." Some say that Hitler's name should be blotted out forever. That feeling has its point, but when Wiesel wrote for *Time*, a different theme reverberated, one that Rosenbaum, Redlich, Hamann, and Kershaw would surely endorse as well. Precisely because Hitler has not been explained—at least not completely—and probably never will be, the world can ill-afford to forget him.

Even if unintentionally, Redlich, Hamann, and Kershaw joined Wiesel and Rosenbaum to advance the case for making Hitler the Person of the Twentieth Century. The twenty-first may eclipse it, but the twentieth century was, after all, the bloodiest in human history. No events did more to produce that outcome than World War II and the Holocaust. No person had more to do with those catastrophes than Hitler. All five of these interpreters also indicate that neither World War II, the Holocaust, nor the Hitler who became *Hitler* were inevitable. Hitler and the havoc he wreaked emerged from deliberate decisions made by human beings. Those decisions were not predestined or unavoidable. The comprehensive work of these five interpreters leads to two conclusions that are crucial for sound Holocaust politics and its interrelated tensions about uniqueness, comparability, and comprehension. We ought not to claim that full comprehension of the Holocaust is humanly possible, but we must share the moral commitment and cooperate in the ethical work that are necessary to affirm that nobody like Hitler shall ever again merit consideration as the Person of the Century.

Chapter Three

How Is the Holocaust Best Remembered?

If we stop remembering, we stop being.
Elie Wiesel

Traffic and business stop when the sirens scream; two minutes later, an Israeli morning goes on as usual. But not entirely, for it is Yom Hashoah, the spring day that annually commemorates the Holocaust. In their particular and related ways, the Israeli sirens and the observance of Yom Hashoah bear witness to Elie Wiesel's conviction: "If we stop remembering, we stop being."[1] However, neither that reality nor the warning that Wiesel takes from it can be comprehended well unless careful consideration is given to the fact that memory, memories, and remembering are human realities that raise crucial questions.

Memory is not purely or simply good. It can be a source of great evil. Antisemitism, racism, and hate are impossible without memory in general and without specific memories in particular. Memory was a condition for the Holocaust itself; if memory had been wiped out before the Holocaust took place, there could have been no Auschwitz. But if memory were destroyed, human life and history would be impossible. Thus, it is crucial to ask, Can we keep memory alive and well? Which memories most deserve attention? What purposes should remembering serve, and how does remembering best serve them? These are some of the questions that swirl in, through, and around what I shall call the ethics of memory. In paying attention to issues about history, morality, and religion, this chapter considers aspects of those questions by moving back and forth in time. That method will involve stories and vignettes more than arguments and theories, but in one way or another all of these approaches to the topic "How Is the Holocaust Best Remembered?" will aim to underscore, first, that events are not finished when they end, nor does history close when it concludes, and, second, that if we stop remembering, we stop being.

Asking how the Holocaust is best remembered requires recalling what the Holocaust was. That recollection, in turn, leads one to consider how the disaster came to be. These encounters with the past involve details and the relations among them. No remembrance of the Holocaust can be adequate without giving those particularities their due. Note, then, that the Holocaust's deadliest year was 1942. Holocaust scholar Raul Hilberg's conservative estimates indicate that Nazi Germany destroyed 2.7 million Jews in that year alone.[2] Keeping that fact in mind, it can be illustrative and instructive to remember two other Holocaust years: 1937 and 1946, the quiet before the storm and the pursuit of justice after it.

Moving Toward a Hideous Catastrophe

Holding academic degrees in medicine and anthropology, a twenty-five-year-old German doctor started his research assistantship at the University of Frankfurt's prestigious Institute of Hereditary Biology and Racial Hygiene on January 1, 1937. Soon he joined the Nazi Party and the SS. Six years later, on May 30, 1943, his career in the service of Nazi Germany's antisemitic policies of racial purity would reach its climax by taking him to Auschwitz and placing him at the center of the Final Solution. Specifically, during his twenty months at Auschwitz, this Nazi doctor conducted notorious medical experiments and presided at "selections" that determined who would be gassed and who would be spared, however briefly, for slave labor. His name was Josef Mengele.[3]

Despite rebelling against his strict religious upbringing, Mengele identified himself as a Catholic. It is worth noting, therefore, that as Mengele began his research at the University of Frankfurt, Achille Ratti, age 79, who had earned a triple doctorate in philosophy, theology, and law, was working in Rome. Ratti would die before World War II began, but in the relative quiet before that genocidal storm, he faced important decisions about his relationship to Nazi Germany. No mere research assistant, Ratti had responsibilities in 1937 that were far greater than any Mengele could imagine, for Ratti's better known identity was Pope Pius XI, leader of the Roman Catholic Church.

Pius XI and Josef Mengele never met. Nevertheless, the pontiff knew about his ilk and their projects of "racial hygiene." From the beginning of Hitler's power, Pius XI had recognized two other realities as well. First, he understood that Nazism jeopardized the Catholic Church's authority. Second, he knew that Germany's Jews were besieged with difficulties. Pius XI's decisions about those matters, and the ones that he might have taken had he lived longer, illustrate that 1937 fitted the description that another key leader, Winston Churchill, offered on April 14. "We seem to be moving," he told Britain's House of Commons, "towards some hideous catastrophe."[4]

Realizing that official Vatican recognition of his authority could be politically valuable at home and abroad, Adolf Hitler sensed correctly that the papacy would consider it wise to safeguard the Roman Catholic Church's status in Germany. In the spring of 1933, Nazi inquiries were favorably received by the Vatican's secretary of state, Cardinal Eugenio Pacelli, a former papal diplomat to Berlin. During an elaborate ceremony on July 20, 1933, a Concordat between the Holy See and the German Reich was officially signed and sealed by Vice Chancellor Franz von Papen and Cardinal Pacelli. It affirmed legal status and protection for the Catholic Church and its organizations in Germany if—but only if—they were dedicated to purely religious activities.

The Concordat gave no comfort to Germany's Jews, for this treaty conferred important international legitimacy on the Third Reich. Hitler himself took the Concordat to provide significant help in the Reich's battle against the Jews. Meanwhile, the Nazis' anti-Catholic pressure did not relent, and by 1937 a mounting list of falsely arrested nuns and priests, closed convents and monasteries, and harassed parochial schools led Pope Pius XI to write *Mit brennender Sorge* (*With Burning Dismay*). Issued on March 14, this encyclical protested the Catholic Church's difficulties in Germany, accused the Nazi government of violating its word, and warned against the deification of race, nation, and state. Smuggled into Germany, printed secretly, and distributed to the clergy, it was read from Catholic pulpits throughout the Reich on March 21, Palm Sunday.

Mit brennender Sorge spoke of "God-given rights" and invoked a "human nature" that went beyond national boundaries. It even stated that rejection of the Old Testament, which some leaders—religious as well as secular—advocated in Nazi Germany, was blasphemous. Yet in failing to mention the racist Nuremberg Laws that had stripped civil rights from Germany's Jews in 1935, it offered no condemnation of the persecution of German Jews. Indeed, instead of protesting antisemitism, *Mit brennender Sorge* referred to "the chosen people" as those who were "constantly straying" from God and who had crucified Christ.

Pius XI's pronouncements sent mixed signals about the Jewish question, but he became an increasingly strong critic of the Nazi state. In June 1938, he summoned Father John LaFarge, an American Jesuit priest, to confer with him. Impressed by LaFarge's antiracist work in the United States, including his book *Interracial Justice*, Pius XI, increasingly frail from heart disease, went outside the usual Vatican personnel and assigned LaFarge to draft *Humani Generis Unitas* (*The Unity of Humankind*), an encyclical that would denounce racism and the persecution of Jews by advocates of racial purity. As the fate of German and Austrian Jews worsened under the Nazi grip, LaFarge and a few trusted colleagues worked in Paris, writing and revising a text that grew to almost one hundred pages.[5]

A heart attack took the life of Pius XI during the night of February 9, 1939. LaFarge's draft of *Humani Generis Unitas* was reportedly on the pope's desk at that time. Delayed for several months—perhaps intentionally—by the Vatican's bureaucracy, it had reached him too late to be of consequence. Cardinal Pacelli, who feared Communists more than Nazis, succeeded him on March 2, taking the name Pius XII. His leadership record during the Holocaust years would be problematic at best. Six months later, World War II began. *Humani Generis Unitas* was shelved in church archives. Nothing much was heard of it until long after the Holocaust took place.

Had the encyclical appeared in the late 1930s, it alone would not have been sufficient to prevent the Final Solution. One reason is that even as LaFarge's text attacked racism and racially motivated persecution of Jews, it did not entirely reject the traditional anti-Jewish teachings that had been part of Christian tradition for centuries. Nevertheless, the disappearance of *Humani Generis Unitas* stands out as a significant example of lost opportunities that might have brought pressure to bear on the Nazi state.

Not every opportunity to thwart Hitler's ambitions was lost in 1937, but neither were any of them sufficient to stop his march. On March 15, the day after Pius XI issued *Mit brennender Sorge*, an anti-Nazi protest rally, sponsored by the American Jewish Congress (AJC) and the Jewish Labor Committee, took place in New York's Madison Square Garden. Inside Germany, David Glick, a Pittsburgh lawyer who had connections with the American Jewish Joint Distribution Committee, successfully negotiated the release and emigration of 120 of the three hundred Jews who were then in the Dachau concentration camp. In late December 1937, the official leadership of German Jewry publicly urged their people to carry on with resoluteness and self-confidence.

Noble though they were, such efforts were too little to check the power they faced. They lacked support from a larger collective will—inside Germany and internationally as well—that would have been necessary to check the Jewish persecution, which was beginning to spread beyond German borders. In the month of August 1937, for example, 350 attacks on Jews were recorded in Poland.[6] Earlier in the year, on June 11, 1937, less than three months after *Mit brennender Sorge* defended a common human nature and God-given rights, the few remaining legal protections given to German Jews were further stripped away when Jews were prohibited from giving testimony in German courts. Five months later, the German Interior Ministry required Jews to carry special identity cards for travel inside the country.

The Nazis also stepped up arrests to enforce the laws forbidding sexual relations between Germans and Jews. Those arrests often resulted in concentration camp sentences. That summer the Nazi concentration camp system expanded, most significantly with the opening of Buchenwald, which became operational on July 16. Three days later, a Nazi exhibition on "Degenerate Art" opened in Munich. Ordered by Hitler himself, this exhibition denigrated innovative art, including many works by Jewish artists. The Nazis eventually destroyed some of this art, but much of it was auctioned off for foreign currency that the Third Reich needed to advance its ambitions. A few months later, on November 8, Munich witnessed the opening of another destructive exhibition. This time it was "The Eternal Jew," an antisemitic art and poster show sponsored by the Nazi Party.

In 1937, Nazi ambitions included a more solid relationship with Italy, which opened the way for German annexation of Austria in 1938. They also encompassed an alliance with imperial Japan and the rapid growth of military forces, which would be needed for the even larger territorial expansion to which Hitler's talk increasingly referred. They embraced as well young Dr. Mengele's research. All too soon, it would take him from the Institute of Hereditary Biology and Racial Hygiene to the racially inspired experiments and "selections" that destroyed millions of Jews and other defenseless people who were branded less than fully human. In that world, there was little concern for the "God-given rights" that Pope Pius XI had in mind.

If 1937 was one of the Holocaust's quieter years, it was certainly ominous enough. The storm's full force was not far off. No papal encyclical, protest rally, or emigration project would be enough to keep it at bay. Churchill was right. The "hideous catastrophe" that he anticipated was fast approaching.

In 1942, the hideous catastrophe reached its zenith. By the end of that year, the tides of war began to turn against Nazi Germany and eventually that genocidal regime was brought to its knees. But history does not stop with the end of a particular event, and the year 1946 was one in which memory and memories tried to serve the cause of justice.

Pains That Will Not Go Away

As a snowstorm gathered on a late November day in 1946, a Jewish woman named Gerda Weissmann Klein headed home after finishing her grocery shopping in Buffalo, New York. Grocery shopping was important to her. Words and pictures on product labels were helping her to learn English. Shelves stocked with food reassured her; their apparently unending abundance meant that she would never again be consumed by hunger. Nevertheless, after unpacking her groceries that day, Klein took the bread she had purchased, sat by a window in her living room, and, as she watched the storm swirl, began to eat the loaf. Fresh though it was, the bread seemed salty and soggy. Those sensations combined with feelings of sadness that made her wonder what was wrong.

Holocaust survivor Gerda Klein, whose remarkable story became the subject of an Academy Award–winning documentary called *One Survivor Remembers*, recounts this episode in her memoir, *All but My Life*. As she ate, memory told her what was wrong. "During the long years of deprivation," she recalled, "I had dreamed of eating my fill in a warm place, in peace, but I never thought that I would eat my bread alone."[7] Married to Kurt Klein, a former U.S. Army lieutenant, Gerda was not alone in late November 1946— and yet she was. Born in 1924, Gerda Weissmann had witnessed the German occupation of her hometown, Bielitz, Poland, in 1939, spent years in Nazi forced labor camps—Bolkenhain, Märzdorf, Landeshut, and Grünberg among them—and endured brutal Nazi death marches in 1945 before American troops, including Kurt Klein, liberated her in early May at Volary, Czechoslovakia.

Kurt Klein and his siblings had escaped Nazi Germany by emigrating to the United States before the war. Valiantly they tried to rescue their parents, but long-delayed U.S. immigration clearance came too late. Kurt's parents had already been gassed at Auschwitz. After Kurt and Gerda met in Volary and fell in love, they married, came to Buffalo in September 1946, and began a long and successful life together. Nevertheless, what Gerda calls "a stabbing memory" or, in particular, "a pervasive loneliness" still inflicted "pains that will not go away," for she lost most of her family and many friends in the Holocaust.[8]

Stabbing memories, pervasive loneliness, pains and losses that will not go away—while Gerda Klein did her grocery shopping in the late autumn of 1946, aspects of those realities also focused the attention of U.S. Brigadier General Telford Taylor. A skilled lawyer, Taylor had been part of the legal team assembled the year before by Robert H. Jackson, the U.S. Supreme Court justice who served as the chief American prosecutor at the International Military Tribunal (IMT). Including representatives from France, Great Britain, and the Soviet Union as well as the United States, the IMT had spent twelve months pursuing justice against twenty-four of the most significant Nazi leaders.

During trials held in the German city of Nuremberg, where the Nazis had held their annual rallies and announced the notorious Nuremberg Laws in 1935, the IMT brought four charges against the defendants: (1) crimes against peace, (2) war crimes, (3) crimes against humanity, and (4) conspiracy to commit any of the foregoing crimes. Making no mention of the *Holocaust* or the *Shoah*—such terms were not yet widespread—these indictments did not identify specifically what had happened to the Jews or to other civilian populations targeted by the Nazis and their collaborators. However, Article 6 of the IMT's charter defined crimes against humanity to include "murder, extermination, enslavement, deportation, and other inhumane acts committed against any civilian population, before or during the war, or persecutions on political, racial or religious grounds in execution of or in connection with any crime within the jurisdiction of the Tribunal, whether or not in violation of the domestic law of the country where perpetrated."

At first, Taylor's IMT assignment made him Justice Jackson's liaison to the Russians, but Taylor's role grew when he was handed responsibility for leading the prosecution's case against the German High Command, the generals and admirals who directed Nazi Germany's military conquest. That conquest put vast numbers of European Jews under Nazi domination and enabled the *Einsatzgruppen*, the SS, various police units, and the German army itself to carry out "the war against the Jews," as the Holocaust has sometimes been called. Without the military victories that subjected nearly all of Europe to German control, the Holocaust, which epitomized the Third Reich's crimes against humanity, would not have taken place, or at least its scope would have been greatly diminished. Although Taylor's explicit task was not to show that members of the German High Command were also Holocaust perpetrators, his aim was to document that Nazi Germany's military professionals had waged war in criminal ways.

Before the IMT's proceedings began in Nuremberg on November 20, 1945, one of the defendants, Robert Ley, head of the German Labor Front, had followed Adolf Hitler and Heinrich Himmler by committing suicide. Another defendant, Gustav Krupp, head of the Krupp armaments industries, was found medically unfit to stand trial. When the verdicts were announced on October 1, 1946, nineteen of the Nuremberg defendants—including Martin Bormann, head of the Nazi Party chancellery, who was tried in absentia—were found guilty. Three men were acquitted: Hjalmar Schacht, former minister of economics; Franz von Papen, first vice-chancellor of the Nazi government; and Hans Fritzsche, chief of the Propaganda Ministry's radio division. Taylor achieved his goal, however, when the guilty verdicts included Nazi military leaders such as Wilhelm Keitel, chief of staff, *Wehrmacht* High Command, and Alfred Jodl, chief of the *Wehrmacht* Operations Staff. Seven defendants got prison sentences that ranged from ten years to life. Twelve defendants, Keitel and Jodl among them, were condemned to death by hanging. Ten executions took place in the early hours of October 16, 1946. (Having been tried in absentia, Bormann was missing. Shortly before Hermann Göring was to be hanged, the commander-in-chief of the *Luftwaffe*—he was also the best known surviving Nazi war criminal—escaped the gallows when he killed himself by swallowing cyanide.)

The pursuit of justice at Nuremberg did not end when the IMT concluded its work in the autumn of 1946. Among thousands of Nazi war crimes trials that took place in numerous countries before and after those conducted by the IMT, the Subsequent Nuremberg Proceedings began in December 1946. Lasting until April 1949, they consisted of twelve trials under American jurisdiction. Now chief counsel for the prosecution, Telford Taylor played a key part in these proceedings, which ultimately focused on 177 Nazi doctors, jurists, industrialists, military and SS leaders (including *Einsatzgruppen* personnel), and other professionals and government officials whose indictments specified crimes ranging from abusive medical experimentation and participation in Nazi Germany's "euthanasia" program to exploitation of slave labor, the administration of concentration camps, and mass murder.

Among the 142 defendants who were found guilty (25 received death sentences, but only 12 were carried out) was Otto Ohlendorf, leader of *Einsatzgruppe D*. In 1941–42, this killing squadron, which was attached to Nazi Germany's Eleventh Army, was instrumental in the murder of 90,000 men, women, and children, mostly Jews, in the Ukraine, the Crimea, and other regions in the southern end of the war's eastern front. A well-educated man in his late thirties, Ohlendorf, a former SS major general, had studied at three universities, earned a doctorate in jurisprudence, and also specialized in economics. In his testimony as a prosecution witness during the initial Nuremberg Trials, Ohlendorf stated that it was "inconceivable that a subordinate leader should not carry out orders given by the leaders of the state."[9] Brought to trial himself in the Subsequent Nuremberg Proceedings, Ohlendorf contended that the killing of Jewish children was unavoidable "because the children were people who would grow up, and surely, being the children of parents who had been killed, they could constitute a danger no smaller than that of the parents."[10]

Sentenced to death in April 1948, Ohlendorf spent more than three years in detention before he was hanged in Landsberg prison on June 8, 1951. By that time, however, more than half of the 142 convicted defendants from the Subsequent Nuremberg Proceedings had been set free and others had their sentences reduced as the new political climate of the Cold War brought pressure to strengthen West Germany as a check against Soviet expansion. Many of the ex-convicts, especially the industrialists and other professionals, resumed their careers and then went on to receive retirement pensions for their services.

Even if all of the sentences meted out to Nazi war criminals had been fully carried out, the pursuit of justice through legal proceedings could not begin to

prosecute and punish all those who were responsible
for the stabbing memories, pervasive loneliness, pains,
and losses that will not go away for survivors such as
Gerda Weissmann Klein. Nor could the pursuit of
justice do anything to bring back the millions of
defenseless people—Jews and non-Jews—who were
murdered during the Holocaust. Nevertheless, the
trials that took place in 1946 and thereafter remain
significant for reasons that Telford Taylor emphasized
on December 9 of that year when he made the prosecution's opening statement in the Doctors' Trial, the
first of the Subsequent Nuremberg Proceedings:

> It is our deep obligation to all peoples of the
> world to show why and how these things hap-
> pened. It is incumbent upon us to set forth with
> conspicuous clarity the ideas and motives which
> moved these defendants to treat their fellow men
> as less than beasts. The perverse thoughts and
> distorted concepts which brought about these
> savageries are not dead. They cannot be killed by
> force of arms. They must not become a spread-
> ing cancer in the breast of humanity. They must
> be cut out and exposed, for the reason so well
> stated by Mr. Justice Jackson in this courtroom a
> year ago: "The wrongs which we seek to con-
> demn and punish have been so calculated, so
> malignant, and so devastating, that civilization
> cannot tolerate their being ignored because it
> cannot survive their being repeated."[11]

As Taylor spoke those words, Gerda Klein's life in
Buffalo, New York, went on. Nearly half a century
later, she returned to Volary, Czechoslovakia, the site
of her liberation. "I paused," she writes in *All but My
Life*, "at the graves of my beloved friends who were

never privileged to know the joy of freedom, the security of a loaf of bread, or the supreme happiness of holding a child in their arms." Her memory of the Holocaust's dead, she adds, "brought up the unanswerable question that has haunted me ever since the day I left them there: Why?"[12] Because no pursuit of justice can ever put it to rest, that question will continue to cry out whenever the Holocaust is remembered.

It's Not So Easy

It is as hard to remember the Holocaust as it is important to do so. There is so much detail, so much particularity that needs to be recollected if we are to avoid making memory so general and abstract that it becomes shallow and superficial, routine and merely ritualized. How hard and how important it is to remember the Holocaust can be illustrated further by the telephone call I received late in the summer of 1994 from a resident of Pasadena, California, whose name is Joseph Freeman. Aware of my work on the Holocaust, this Jewish survivor asked me to read and comment on the autobiographical manuscript he had written. From time to time, Holocaust survivors send me such requests. Each time I am moved by what I read, but for three reasons the impact of Joseph Freeman's words was especially strong.

First, Freeman used language with the clarity, simplicity, and compactness that identify a good writer. Second, his memoir was carefully researched. Drawing on his personal experience, Freeman had also contextualized his story within the Holocaust's larger history. Third, parts of Freeman's chapters provided glimpses into an aspect of the Holocaust that has been discussed much less—even in survivor testimony—than what happened, for example, to Jews in ghettos or camps. I refer to the infamous death marches that took place in the last months of World War II, well after the military tide had turned against Nazi Germany and its killing centers on Polish soil—Auschwitz-Birkenau among them—had been shut down and evacuated. Especially with respect to Freeman's account of the death marches, I sensed that there was more to his story than he had told. I urged him to turn the glimpses into a more detailed narrative. He promised to do so in a second book.

Two years after Freeman contacted me, his first manuscript was published. He titled it *Job: The Story of a Holocaust Survivor*.[13] Pleased as I was when Freeman sent me an inscribed copy of that book, I was even more impressed when he handed me his second manuscript. This death-march sequel—Freeman calls it *The Road to Hell*—appeared in 1998.[14] In turning glimpses of too-little-studied aspects of the Holocaust into a succinctly detailed narrative, it helps to document how cruel and systematic, how brutal and unrelenting the Third Reich's destruction of the European Jews turned out to be.

When Joseph Freeman speaks to my classes, as he often does in the company of his wife, Helen, who is also a survivor, the students and I always notice two of his characteristics. First, in spite of the inhumanity he has experienced, he has a firm commitment to mend the world. Second, he often repeats the phrase, "It's not so easy." The phrase and the commitment belong together where the ethics of memory is concerned.

"It's not so easy"—when Joseph Freeman uses those words, he is doing what Holocaust scholar James E. Young calls "memory-work."[15] In cases such as Freeman's, memory-work has two crucial dimensions. First, this memory-work must not only recall catastrophe but bring it back to life in the present so that what happened can be described and analyzed. Horror experienced once must be relived—again and again. Even that mandate, however, is incomplete. For the required memory-work, description and analysis alone will not suffice. The description must be detailed and accurate, the analysis honest and truthful. Those requirements permit neither cheap optimism nor easy hope.

Second, Freeman's memory-work requires him to communicate what he experienced. But the communication work is not so easy because his audience can scarcely imagine what he tries to describe. My students and I, for example, do our best. We work to comprehend what we are hearing when Freeman speaks to us, but the more we listen, the more we realize how far his experience is removed from ours.

My students and I do not doubt that Freeman speaks the truth. We also know that we were not "there." Try as he might, Freeman cannot bridge completely the gulf that separates him from us. We come to understand how much he feels this gulf as he keeps telling us, "It's not so easy." What he means is that he wants so much for us to grasp what happened, even as he realizes that he cannot find the words to bridge the gap, for there are none that can do so completely. Yet, even though we cannot comprehend fully, perhaps our learning is deepest, our grasp as great as it can be, just when we see how much he struggles to make clear and vivid what we can only glimpse from afar. Thus, in spite of the difficulty of communication, Freeman's memory-work makes unforgettable connections.

Since the Holocaust happened more than fifty years ago, its survivors are a rapidly dwindling number. How much longer will Joseph or Helen Freeman be able to visit my Holocaust class? Indeed, how much longer will there be a course on the Holocaust on my own campus? At the beginning of the twenty-first century, those Holocaust-related questions are on my mind. It is right that they should be, for memory of the Holocaust refers increasingly not to a living person's firsthand experiences from 1933, 1935, 1938, 1942, 1945, or any other explicit time when Nazi Germany unleashed its unprecedented intentions against the European Jews and the millions of other people who found themselves trapped in that web of mass death. More and more, memory of the Holocaust refers to history that recedes further and further away from anyone's living present.

What will happen to memory of the Holocaust? Why should that question be of any concern? What difference would it make if nobody remembered the Holocaust anymore? What dangers would await us if Auschwitz and Treblinka become forgotten places or if Holocaust years such as 1937, 1942, and 1946 are largely forgotten? Are there reasons—moral imperatives—that enjoin us, whether we are Jewish or not, always to remember the Holocaust's history?

My short responses are, first, that memory of the Holocaust is obviously destined to be less strong, less intense, in 3001 than it has been in 2001. Second, questions about the fate of Holocaust memory should concern us—particularly if my initial response is valid—because the quality of human life depends greatly on what we remember, how we remember, and why we remember. The presence or absence of the Holocaust in our remembering affects those dimensions of life, each and all. Third, to the extent that memory of the Holocaust disappears, indifference to the wasting of human life will become more prominent. In a world with increasing population pressures, the likelihood of repeated genocide will also expand. Fourth, to the extent that Auschwitz and Treblinka become forgotten places, we will lack warnings that are essential to keep us from a complacency that takes good things for granted. Hence, there are indeed reasons—moral and religious imperatives—to remember the Holocaust's history. Those short responses help to identify what I mean by the ethics of memory.

The Ethics of Memory

Holocaust survivor Primo Levi, one of the most perceptive witnesses to that event, reminds us that "human memory is a marvelous but fallacious instrument."[16] Memories (I use the plural consciously so as to include our remembering of particular things) can blur and decay. They can become selective, stylized, embellished, and influenced by later experiences and information. In addition, memories can be confused, distorted, repressed, or denied. Still further, they can breed, inflame, and intensify hate.

Writing with the extremity of Holocaust memories in mind—the survivor's and the perpetrator's—Levi noted that "a person who has been wounded tends to block out the memory so as not to renew the pain; the person who has inflicted the wound pushes the memory deep down, to be rid of it, to alleviate the feeling of guilt."[17] Nevertheless, memories can also be as accurate as they are painful, as clear as they are irrepressible. They can be sharpened, recorded, intensified, documented, and even corrected so that they bear witness to the truth with penetrating insight.

Memories are not entirely in our control. For one reason or another—physiological or psychological—we may lose them. Without memories we could scarcely be moral creatures, for history would dissolve and we would be able neither to identify one another as persons nor to make the connections on which moral decisions depend. But given the fact that we do have memories, we are creatures who cannot avoid responsibility and moral responsibility in particular.

If ethics cannot exist without memory, it is also true that ethical judgment comes to bear on memory. How are we taking care of our memories? Are we doing our best to keep them sharp, clear, documented, and honest? What actions do our memories lead us to take? Do our memories serve good purposes or destructive ones? Such questions stand at the heart of the ethics of memory. Just as our memories say much about who we have been, the uses to which our memories are put say much about who we are and will become.

The points I have made thus far lead to a paradox about Holocaust memories, which can be stated as follows: At the very time when attention to the Holocaust is more prominent and unavoidable than ever, the Holocaust—sooner or later—may also be destined for low-intensity, inconsequential remembrance, if not to being largely forgotten.

To understand the existence of this tension, consider, first, that in the late 1990s hardly a month passed without attention being called to Holocaust history. One only need think of the 2000 Academy Awards, which honored Roberto Benigni and *Life Is Beautiful*, or a much more powerful film—one that avoids sentimentalizing, to say nothing of trivializing, the Holocaust as *Life Is Beautiful* arguably does. I refer to *The Last Days*, which was honored by the Academy as the best documentary feature film in 1999, a study of the destruction of Hungarian Jewry in 1944 and the lives of a few men and women who survived that onslaught.[18] Still other examples are easy to find. Writing in the April 12, 1999, issue of *Time*, for instance, Roger Rosenblatt titled his essay "Paying for Auschwitz." Noting that Swiss banks have agreed to pay $1.25 billion in Holocaust-related claims and observing that firms such as Siemens and I.G. Farben were facing lawsuits from Holocaust survivors and that ex-slave laborers had initiated proceedings against Volkswagen, Krupp, and Daimler-Benz, Rosenblatt went on to mention that Deutsche Bank, Germany's largest bank, had released documents verifying that it extended substantial lines of credit to the builders who constructed the Nazi concentration camp and killing center at Auschwitz. Holocaust-related lawsuits were being brought against Deutsche Bank too, but Rosenblatt underscored something very important about the ethics of memory: "The Holocaust cannot be compensated for."[19] During and after the Holocaust, as Lawrence Langer emphasizes in his 1999 book, *Preempting the Holocaust*, the pursuit of justice was less than successful. During the Holocaust, injustice prevailed. After the Holocaust, we continue to face a wrong that can never be set right. History does not stop when a particular period is over.

Another sign that Holocaust history does not stop can be signified by the name of a place that has been in the news at the turn of the century. I refer to Kosovo. One could scarcely watch television reports about the "ethnic cleansing" and "identity elimination" that Slobodan Milosevic and his criminal Serb regime inflicted on Kosovo's ethnic Albanian population without sensing that there are links between

Kosovo and Nazi-occupied Europe nearly sixty years earlier.[20] Although it is important to avoid facile comparisons that inaccurately equate Milosevic with Hitler or Milosevic's goal in the Balkans with the Nazi intention to kill every Jew in Europe, if not the world, it is nevertheless sobering to consider that the genocidal success of Nazi Germany meant that boundaries were crossed that may have made it easier for Milosevic and his followers to do their dirty work. We live in a post-Holocaust world where the truth of the cry "Never again!" is far from self-evident.

As these examples suggest, the Holocaust magnifies issues about the ethics of memory. That magnification occurs because so much information, so much responsibility, so much guilt, so much pain, anguish, and suffering have been hidden, obscured, evaded, repressed, silenced, rationalized, denied, or more-or-less consciously forgotten. Those patterns, however, have not only been noticed but also resisted by individuals and groups. Holocaust survivors have exercised energetic leadership in this regard. Engaging in their special "memory-work," the survivors have been joined by a significant number of scholars, teachers, writers, and artists who, together with the survivors, have mustered their resources, testimonies, research efforts, pedagogical plans, and creative expressions to bear witness to what happened during the Holocaust years, to document and to commemorate what happened *then* so that forgetfulness will not triumph *now* or *ever*.

At least in the United States, the commitment to fostering memory about the Holocaust is growing as the twenty-first century begins. It is doing so because that memory is becoming increasingly institutionalized. Millions of people annually are visiting Holocaust museums such as the U.S. Holocaust Memorial

Museum in Washington, D.C., and the Museum of Tolerance at the Simon Wiesenthal Center in Los Angeles. Many millions more have seen the film *Schindler's List* in theaters or on television. Tens of thousands of videotaped testimonies from Holocaust survivors have been gathered internationally by the Survivors of the Shoah Visual History Foundation in Los Angeles. Publications and classes about the Holocaust continue to proliferate. Ironically, even those who deny that the Holocaust happened have produced results that they could scarcely have intended, namely, redoubled efforts to document ever more thoroughly and in growing detail that there can be no reasonable doubt about the Holocaust's reality.[21]

Nevertheless, at the beginning of the twenty-first century, nagging doubts remain about the future of Holocaust memories. Those doubts, which include concerns that "Holocaust fatigue" may diminish interest in the event, shadow the sense that either new discoveries about the Holocaust's history or ongoing efforts to institutionalize Holocaust memory are themselves sufficient to withstand the corrosive effects of time's passage. Unquestionably, the vast outpouring of resources to document the Holocaust has been fueled by awareness that the generation of eyewitnesses, especially Holocaust survivors, is dying out.

Institutionalization of the Holocaust cannot guarantee deep memory about it. Soon the survivor generation will be gone. The intensity of concern about the Holocaust may diminish once that generation disappears. As time passes, what will happen to our observances of Yom Hashoah? If they exist in the twenty-second century, how many participants will there be? Who will those people be? Why will they have come? What difference will their presence make? And if Yom Hashoah goes on for a hundred years, what about the vast numbers who will not care in the least because they are indifferent about the Holocaust's history, even if they know something about it?

To focus further on the United States, we Americans are hardly noted for the depth and persistence of our historical consciousness. In our country, an unrelenting invasion of forgetting succeeds too well in putting the past "behind us." It is quite conceivable that even the extensive contemporary American commitments to Holocaust memorialization, education, scholarship, publication, film productions, and oral history and museum projects will all turn out to be rearguard actions against senses of time that in the United States (and in most modern societies) place more attention on the present and the future than on the past. Such thinking at the threshold suggests that, high though it now may be, the Holocaust's impact on American life will gradually decline.

While experiences and events accumulate, even the Holocaust's immense historical significance may not be able to hold its own in the competition for human attention. Hence there is a paradox about Holocaust memory: At the very time when attention to the Holocaust is more prominent and unavoidable than ever before, there are also concerns that the Holocaust—sooner or later—will be substantially obscured.

My thinking often concentrates on that paradox. I have had a small part in increasing attention to the Holocaust, which I believe to be the most important work that I do. Yet I wonder where this effort will lead, given the fact that, in one way or another, memory loss is not only inevitable but widespread in human experience and that, for all but a few, the passion of human attention is focused on what happens in the present or what may happen in the future much more than on what happened in the past.

The ethics of memory involves deciding what we ought to do with what we have experienced and with what we know. In my case, that issue leads to renewed commitment to teach and write about the Holocaust precisely because the threat of forgetting looms so large. When discouraged moods conspire to make me think that the struggle against forgetfulness is likely to be a losing battle, I find myself saying "and yet." And yet . . . it does not follow that America's encounters with the Holocaust will be insignificant and inconsequential or that the concerted efforts to keep Holocaust awareness alive and vital will be without lasting success. To the contrary, even if the tides of forgetfulness cannot be reversed permanently, they may be checked or at least resisted in ways that permit Holocaust encounters to mark American consciousness in decisive ways. To elaborate on this outlook, it can be helpful to relate our theme about the ethics of memory to the idea of *encounters* with the Holocaust.

Holocaust Encounters

Encounters are meetings. They are meetings that take place by chance, face to face, as conflicts, or as some combination of those elements. American life and culture have encountered the Holocaust in all of those ways. As we have noticed already, some of those encounters took place directly during the Holocaust years. Most contemporary encounters with the Holocaust, however, are post-Holocaust meetings with that history's defining places, persons, and processes of destruction. Removed as they are from actual events that others lived through directly in earlier times, such encounters are experiences at secondhand.

Whether they are firsthand or secondhand, encounters with the Holocaust do not happen in general. They take place through the particularities of an individual's experience. When I think about that fact, I am led to three main clusters of ideas regarding encounters with the Holocaust and the ethics of memory. After identifying those clusters, I will illustrate how they work by sharing some of my own post-Holocaust experiences.

The first point to make is that no one can be sure in advance who will be deeply and profoundly affected by the Holocaust. In that sense, encounters with the Holocaust are matters of chance.

Second, such encounters may not be matters of chance alone. In fact, they typically depend on face-to-face meetings. Such meetings are not matters of a fleeting glance, a momentary acknowledgment, or a casual acquaintance. Face-to-face meetings, at least of the kind I have in mind, are sustained, thorough, and profound. They encourage study and invite reflection. They change one's life. Where post-Holocaust encounters with the Holocaust are concerned, these meetings depend especially on teaching and learning. In particular, they depend—not exclusively but centrally—on Holocaust education in museums, universities, colleges, and libraries, the places where there is time for study, opportunity to engage in sustained reflection, and an insistence on immersing oneself, at least for a time, in the vast and overwhelming detail of the Holocaust's history.

Third, if post-Holocaust teaching and learning about the Holocaust take place to the best of our abilities, memory of the Holocaust still will fade, but it will not disappear without a trace. The traces will leave behind a crucial and perhaps lasting impression. That impression will be rooted in conflict that encounters with the Holocaust produce.

The key conflict is ethical. Building on the awareness that the Holocaust was morally wrong—or nothing ever could be—the right kind of post-Holocaust encounters with the Holocaust can sensitize the conscience of individuals and help to make them more humanely conscientious than they would otherwise be. That outcome will not necessarily produce agreement about what a nation's domestic or foreign policies should be. It should mean, however, that questions otherwise unasked will be raised, that silence otherwise unbroken will be lifted, that indifference otherwise unchallenged will be disputed, that protest, resistance, and compassion otherwise unexpressed will find expression.

To illustrate those points briefly, I need to mention that I spent a recent sabbatical on a Fulbright fellowship in Norway. Norway's chapter in the history of the Holocaust may seem comparatively small, even insignificant, but for me, neither description is accurate. True, Norway's Jewish population was minuscule compared, for example, to Poland's. Still, the destruction of Jewish life in Norway was more thorough than in many other Nazi-occupied territories.

Quite by accident, my Oslo apartment, which was in a building constructed in the late 1930s, stood not far from Kirkeveien 23. A relatively new apartment building exists there today, and the address meant nothing particular to me until I learned that Kirkeveien 23 was the place where hundreds of Norwegian Jews were initially confined when roundups took place around the country in late October 1942. Later, many of those same Jews were imprisoned at the Grini concentration camp, which was located about an hour's train ride away from my flat.

As I did my Holocaust studies in Norway, I also visited the country's secondary schools to consult with teachers who have responsibilities for teaching American history and literature to Norwegian students. Typically, those schools contain memorials to Norwegian students who were killed by the Nazis. Among their names are those of Jewish students—Feinberg and Jaffe, for example—who were taken away from their schoolrooms by Norwegian police while their classmates and teachers stood by.

Accidental though some of these encounters were at first, my scholarly interests in the Holocaust were deepened by my further study of these Norwegian events, places, and persons. That study has sharpened my awareness of the Holocaust and deepened my commitment to let it affect me more. So I ponder the fact that there were not very many Jews for the Nazis and their collaborators to arrest in Norway. At the time of the Nazi invasion on April 9, 1940, less than two thousand Jews—about 0.07 percent of a total population of 2.8 million—lived there. That number included between two hundred and four hundred refugees from Germany, Austria, and Czechoslovakia.[22]

The raw numbers of the Holocaust's death toll on the Norwegian Jews are much smaller than in other European countries, but the percentages are not. In one of the relatively remote areas of the European continent, the Final Solution was quite thorough. About 45 percent of the Norwegian Jews were killed by the Nazis and their collaborators in Norway and elsewhere. By comparison, in France and Italy the rates of Jewish death were about 22 and 17 percent, respectively.

Some American visitors to Norway take time to visit the Resistance Museum in Oslo, but probably few Americans who visit or live in Norway know or care very much about its Holocaust history. As I think about my own experience, it is almost by chance that I have come to know and to care a great deal about that history myself. Yet not a day, indeed hardly even an hour, of my time in Norway—or anywhere else for that matter—has passed without thoughts, feelings, imaginings, visions, and memories that create post-Holocaust encounters with the Holocaust for me.

Among other things, I have come to see that the Holocaust stalks the best parts of the American tradition. The Holocaust's "truths" denied basic human equality and human rights; those "truths" were the antithesis of life, liberty, and the pursuit of happiness. Nazi Germany's antisemitism and racism unleashed a nightmare that identified "life unworthy of life" and then targeted it for annihilation. My study of the Holocaust has also driven home to me the incredibly high and lethal price that human life has paid for racial classifications and the almost unavoidable racist thinking that follows from them. In that context, I often think of a Norwegian city called Tromsø, which sits far above the Arctic Circle. Only a very few Jews lived in this remote place, but today in Tromsø there is a memorial stone on which the names of seventeen Tromsø Jews, most of them from three or four families, are inscribed. All of them were killed in the Holocaust. More than any other object I know, that memorial stone in Tromsø sums up for me what the Final Solution was all about.

My awareness of these things leads me to take Elie Wiesel's warning very seriously: "If we stop remembering," he says, "we stop being." No tradition emphasizes memory more than the Jewish tradition from which Wiesel comes. That fact helps to explain why one of his novels, *The Forgotten*, focuses on the struggle of a Holocaust survivor who strives to transmit his story before the devastation of Alzheimer's disease takes its irreversible toll upon his memories. Especially as we age, we can understand Wiesel's point in our personal lives. We dread memory loss; it means an enfeebled life. And at the end of the day, there is definitely a sense in which we stop existing when we can no longer remember. Wiesel fears that the loss of Holocaust memory threatens the very existence of human society. That loss would leave us bereft of much needed warnings about the destructive power of blindness, arrogance, hatred, and dogmatic convictions that we are right and everyone else is wrong.

The existence of memory, however, is not enough. Memory alone is insufficient for our needs. Everything depends on having *good* memory. Good memory depends on vivid recollection and on lucid connection; it requires recalling details with candor, documenting what is recalled, and discerning patterns of action with honesty. But good memory goes beyond those essential qualities too. It involves questions not only about what we remember but also about how we remember, what we do with what we remember, whether we turn memory into something that hurts or something that heals. In those dimensions, good memory compels us to be courageously committed to tell and validate the truth in the best ways we know.

Experience teaches us that memory can be potent. It can hurt and harm. It can incite us to revenge. But memory, especially good memory, can also lead us to protest against injustice, to document what is true, to reach out to help others, and to link people together in friendship. Wiesel often suggests that one of the things we need to learn is how to use memory against itself, how to turn memory away from bitterness, revenge, hate, despair, and silence and toward testimony that finds ways to affirm life.

In saying such things, I want to encourage good memory. To do so with the awareness that the ethics of memory enjoins, I also have to underscore that encounters with the Holocaust, especially when they take place by reading or listening to the testimony of survivors, require what Holocaust scholar Lawrence Langer calls "an experience in *un*learning."[23] What has to be *unlearned* is our tendency to hope too easily that all brokenness can be mended, that all suffering has meaning, that all evil can be overcome and redeemed, that the fragmentation caused by disaster can be repaired, that the human spirit always triumphs. When Holocaust survivor and writer Ida Fink speaks about "the ruins of memory," ethical listening requires us to let those words say what they say.[24]

Especially those of us who encounter the Holocaust at secondhand have to learn how to listen and read so that we will approach the ruins of memory without shallow optimism or false hope or glib statements about "the triumph of the human spirit," which all would deceive us. And yet it remains true that survivors such as Ida Fink, Elie Wiesel, and Primo Levi do use memory against itself in other ways too—to bear witness, to share, to help others, to warn, to touch and influence people they never met and will not know. Where encounters with the Holocaust are concerned, the ethics of memory urges us to do the same.

Post-Holocaust encounters with the Holocaust, including the conflicts those encounters may entail, should keep stalking our souls. If those encounters do not happen, the failure will mean that important questions remain unasked, that silence in need of breaking will not be broken, that indifference will not be challenged enough, that protest, resistance, and compassion will ignore or miss needs that should be served.

In particular, encounters with the Holocaust should make us remember how deadly it can be for racial thinking and racism to reassert themselves, for hate and violence to continue their destructive work, for the insidious perceptions to exist that wealth or class determines justice and that might makes right. If such inquiry into the Holocaust does not have a high priority in contemporary life, then not only will the Holocaust be forgotten more quickly but also the quality of human life may be endangered even more in the twenty-first century than it has been in the bloody twentieth century.

No one knows in advance who might be permanently affected by a post-Holocaust encounter with the Holocaust or how that impact might change a person's life. At least in some cases, those encounters may move people—as nothing else can—to try to mend the world. To a considerable degree, such encounters with the Holocaust may originate as matters of chance. By no means, however, should such encounters be left to chance alone. Only as opportunities for sustained, face-to-face study are ensured in the twenty-first century will it be possible to say that the Holocaust is being remembered well. Meeting that challenge creatively and constructively is one of the best things that Holocaust politics can possibly do.

Chapter Four

How Is the Holocaust a Warning?

The Holocaust demands interrogation and calls everything into question. Traditional ideas and acquired values, philosophical systems and social theories—all must be revised in the shadow of Birkenau.

Elie Wiesel

One of the remarkable friends who has enriched my life is the Belgian diplomat Wilfried Geens. We met in 1973 when my faculty appointment in a study abroad program at Claremont McKenna College took me to Franklin College in Lugano, Switzerland. At the time, Geens was dean of the faculty there, but he was also preparing for the Brussels examinations that would enable him to enter his native country's diplomatic corps. When he invited me to travel in Belgium, I had an excellent teacher. I learned as much as I saw in an old European country that was new to my young American eyes.

In 1973, my focus on World War II and the Holocaust was sharpening. When Geens took me to Ypres and other First World War sites, my understanding of that war's impact on Adolf Hitler deepened. As the two of us hiked in the late February winter in the Ardennes forest and went to the monument at Bastogne that commemorates the Battle of the Bulge, I sensed in ways I had not known before how Europe and the United States are linked. After 1973, Geens and I saw each other infrequently, but we kept in touch while my periodic sabbatical leaves took me to Austria, Japan, Israel, and Norway, and his diplomatic postings took him to places as far afield as Pakistan and the United Nations. So it was that an e-mail message from my Belgian friend appeared on my computer screen in October 2000. It not only announced his latest assignment as Belgian ambassador to Israel but also reflected on the violent turn of events in the Middle East.

My friend's message emphasized the high hopes for a just and lasting peace between Israelis and Palestinians that he had optimistically exchanged with Israeli leaders when he officially presented his diplomatic credentials to them on September 12. Noting the sounds of violence nearby as he wrote to me, Geens lamented that this dream would be deferred if not dashed beyond repair.

As the year 2000 drew to a close, such judgments were not his alone, nor were feelings of lamentation by any means the only ones that found expression as the cycle of provocation, attack, and reprisal defied attempts to break it, revealing that the "peace process" attempted since the 1993 Oslo Accords had negotiated much but settled little. On October 7, for example, by a vote of 14–0, with the United States abstaining, the United Nations Security Council condemned the violence that had broken out on September 28. Singling out what it called "the excessive use of force" against Palestinians, the Security Council called for "the immediate cessation of violence." Five days later, on October 12, the *New York Times* reported that an estimated 15,000 people gathered at the Israeli consulate in Manhattan to protest Palestinian violence and support Israel. The speakers included Elie Wiesel, who expressed outrage at what he identified as the Security Council's "hypocritical vote," which in his view had failed to "condemn Palestinian excessive reactions but condemned Israel's response to them."[1]

In cadences reminiscent of Martin Luther King's "I Have a Dream" speech, Wiesel declared that "we had dreams of Israeli and Palestinian children playing together, studying together, laughing together, and discovering each other's worlds." The Holocaust was at least in the background when he lamented that "our dreams of peace have gone up in the smoke of ransacked synagogues, in the lynching of Israeli prisoners and of blood-thirsty mobs shouting their version of a Jerusalem without Jews and a Middle East without Israel." As Wiesel saw it, responsibility for the destruction of those dreams belonged, first and foremost, to the Palestinian leader Yasser Arafat. Attacking him as "ignorant, devious and unworthy of trust," Wiesel stated that all of Arafat's "promises were lies; all his commitments were false." In addition, Wiesel said that Arafat had "betrayed the highest honor society can bestow upon a person," a reference to the Nobel Peace Prize that Wiesel had won in 1986 and that Arafat had shared with Shimon Peres and Yitzhak Rabin in 1994 for their efforts to create peace in the Middle East.

Scorching though it was, Wiesel's widely reported and broadly disseminated speech did nothing to deter the United Nations General Assembly. On October 20, that body followed the earlier Security Council resolution and condemned Israel's "excessive use of force" against the Palestinians. It also demanded that the violence end immediately. Although denounced by the United States and Israel, this UN resolution passed by a vote of 92–6, with 46 nations abstaining.[2] Resolute though it was, the UN's action seemed to have little effect. By mid-December, there were more than three hundred dead: by mid-April 2001, the death toll had reached 469, including 386 Palestinians, 64 Israeli Jews, and 19 others. Thousands more were wounded, many of them permanently maimed. The continuing violence ensured that those hate-inflaming statistics would rise.

Although most of the dead were Palestinians, Jews had plenty of reasons for mourning and rage as well. On November 20, 2000, to cite only one instance, an armored school bus was traveling between Israeli enclaves in the Palestinian-ruled Gaza Strip when it was bombed. An Israeli teacher and a maintenance man were killed. The blast also dismembered several Jewish children.[3] When Israel responded with a punishing strike by rocket-firing helicopter gunships, the U.S. State Department issued its attempt at an even-handed statement by condemning the "heinous attack" on the school bus and underscoring that "the Israelis also need to understand that the excessive use of force is not the right way to go."[4] Arguably less evenhanded was the action taken by Egypt, which reacted to the violence by recalling Mohammed Bassiouny, its ambassador to Israel, or the step taken by Israel, which handed foreign governments and news agencies a 48-page English-language report contending that the Palestinians had repeatedly broken peace and cease-fire agreements.

On November 22, 2000, the eve of the American holiday of Thanksgiving, no one could say how the current tensions between Israelis and Palestinians would play out, let alone be resolved, a judgment that remained valid as Passover and Easter came and went in the year 2001. The two sides, to use Deborah Sontag's phrase, seemed to be "trapped in and perpetuating a cycle of violence and retribution" with no relief in sight.[5] Sontag's observation was included in her report about a car bomb detonated beside a bus on a crowded street at rush hour, killing two Israelis and wounding dozens more in the coastal city of Hadera. By the end of that November day, which at the time was the deadliest since Intifada II began in late September, at least twelve persons were dead—three Israelis and nine Palestinians—while more violence broke out in Israel and Gaza. As Ehud Barak, the Israeli prime minister at the time, promised that Israel would "get even" for the Hadera attack, a statement he later moderated, Yasser Arafat, who was then in Egypt, launched a verbal attack on the United States. Sontag's *New York Times* report quoted him as saying, "The weapons used are American—American helicopters, American fighter planes, American armored cars, American missiles, American shells, American bombs. The responsibility for this lies with America, the main sponsor of the peace process."

As Thanksgiving came and went, Barak announced his December 10 resignation as Israel's prime minister, gambling that his action would give him the advantage in new elections by denying Benjamin Netanyahu, his Likud rival, the necessary parliamentary status to run against him. The unintended consequence of Barak's political maneuvering was that Ariel Sharon, the hawkish warrior-turned-politician whose name is associated with some of the bloodiest aspects of Israeli history, swamped Barak in the February 6, 2001, elections and became the nation's prime minister. His campaign slogan, "only Sharon can bring peace," raised more questions than it answered as Israelis and Palestinians hunkered down for a long struggle.[6]

Meanwhile, as some Americans had Israel on their minds in November 2000, others noted that a ruling by U.S. District Judge Edward R. Korman seemed to conclude a lengthy dispute about the distribution of the $1.25 billion settlement that Swiss banks have made with Holocaust victims and their heirs.[7] For most Americans, however, news from the Middle East or about Holocaust reparations was dwarfed by national wonder about how the 2000 presidential election would turn out, as issues about the razor-thin vote margin separating George W. Bush and Al Gore in the decisive state of Florida found their way through multiple recounts and courts of law. The decisive moment in that struggle came on the night of December 12, five weeks after election day, when the United States Supreme Court's 5–4 decision ensured that Bush would be the nation's forty-third president.

Prior to the court's historic decision, absentee votes cast by Floridians in Israel loomed larger than usual as the election came down to the wire. Those ballots were in the spotlight partly because of an unprecedented event in American politics, one that connects with what has been called the American Dream, a theme to which I will return shortly. For the first time in American history, a Jew was potentially a few hundred votes and a fatal heartbeat away from becoming president of the United States. More than that, Hadassah Lieberman, the wife of Senator Joseph Lieberman, Al Gore's running mate, is the child of

Holocaust survivors. In accepting his party's vice-presidential nomination in Los Angeles on August 16, 2000, Lieberman recounted his wife's family history: "Her family was literally saved by American GI's who liberated the concentration camps," said Lieberman. "Then her parents escaped Communism and were welcomed as immigrants to America and given a new life. The fact that half a century later, their daughter, would be standing on this stage is a testament to the power of the American Dream."[8] With her distinctive, Holocaust-related legacy, Hadassah Lieberman stood as close to being the nation's first lady as her husband did to occupying the White House. Even with the defeat of the Gore-Lieberman ticket, the significance of those images contains much for Americans to ponder.

When the Battle of the Bulge was under way in Belgium during the winter of 1944–1945, such possibilities, political and symbolic, were not even remote. Owing in part to American antisemitism, they were unthinkable, a judgment whose validity would not have lost much of its credibility in 1973, when I visited Bastogne with Wil Geens, my Belgian guide. By contrast, the existence of the State of Israel and its volatile relations with Arabs and particularly Palestinians, which have been practically inseparable from its founding, history, and future, were much more conceivable in 1944. By 1967 and 1973 they were definitely real as outright warfare seriously threatened Israel's existence for a time.

The twenty-first century's arrival brought possibilities that were unforeseen, if not unforeseeable a generation or two ago. In cases of the kind that the opening of this chapter has identified, they are linked—indirectly, if not directly—to the Holocaust.

As this chapter explores that proposition, it also takes up questions that are central for Holocaust politics. For example, as the cry "Never again!" suggests, the Holocaust appears to be a warning. If the Holocaust is a warning, how does the warning work? What is warned against? How are Holocaust warnings best communicated? What would it mean to heed them? If they are ignored, will it make any difference? Holocaust politics is reflected in and provoked by such questions. Responses to them do much to determine what the quality of that politics will be. This chapter responds to questions of that kind by considering basic moods and attitudes that are fundamental for converting dreams into good realities that can help to mend the world. It stresses moods and attitudes because Holocaust politics finds its grounding in feeling and emotion as much as in thought and policy. These elements, of course, are rarely separable, but as they mix and mingle, it can be worthwhile to emphasize the dispositions and temperaments that are likely to be most helpful for constructive Holocaust politics. Fitting what I will attempt to do, the emphasis will not consist of a set of propositions or a list of virtues. Even less will it offer a theory. Instead the emphasis will be made by trying to set a tone, by calling forth the very moods to which it alludes by telling stories, recounting history, and asking questions. Let us see what may happen as those elements interact.

Converting Dreams into Realities

On January 17, 1896, the *Jewish Chronicle*, a London weekly, published Theodor Herzl's preview of his book, *The Jewish State*, which appeared a few weeks later. Calling for "the restoration of the Jewish State" as the only practical answer to "the Jewish Question," Herzl, the father of secular Zionism and the founder of the World Zionist Organization, emphasized that his idea was not new but very old. "It is remarkable," his *Jewish Chronicle* essay went on to say, "that we Jews should have dreamt this kingly dream all through the long night of our history. Now day is dawning. We need only rub the sleep out of our eyes, stretch our limbs, and convert the dream into a reality."[9]

Converting dreams into realities—the histories of the United States and the State of Israel are intertwined, even interdependent, but one of the most important links involves the ways in which dreams have governed their realities, and how both their dreams and their realities have been affected by Holocaust politics and the questions it entails. Here I develop parts of that theme by concentrating on aspects of American experience, but I will do so with references and allusions that bring to mind Israeli dreams as well.

A personal American dream was converted into reality in 1982 when I had the opportunity to spend a sabbatical leave as visiting professor of Holocaust studies at Israel's University of Haifa. Among my most memorable experiences in Haifa, I remember particularly a brief but striking conversation with a student while the two of us waited for our buses home one spring evening. I did not learn the student's name, but I have not forgotten what he said.

Older than my students in the United States, this *sabra* was dressed differently as well. Army duty necessitated that he and significant numbers of his peers periodically came to the university in military garb, carrying weapons along with their books. This particular student-soldier talked tougher than he seemed. Was there some ambivalence within him, symbolized perhaps by his simultaneous toting of scholarly books and weapons of war?

When he learned that I was a visiting professor, a Christian from California, he asked what I taught. I told him about my work in the university's Holocaust studies program and explained how my courses dealt with the Final Solution. Thereafter I mostly listened, because the student-soldier was more irritated than impressed. Such courses, he stressed, were of little use to him. He already knew what the Holocaust taught, namely, that weakness is a recipe for disaster. Since the establishment of the State of Israel in 1948, he continued, there had been more than enough struggle to occupy his attention. Concern about the Holocaust seemed unhelpful. How much better it would be, he insisted, to move beyond that sad catastrophe of powerlessness and to concentrate instead on the happier lessons of Israel's strength, its determined and successful self-defense in a post-Holocaust world.

The quick rush of his words, their apparently unquestioning delivery, have made me wonder. Was he reassuring himself of their truth? Does he still believe them? Our respective bus departures cut the conversation short. Time permitted no answer. Still, the young man's "last word" has remained with me. "If Jews had possessed a state of their own," he asserted on the run, "there would have been no Holocaust."

Although Theodor Herzl died in 1904, decades before the twentieth-century's unprecedented genocidal horrors began, that student-soldier in Haifa might have echoed Herzl's intuitions. Be that as it may, I still wonder whether the young man ever had second thoughts about his last words to me. Certainly I have had them, because no more now than then do those last words seem entirely convincing. Not only does such a proposition fail to emphasize how tragically complicated the relations between the Holocaust and Israeli independence turned out to be, but also the claim's implications treat the victims of the Final Solution unfairly by emphasizing their powerlessness to the exclusion of their determination to survive against overwhelming odds.

If not fantasy, moreover, it can be only fiction—based on a counterfactual analysis that a close reading of history makes speculative at best—to think that in the first half of the twentieth century there could have been a Jewish state capable of preventing what Nazi Germany did to European Jewry. Even to absorb successfully in Palestine the flood of Jewish refugees that would have materialized—if by some miracle, for example, the Wannsee Conference of January 20, 1942, had not ratified the Final Solution that was already under way but facilitated Jewish emigration from all Nazi-controlled territory instead—is to fantasize possibilities that strain credulity at every turn.

That said, the Haifa student-soldier's parting word still makes its case. Statelessness can mean helplessness and hopelessness. Defenselessness is unsound strategic policy. National power does make one's opponents think twice before tampering with it, and anyone who tampers with Israel's security, or with Jewish well-being anywhere in the world, should not expect to do so with impunity. I will return to points related to these themes of power and powerlessness, confidence and ambivalence, might and right, but first let us consider some other realities that can make us think about dreams and Holocaust questions.

Surviving the Holocaust

After Nazi Germany surrendered in May 1945, about eleven million homeless and uprooted people in central Europe—non-German former prisoners of war, former forced laborers, and concentration camp survivors—were classified by the Allies as "displaced persons" (DPs).[10] About seven to eight million of the DPs were in Germany and the territories of its former allies. Most of those people eventually returned to their native lands. By the end of September 1945, however, nearly 1.5 million DPs remained in Germany and Austria. They included about 50,000 Jews, mostly from Eastern Europe, as well as hundreds of Roma and Sinti (Gypsies), who had recently been liberated from Nazi camps. These people lived in DP camps that were often former concentration camps, still enclosed by barbed wire. Here the living conditions for the DPs were poor. Food was meager, the living quarters overcrowded, and sanitation inadequate. Lodged together with non-Jewish DPs, including at times Nazi collaborators and former enemy prisoners of war, the "liberated" Jews were still targets of antisemitic outbursts. Not until late in 1945 did some DP camps become specifically Jewish camps, where the needs of the Jewish survivors could be better served.

Relief agencies such as the United Nations Relief and Rehabilitation Administration (UNRRA), the Jewish Brigade, the American Jewish Joint Distribution Committee (the "Joint"), and the Organization for Rehabilitation through Training (ORT) worked to improve living conditions and to provide educational and occupational training for the Jewish survivors in the DP camps. As the months passed, Jewish life began to renew itself, even in the ruins. Survivors married and new families formed as the Jewish DPs made new beginnings. Nevertheless, the DP camps were never very happy places.

Many Jews died in the DP camps, victims of the abuse they had undergone during the war. Others tried to return to their former homes, only to find that their property had been looted or confiscated. In fact, because of intensified antisemitism in Poland and other parts of Eastern Europe, the population of the Jewish DP camps greatly increased as 1945 ended. By the time the majority of the Jewish DP camps closed in 1952, nearly 250,000 Jews had lived in them while waiting for the opportunity to emigrate. Eventually, the Jewish DPs found homes: 142,000 went to Israel, 72,000 to the United States, 16,000 to Canada, 8,000 to Belgium, 2,000 to France, and about 10,000 to Latin America and other places.[11]

The goal for tens of thousands of Holocaust survivors was emigration to Palestine, where they hoped to establish and live in an independent Jewish homeland.[12] But the British controlled Jewish immigration to Palestine. Fearing that a flood of Jewish refugees would alienate the Arab world, the British were unwilling to permit large-scale Jewish entry. They permitted a meager legal quota of 1,500 Jews per month and clamped down on "illegal immigration." Nevertheless, between 1945 and 1948, tens of thousands of Jews tried to flee to Palestine, crossing borders in any way they could. During that period, about seventy thousand Jews made the journey by sea on sixty-four ships. Often, the ships carrying Jewish refugees were intercepted by the British blockade. As a result, about 52,000 Jews spent up to two years in British detention camps on the island of Cyprus.

International pressure encouraged the establishment of a Jewish homeland. On May 14, 1948, several months after the United Nations voted to divide Palestine into a Jewish and an Arab state and the British had begun their withdrawal from Palestine, David Ben-Gurion, head of the provisional government and subsequently the nation's first prime minister, proclaimed the establishment of the State of Israel. Even if its earlier arrival could have done so, however, Israel's independence came too late to save the Jews of Europe from the Holocaust. In addition, Israel's existence does not undo the horror of the Final Solution. Some opinions emphasize that Israel's existence means that Hitler did not win; other opinions sometimes add that the State of Israel is even a sign of God's faithfulness to the covenant made with God's chosen people. Those views often inflame Holocaust politics because they collide with the persistent theme that nothing, the State of Israel included, should or can be an "answer" to the Holocaust. At the same time, as the Jewish homeland, Israel has given many survivors a chance to rebuild their lives. Its existence provides a sense of security for Jews worldwide. Its reality underscores that Hitler did not get his way, at least not completely.

Meanwhile, although immigration restrictions did not make it easy for Holocaust survivors to enter the United States, tens of thousands of them did reach America after the end of the war. They did not, however, have an easy time in the land of the free. They often arrived poor, jobless, without knowing English, and haunted by immensely difficult memories. Their feelings about their new homeland, moreover, were complicated when they learned that the United States had not done all it could have done to help Jews during and after the Holocaust.[13] Moreover, American life is not free, even now, from antisemitism. Nevertheless, Holocaust survivors in the United States are deeply devoted to their adopted country, and many of them have been able to rebuild their lives successfully here.[14] Their presence in America is a gift, a warning, that should make us remember how precious—and how precarious—the rights to life, liberty, and the pursuit of happiness really are.

Precious and Precarious Beliefs

Beliefs about rights to life, liberty, and the pursuit of happiness are at the heart of American dreams. Indeed, versions of those beliefs inform the best of human dreams, but the Holocaust raises questions about those same rights and beliefs about them. Those questions issue warnings about the difficulties of converting dreams into realities. With those themes in mind, consider that President Bill Clinton issued his 1998 Labor Day message on September 7 from Dublin, Ireland. An ocean away from Monica Lewinsky and from Kenneth Starr's grand jury inquiry, he paid tribute to "America's working men and women." As he did so, Clinton stressed that "our nation is enjoying unprecedented growth and prosperity. Our economy is the best it has been in a generation." Then the President listed goals that he wanted Americans to pursue: a higher minimum wage, better training and continuing education for American workers, and affordable health care, to mention a few. His message closed by urging that "we can make the American Dream a reality for all our people and build a brighter future for our children."[15]

Americans dream. To borrow a line from Arthur Miller's *Death of a Salesman*, doing so "comes with the territory."[16] Frequently we Americans sum up our dreams—or at least our political leaders do—by referring to the "American Dream." Bill Clinton liked that concept a lot. So do Al Gore and George W. Bush, the latter incorporating the concept into his first speech as President-elect, when on the evening of December 13, 2000, he spoke of creating "an America that is open, so every citizen has access to the American Dream." Meanwhile, notice a few more points about American dreams and the American Dream. In 1931—during the Great Depression and only a short time before Hitler's rise to power—an American historian named James Truslow Adams first published a widely read and often reprinted book called *The Epic of America*. One of the first to popularize the concept of the American Dream, Adams contended that, apart from the Dream, the glory of America's epic would be lost. Indeed, he believed this Dream was "the greatest contribution" the United States had "as yet made to the thought and welfare of the world."[17] Adams summed up his vision by referring to

> that dream of a land in which life should be better and richer and fuller for every [person], with opportunity for each according to his [or her] ability or achievement. . . . It is not a dream of motor cars and high wages merely, but a dream of a social order in which each man and each woman shall be able to attain to the fullest stature of which they are innately capable, and be recognized by others for what they are, regardless of the fortuitous circumstances of birth or position.[18]

As inviting, elusive, and ambiguous, as tantalizing, ambitious, and yet frustrating as those ideas remain, the Dream appears again and again in American culture. Advertising and political rhetoric are only two sources, suggesting that "the American Dream," at least as a concept, still has plenty of life. Real estate commercials often equate the American Dream with home ownership. During the 1996 presidential election, the Republicans titled their party's platform "Restoring the American Dream." Bill Clinton spoke for presidents before and after him when he proclaimed that "we can make the American Dream a reality for all our people."

Turning in a different direction, book titles are another prolific source for American Dream references. A quick web site check at Amazon.com, for instance, will turn up several hundred titles that use the phrase, more than a few of them published in the last year or two. Among the more intriguing titles I have found are *Denim: An American Dream*, *Crime and the American Dream*, and one of my favorites, Bob Garfield's *Waking Up Screaming from the American Dream: A Roving Reporter's Dispatches from the Bumpy Road to Success*. As some of the book titles indicate, the American Dream provokes diverse reactions. In fact, *re-* words are often associated with it. Literally you can fill in the blank, _____ *the American Dream*, with words such as *Recapturing*, *Reclaiming*, *Redefining*, *Redesigning*, *Reinterpreting*, *Reinventing*, *Remembering*, *Rescuing*, *Reviving*, and even *Re-manufacturing*.

Coupled with James Truslow Adams's idea that the American Dream is about a "better and richer and fuller" life, the variety of book titles suggests that the contents of the American Dream are not simply identified, let alone easily reconciled or smoothly put into practice. How, for instance, will Americans interpret the words when the Dream is defined to mean a "better and richer and fuller" life for every American? How should we Americans interpret words like those?

One of the fascinating and potent features of the American Dream is that this concept is and always has been composed of many dreams. Many of those dreams are basically economic or materialistic—owing a house, buying a car, finding a well-paid job—the elements promoted most by advertising, in which the concept of the Dream is often used to create visions of success defined in terms of wealth, power, and the creature comforts of an upwardly mobile standard of living. Other versions of the Dream stress moral, political, and religious ideals. They champion human rights, freedom, justice, integrity, character, and honor. Usually these diverse ingredients mix and mingle, but not always clearly, coherently, and harmoniously. The material aspects of the Dream tend to take priority, partly because they are connected to the ideal dimensions. Nevertheless, the ideal dimensions of the Dream cannot be reduced to material considerations. To the contrary, the material aspirations that drive so many of us Americans depend upon ideals that are integral to the Dream but that are too easily and too often taken for granted.

Not a Day Goes By

American dreams and Holocaust questions converge, even collide, when we think about ideals that are integral to the Dream but that are too easily and too often taken for granted. We can draw closer to that intersection by observing that moviegoers were brought to tears by Steven Spielberg's *Saving Private Ryan*. As you may recall, the film opens with a shattering reenactment of the Allies' D-Day invasion at Normandy on June 6, 1944. Then it narrates how Captain John Miller, a high school English teacher from Pennsylvania, and his small unit save James Francis Ryan, the Iowa farm boy whose three older brothers have already been killed in action.

D-Day was essential to destroying Nazi Germany's domination of Europe. The Nazi grip that D-Day helped to break included the Holocaust. D-Day also played a part in events that brought the State of Israel into existence. Now we remember the Holocaust decades after the founding of the Israeli state. Rosh Hashanah and Yom Kippur, the Jewish tradition's High Holy Days, are annually observed without anything approaching the catastrophic conditions in which those sacred times were marked in the Warsaw ghetto in 1942 or in Auschwitz in 1944. Had the Nazis succeeded, however, there would have been no celebration of Israeli independence and those Jewish religious observances would have become things of the past.

Saving Private Ryan covers seven days of the Normandy campaign. The story's wartime part ends on June 13 when Captain Miller and most of his men are overrun and killed as they try to stop German troops who have been ordered to turn back the Allies' advance. Private Ryan survives. Some critics have said that Spielberg's film—drenched in male blood as it is—definitely belongs in the "guy movie" category. Perhaps it does, but I have not forgotten a scene filled with women seated at row upon row of typewriters. Their keystrokes wrote official words of condolence that did little to assuage grief but much to document war's toll, which included the wasting of dreams worth having. Day after day those women prepared letters that announced the death of husbands, fathers, sons, and brothers. Those letters, however, were received, read, and probably saved primarily by women—wives, mothers, and daughters among them. Although in different ways, life and death—especially in wartime—separate and bind us together in relations and feelings so deep and mysterious that they all but elude any words we can muster.

Its story told from an American perspective, *Saving Private Ryan* has a subplot that takes us inside the lives of the men in Captain Miller's unit. Between battles, they talk in moments of reprieve. More specifically, they gripe, they remember, they ask about each other's lives before the war, they listen to each other's stories, and they wonder how the war will end for them and what will happen when it is over. By no means are they convinced that the future holds for them a "better and richer and fuller" life, but their lives are on the line for dreams of that kind nonetheless. For the most part, Captain Miller's men give him their allegiance, even their admiration and affection, but he is something of an enigma. He says that ninety-four men have been killed under his command. His men see his right hand shake; they do not see him weep, although he does. Sometimes they worry about him, sensing that their destiny is peculiarly dependent on his. Captain Miller accepts the orders he is given; he is even prepared to lead his unit to take avoidable risks and to make voluntary sacrifices to keep people they do not know from falling into harm's way.

Captain Miller's men have a lottery to see who can correctly identify where he comes from and what he did before war's cruelty—not of their own choosing—forged links of life-and-death interdependence among them. A conversation between the captain and one of his men shows that he knows the writings of Ralph Waldo Emerson, an American writer who dreamed of self-reliance, but when John Miller finally reveals that he is a family man who has been a high school English teacher and a baseball coach as well, his men are surprised, although perhaps not entirely, for *Captain* Miller is also a teacher and a coach.

Saving Private Ryan does not begin with D-Day but with an aging man on a pilgrimage fifty-four years later. On June 6, 1998, he is on his way to a military cemetery, but before the particularity of his visit is revealed, our eyes are drawn into his—and then the carnage on Omaha Beach engulfs us. It is "only a movie," we remind ourselves, and yet we can hardly bear to watch. We want to stop our ears against the sounds of violence and death that surround us, even if they are only in Dolby-digital.

Three days after helping to secure the Normandy beachhead, Captain Miller and his men get another mission: They must save a very particular Private Ryan—not one with a similar name who hails from Minnesota but James Francis Ryan from Iowa. It is not clear to anyone in the captain's unit how much sense this mission makes in the wake of all that has been and surely will be lost.

James Francis Ryan makes it home again. Years later, he returns to Normandy with his family. He has come to pay respects to Captain Miller and the men who saved him. Finding the white cross inscribed with the captain's name and his date of death, June 13, 1944, Private Ryan kneels and his eyes fill with tears as he remembers.

On June 13, 1944, Private Ryan heard the last words that Captain Miller spoke as he lay dying. "Earn this," Miller had said to Private Ryan softly. Then, in a voice that revealed his life was leaving, the captain repeated those words—"Earn this"—and Private Ryan heard them as an order, Captain Miller's last.[19]

More than fifty years later, Ryan speaks to the man he scarcely knew but who had saved him nonetheless. "Not a day goes by I don't think about what happened on that bridge. About what we did, and what you said to me. . . . I've tried," he goes on to say. "Tried to live my life the best I could. I hope that's enough. I didn't invent anything. I didn't cure any diseases. I worked a farm. I raised a family. I lived a life. I only hope, in your eyes at least, I earned what you did for me." For James Ryan, not a day goes by without remembering what happened *then* and without asking, as a result, what should happen *now*. Not a day goes by without the challenge of converting good dreams into the best realities one can produce. Such reflection should govern the actions that Holocaust politics takes.

Ryan's words contain dreams. They also contain doubts, perhaps some survivor guilt. How could they not, for what could one do that would be enough to compensate for the gift of life that Captain Miller and his men had bestowed upon him? Modesty and humility of that kind have a place in Holocaust politics too, lest it become a clash for domination over others. Sensing his anguish, perhaps even his unspoken plea for reassurance, Ryan's wife, Alice, approaches, and she listens as he asks her: "Alice . . . have I lived a good life? Am I a good man? . . . Just tell me . . . tell me if you think I've earned it."

"Oh, yes," she answers. "Yes, you have." Where Holocaust politics is concerned, such assurance must really be earned, not taken for granted. Furthermore, Ryan's questions should take precedence over his wife's assurance, for they quicken the interrogation of our assumptions and the revision of our policies that the shadow of Birkenau will continue to require.

American life can be deceptive. Its success can lull us into forgetfulness or indifference about the costs of dreams. Americans tend to think, for example, that new beginnings are always possible. That belief has long stood at the heart of the American Dream; it reflects better than any other the optimism that is so characteristically American and helps to explain why rhetoric about the Dream caught on in the United States. That strand of thought has been strengthened by other hopeful beliefs, including affirmation of the unalienable rights enshrined in the Declaration of Independence, trust in the Constitution, conviction that opportunities still remain for individuals to achieve material prosperity and their own versions of happiness, confidence that the United States can successfully meet any challenge, and faith that the nation is sincerely dedicated to human equality, respect for diversity, justice, and freedom of choice. But what grounds these beliefs? What makes us confident about them? Or, if we are losing confidence about them, why is that the case? How well do we practice what we preach? To what extent can we Americans do what our dreams say? What do we too easily take for granted? About what do we fail to care enough? Dilemmas, betrayals, misgivings, skepticism, and cynicism stalk American dreams because the answers to such crucial questions are not always reassuring. Part of *Saving Private Ryan*'s impact has been that it can make us think about those issues, especially the one about taking good things for granted.

The Fatal Dependence of All Human Actions

Considering the importance of not taking good things for granted, let us turn next to a phrase that has long governed my thinking and teaching, a concept that focuses further how the Holocaust is a warning. The phrase was coined by the scholar-journalist Gitta Sereny. Her encounters with a man named Franz Stangl drove home to her what she calls "the fatal interdependence of all human actions."[20]

Formerly the commandant of Nazi death camps on Polish soil at Sobibor and Treblinka, Stangl was sentenced to life imprisonment by a West German court on December 22, 1970. Early in April of the next year, Sereny met him for the first time. The result was a memorable series of interviews not only with Stangl himself but also with his family and many of his associates. These ingredients formed the basis for Sereny's 1974 book, *Into That Darkness: An Examination of Conscience*. It remains among the most instructive studies of the Holocaust.

Sereny's inquiry emerged from hopes that it might reveal, as she put it, "some new truth which would contribute to the understanding of things that had never yet been understood."[21] Specifically, she wondered, could Franz Stangl have left the path that took him to Treblinka? And if he could have left that path, would it have made any difference?

As Sereny probed her findings, she drew the following conclusions: Individuals remain responsible for their action and its consequences, but persons are and must be responsible for each other too. What we do as individuals, contended Sereny, "is deeply vulnerable and profoundly dependent on a climate of life" that reflects "the fatal interdependence of all human actions."[22]

If Gitta Sereny is correct to speak of "the fatal interdependence of all human actions"—and I think she is—then how might that idea advance our thinking about Holocaust politics? One perspective is illustrated by Stingo, the young American dreamer whose "voyage of discovery," as William Styron describes it, fills the pages of Styron's controversial novel, *Sophie's Choice*.[23] Initiated by Sophie Zawistowska, a fictional Polish Catholic who, like thousands of her actual Polish sisters and brothers, experienced Auschwitz, Stingo in 1947 learns about a world very different from his own. As Sophie's story unfolds, Stingo undergoes shocks of recognition, including, as he relates the incident, "the absurd fact that on that afternoon, as Sophie first set foot on the railroad platform in Auschwitz, it was a lovely spring morning in Raleigh, North Carolina, where I was gorging myself on bananas."[24] On that day—Styron says it was April Fool's Day, 1943—Stingo was seventeen. He was desperately trying to make the weight requirement for enlistment in the United States Marines. He squeaked by. He had not heard of Auschwitz.

American dreams and Holocaust questions—in some ways these dimensions of life are as different as the experiences of Sophie and Stingo in April 1943. And yet those realities intersect and challenge each other in ways that can make one wonder. From their inception, American self-images reflected the idea that the past did not bind one irrevocably. Fresh starts could be made, tomorrow promised to be better than today, and progress always seemed possible. In Styron's novel about Sophie Zawistowska, Stingo meets her in "a place as strange as Brooklyn," but their shared experience climaxes in Washington, D.C. "We walked through the evening in total silence," Stingo recalls. "It was plain that Sophie and I could appreciate neither the symmetry of the city nor its air of wholesome and benevolent peace. Washington suddenly appeared paradigmatically American, sterile, geometrical, unreal." Auschwitz, realized Stingo, "stalked my soul as well as hers. Was there no end to this?" he wondered, "no end?"[25] What if Auschwitz stalks our souls too? What would that presence do to American dreams? Should it make them "paradigmatically American, sterile, geometrical, unreal," or should Holocaust questions make something else of those dreams?

Given my American identity, which involves elements akin to Stingo's, such questions strike me as looming large for the United States. But versions of them can be equally real for persons of any nationality who find that Auschwitz stalks their souls too. Elie Wiesel may have had that kind of human interdependence in mind when he wrote that "the Holocaust demands interrogation and calls everything into question. Traditional ideas and acquired values, philosophical systems and social theories—all must be revised in the shadow of Birkenau."[26] Those words ring so true that Holocaust politics should never forget them. Whatever the traditional ideas and acquired values that have existed, whatever the philosophical systems and social theories that human minds have produced, whatever the dreams that have been dreamed, they either helped to pave the way to Auschwitz, failed to block the way to that place soon enough, or left us in a world that continues to be plagued by warfare, ethnic cleansing, and genocide, as well as violence in the Middle East.

Looking back to World War II, American attention could not have been completely focused on the European theater, let alone the Holocaust, because the United States was waging a massive war against Japan in the Pacific. Among the shadows of that campaign, however, something closer to my California home in the United States bears remembering. Authorized by an executive order signed by President Franklin D. Roosevelt on February 19, 1942, just a few weeks after Japan's bombing of Pearl Harbor, the federal government—supposedly to forestall possible attacks by Japanese agents against strategic installations in the United States—took action to "relocate" 120,000 ordinary citizens and immigrants of Japanese descent to ten internment camps. Most of these people lived in California at the time.

The internment's legality was contested, but only in 1944 did the Supreme Court rule on it. Notwithstanding comments about the melancholy resemblance the evacuation bore to some Nazi treatment of the Jews, the Court held that the military, under certain special circumstances, could legally segregate "all citizens of Japanese ancestry." Troubling precedents lurk in that decision, foremost the Court's overriding of constitutional guarantees to equal protection under the law for American citizens.

Manzanar, it must be underscored, was not Auschwitz, and Tule Lake was not Treblinka. American policy was far removed from Nazi genocide. Yet, as John R. Dunne, the Justice Department official who supervised the redress effort, has said, "The injustice of the forced evacuation and detainment of citizens without due process of the law was a constitutional travesty."[27] It still stands as one of the nation's worst violations of individual rights.

Furthermore, even if the history cannot be detailed here, it also bears remembering that historian David S. Wyman hits the target when he writes about "the abandonment of the Jews" by the United States during the Hitler era.[28]

In the late 1930s, restrictive immigration policies meant that the American Dream of Emma Lazarus, a

Jewish poet whose words "Give me your tired, your poor, / Your huddled masses yearning to breathe free" are inscribed on the Statue of Liberty, would be a dream tragically deferred for many of her own people who might have escaped the Holocaust. "Negative attitudes toward Jews," Wyman shows, "penetrated all sectors of wartime America."[29] Even after public governmental acknowledgment in December 1942 that the Jews were being slaughtered en masse, the government was not moved to take action specifically directed at alleviating their plight. Not least of the reasons for that inaction was American antisemitism. According to Wyman, polls taken from August 1940 until the war's end showed that 15 to 24 percent of the respondents "looked upon Jews as 'a menace to America.'"[30] Such ingredients conspired to yield a record less noble than the American Dream might like to envision. But Birkenau's shadow on American ground does not stop there. From 1980 to 1983, for example, Allan A. Ryan, Jr., directed the Office of Special Investigations, a division of the United States Department of Justice, formed in 1979 to identify and prosecute Nazi criminals in America. Ryan hoped the nation's "record in dealing with Nazi war criminals is not entirely beyond salvage," but he also estimated that hundreds, if not thousands, of German and Eastern European war criminals found a haven here after the Second World War. "The record is clear," asserts Ryan. "Preventing the entry of Nazi criminals to the United States was not a high priority, and was not taken seriously."[31]

Black and Blue

Allan Ryan's report would have saddened but not surprised the brilliant African-American novelist Ralph

Ellison. In 1945, he was working on a different narrative when what he identified as "blues-toned laughter" began to dominate his imagination. Eventually the laughter compelled him to give full expression to its voice, which belonged to the "invisible" black man "who had been forged in the underground of American experience and yet managed to emerge less angry than ironic."[32]

Ellison's postponed story was to be about an American pilot. Downed by the *Luftwaffe* and interned in a German POW camp, he was the highest ranking officer there and thus, owing to war's conventions, the spokesman for his fellow prisoners. Like Ellison himself, the American pilot was black. Prisoner of racists and also the "leader" of prisoners who in normal American circumstances would not see him as their equal, let alone as their superior, Ellison's pilot would have to navigate his way between the democratic ideals he affirmed and "the prevailing mystique of race and color." This dilemma, Ellison adds, was to be "given a further twist of the screw by [the black pilot's] awareness that once the peace was signed, the German camp commander could immigrate to the United States and immediately take advantage of freedoms that were denied the most heroic of Negro servicemen."[33]

If Ralph Ellison never finished that story, his pilot's voice, like that of *Invisible Man*, would seem to echo Langston Hughes's poem, "Let America Be America Again": "Oh yes, / I say it plain, / America never was America to me, / And yet I swear this oath— / America will be! / An ever-living seed, / Its dream / Lies deep in the heart of me."[34] *Invisible Man* ends where it begins. Ellison's character is in the underground hideout where American life has driven him. He is awakening from a state of hibernation, as he calls it, and his awakening entails writing. Thus, in the novel's epilogue (making poetry out of invisibility, it is, in my judgment, one of the most insightful writings produced by an American author), Ellison expresses his character's outlook as follows:

> So why do I write, torturing myself to put it down? Because in spite of myself I've learned some things. Without the possibility of action, all knowledge comes to one labeled "file and forget," and I can neither file nor forget. Nor will certain ideas forget me; they keep filing away at my lethargy, my complacency. . . . So it is that now I denounce and defend, or feel prepared to defend. I condemn and affirm, say no and say yes, say yes and say no. I denounce because though implicated and partially responsible, I have been hurt to the point of abysmal pain, hurt to the point of invisibility. And I defend because in spite of all I find that I love. In order to get some of it down I *have* to love. I sell you no phony forgiveness, I'm a desperate man—but too much of your life will be lost, its meaning lost, unless you approach it as much through love as through hate. So I approach it through division. So I denounce and I defend and I hate and I love.[35]

Ralph Ellison's emphasis on diversity and his approach "through division" resonate with Elie Wiesel's insistence that the shadow of Birkenau warns against placing too much confidence in "answers." Wiesel's urging—"the questions," he contends, "remain questions"— is to resist that temptation, especially when it aims to settle things that ought to remain unsettled and unsettling.[36] For if answers aim to settle things, their ironic, even tragic, outcome is that they too often produce injustice and death.

People are less likely to savage and annihilate each other when their minds are not made up but opened up through questioning. The Holocaust shows as much. It happened because human minds became convinced that they could figure everything out. Those minds "understood" that one religion had superseded another. They "comprehended" that one race was superior to every other. They "saw" what nature's laws decreed, namely, that there was *lebensunwertes Leben* ("life unworthy of life"). Thus, they "realized" who deserved to live and who deserved to die. Hitler and his Nazi followers "knew" they were "right." Their "knowing" made them killers. Before it was too late, questioning might have redeemed those who became the killers and their victims.

One can argue, of course, that such "knowing" undermined rationality and perverted morality. It did. And yet to say that much is too little, for one must ask about the sources of such undermining and perversion. When that asking occurs, part of its trail leads to the tendency of human reason to presume that indeed it can, at least in principle, figure everything out.

As Ellison, Hughes, Styron, and others help to show, destructive qualities of mind—certainly not identical but still akin to those that took Elie Wiesel to Auschwitz—also scar American ground. They led Ellison's invisible man to remark (and he speaks for more than himself) that "I'd like to hear five recordings of Louis Armstrong . . . playing and singing all at the same time":

> Cold empty bed,
> Springs hard as lead,
> Pains in my head,
> Feel like old Ned,
> What did I do to be so black and blue?
> No joys for me,
> No company,
> Even the mouse
> Ran from my house.
> All my life through, I've been so black and blue.
> I'm white inside, it don't help my case.
> 'Cause I can't hide what is on my face.
> I'm so forlorn,
> Life's just a thorn,
> My heart is torn,
> Why was I born?
> What did I do to be so black and blue?[37]

The Shadow of Birkenau

The shadow of Birkenau questions American dreams. In William Styron's story about Sophie Zawistowska, an SS doctor gave her what the Holocaust scholar Lawrence Langer calls a "choiceless choice."[38] Such choices are neither normal nor made in circumstances of one's own choosing; they are "choices" that are forced and between options that are unacceptable or worse. Sophie could pick which of her two children, Jan or Eva, should go to the gas. "'*Ich kann nicht wählen!*' she screamed."[39] Sophie could not choose.

And yet, so as not to lose them both, she let Eva go. Limited though it was, Sophie's choice was real. So was her sense of guilt. Set free in 1945, she found her way to the United States. "But," as the lyric from the musical *Les Miserables* so aptly states, "there are dreams that cannot be, / And there are storms we cannot weather." Sophie's "liberation" was no liberation; it left her in the shadow of Birkenau. She found inescapable the conclusion that her own life, even in America where she hoped for a new beginning, was not worth living. In 1947, Sophie let it go too—also by choice.

Had Sophie Zawistowska been a Jew, she would have had no choice, for Hitler's racist antisemitism and the power of his Nazi state destined all Jews for annihilation. Such facts prompted another of America's eminent Jewish thinkers, Richard L. Rubenstein, to write *The Cunning of History: The Holocaust and the American Future*. His reflections make me wonder about the "truths" that Thomas Jefferson taught Americans to hold "self-evident."

None of those truths is more crucial to American dreams than the claim that persons are "endowed by their Creator with certain unalienable Rights." Those rights, Jefferson believed, are not merely legal privileges that people grant to each other as they please. Rather, his philosophy held, reason—rightly used—shows that such rights are "natural." Part and parcel of what is meant by human existence, they belong equally to all humanity and presumably cannot be violated with impunity. Nonetheless, the sense in which rights are unalienable—inviolable, absolute, unassailable, inherent—is an elusive part of Jefferson's Declaration, which states that "to secure these rights, Governments are instituted among Men." Apparently unalienable rights are not invulnerable, but if they are not invulnerable, then in what way are they unalienable?

One important answer could be that what *is* and what *ought to be* are clearly not the same, and reason can make the distinction. To speak of unalienable rights, therefore, is to speak of conditions of existence so basic that they ought never to be abrogated. Persuasive though it may be, such reasoning may still give too little comfort. Rights to life, liberty, and the pursuit of happiness are qualified repeatedly, even by governments that seek to secure them. Far more radically, Auschwitz questions the *functional* status of unalienable rights. In Rubenstein's words, for example, the Holocaust, genocide, and related instances of mass death suggest that "there are absolutely no limits to the degradation and assault the managers and technicians of violence can inflict upon men and women who lack the power of effective resistance."[40]

While it is still true that many say that certain rights must not be usurped, if those rights are frequently violated completely and all too often with impunity—and they are—how can they convincingly be called "natural" or "unalienable"? Is that not one more idealistic illusion, another instance of how the American Dream obscures reality? Rubenstein's proposition is certainly arguable, but he contends that greater credibility is found when one concludes that "*rights do not belong to men by nature*. To the extent that men have rights, they have them only as members of the polis, the political community. . . . Outside of the polis there are no inborn restraints on the human exercise of destructive power."[41]

Although with a different name, as we shall see, a man named Hans Maier has appeared earlier in this book, and he knew too well whereof Rubenstein speaks. Born on October 31, 1912, the only child of a Catholic mother and a Jewish father, more than anything else Maier thought of himself as Austrian, not least because his father's family had lived in that land since the seventeenth century. Hans Maier, however, lived in the twentieth century, and thus it was that in September 1935 he studied a newspaper in a Viennese coffeehouse. The Nuremberg Laws had just been promulgated in Nazi Germany. Maier's reading made him see unmistakably the fatal interdependence of all human actions. Even if he did not think of himself as Jewish, the Nazis' definitions meant that the cunning of history had nonetheless given him that identity.

Maier lacked the authority to define social reality in the mid-1930s. Increasingly, however, the Nazi state did possess such power. Its laws made him Jewish even if his consciousness did not. As he confronted that reality, the unavoidability of his being Jewish took on another dimension. By identifying him as a Jew, Maier would write later on, Nazi power made him "a dead man on leave, someone to be murdered, who only by chance was not yet where he properly belonged."[42]

When Nazi Germany occupied Austria in March 1938, Maier drew his conclusions. He fled his native land for Belgium and joined the Resistance after Belgium was swept into the Third Reich in 1940. Captured by the Gestapo in 1943, the Nazis sent him to a series of camps, including Auschwitz, before he was liberated from Bergen-Belsen in 1945. Eventually taking the name Jean Améry, by which he is remembered, this philosopher waited twenty years before breaking his silence about the Holocaust. When Améry did decide to write, the result was a series of remarkable essays about his experience. One is simply entitled "Torture." Torture drove Améry to the following observation: "The expectation of help, the certainty of help," he wrote, "is indeed one of the fundamental experiences of human beings." Thus, the gravest loss produced by the Holocaust, Améry went on to suggest, was that it destroyed what he called "trust in the world, . . . the certainty that by reason of written or unwritten social contracts the other person will spare me—more precisely stated, that he will respect my physical, and with it also my metaphysical, being."[43]

Jean Améry would wonder about American dreams, their affirmations about unalienable rights and their hopes for new beginnings. "Every morning when I get up," he tells his reader, "I can read the Auschwitz number on my forearm. . . . Every day anew I lose my trust in the world. . . . Declarations of human rights, democratic constitutions, the free world and the free press, nothing can lull me into the slumber of security from which I awoke in 1935."[44]

Far from scorning the human dignity that those institutions emphasize, Améry yearned for the right to live, which he equated with dignity itself. His experience, however, taught him that "it is certainly true that dignity can be bestowed only by society, whether it be the dignity of some office, a professional or, very generally speaking, civil dignity; and the merely individual, subjective claim ('I am a human being and as such I have my dignity, no matter what you may do or say!') is an empty academic game, or madness."[45]

Lucidity, believed Améry, demanded the recognition of this reality, but lucidity did not end there. He thought it also entailed rebellion against power that would make anyone a "dead man on leave." Unfortunately, it must also be acknowledged that Améry's hopes for such protest were less than optimistic. On October 17, 1978, he took leave and became a dead man by his own hand.

Améry's testimony tests assumptions that have long been at the heart of the American Dream. They include beliefs that the most basic human rights are a gift of God and that nature and reason testify to a universal moral structure which underwrites them. But what if there is no God? What if nature is amoral? Granting that reason can make critical distinctions between what is and what ought to be, what if reason also insists that the most telling truth of all is that history is what G. W. F. Hegel, the nineteenth-century German philosopher, called it: a slaughter bench, a realm where unalienable rights are hardly worth the paper they are written on—unless political might ensures them.

Such questions have crossed American minds in the past, but in a post-Holocaust age they cross-examine American optimism more severely than before. It is no longer clear that anything but human power secures a person's rights, and, if rights depend on human power alone, then they may well be natural and unalienable in name only. In such circumstances, to call rights unalienable may still be a legitimate rhetorical device to muster consensus that certain privileges and prerogatives must not be taken away.

No doubt the idea of unalienable rights functions—and will continue to do so—precisely in that way as an ingredient in American dreams. But ideas do not necessarily correspond to facts any more than dreams do to waking life. It appears increasingly that rights are functionally unalienable (which may be what counts most in the long and short of it) only within a state that will successfully defend and honor them as such.

As they continue the tasks of converting dreams into realities, the United States, Israel, and all who take part in Holocaust politics need to deepen memory—even memory of immense and irreplaceable loss—to intensify and broaden appreciation for the preciousness of life. No utopia will ever be forthcoming, nor is the kingdom of God likely to come on earth, but if the Holocaust becomes the warning we should let it be, the twenty-first century need not be a continuing age of genocide, the United States may do better at converting its best dreams into realities, and a just and lasting peace may yet be found in the Middle East.

D-Day and Israeli Independence Day. Captain Miller and Theodor Herzl. Private Ryan and a soldier-scholar from Haifa. Franz Stangl and Gitta Sereny. Stingo and Sophie. New beginnings and the cunning of history. Trust and torture. Omaha Beach, Normandy; Raleigh, North Carolina; Auschwitz, Poland; Washington, D.C.; and Jerusalem. The right to life, a "better and richer and fuller" life, and "life unworthy of life." *Into That Darkness* and "now day is dawning." Loving and hating. Saying yes and saying no. Denouncing, defending, dividing. And yet—and yet. American and Israeli dreams. "Earn this"—"Just

tell me. . . . Tell me if you think I've earned it." Holocaust questions and Holocaust politics. The fatal
interdependence of all human actions.

The earth is woven of many strands. Frayed and
torn, it needs the mending that depends on encountering the shadow of Birkenau with undeceived lucidity and then on resisting its destructive legacy.
Stripped of illusions but not of dreams worth having,
the world still awaits our heeding of the Holocaust's
warnings, our conversion of dreams into realities that
are good.

Chapter Five

Holocaust Politics and Post-Holocaust Christianity

The music which we shall listen to together shall reconfirm our resolve to consolidate the good relations between Christians and Jews so that with the help of almighty God, we can work together to prevent the repetition of such heinous evil.

Pope John Paul II, April 7, 1994

Take virtually any aspect of human life—education, religion, economics, international relations, or the arts, to name a few—and Holocaust politics will not be hard to find. Illustrating that fact, the October 27, 2000, edition of the *New York Times* carried a story about the interruption of a performance by the Rishon Letzion Symphony Orchestra in Israel.[1] According to the *Times* report, as the orchestra began to play under the direction of its conductor, a Holocaust survivor named Mendi Rodan, an elderly man rose in protest by swinging a noisy Purim grogger (noisemaker) around his head.[2] A scuffle ensued, but beefed-up security in the concert hall brought the protest to an end almost as quickly as it had erupted. The protester was identified only as Shlomo—he had declined to give reporters his surname—and also as a survivor whose family had perished in the Holocaust. When asked why he had chosen the Purim noise-maker, he was quoted as saying, "Because I couldn't find a bomb."

The music that provoked protest in Israel, and not just by Shlomo and his grogger, was Richard Wagner's "Siegfried Idyll." A dedicated German nationalist, Wagner (1813–1883) was an antisemite whose music and political writings attracted a large following. Music by Wagner (he was Hitler's favorite composer) aroused emotion at Nazi festivals. Wagner's family contained fervent Nazi supporters, and his art supported the Third Reich's genocidal campaign against the Jews.[3] These realities made his music taboo in Israel. From the late 1980s, Wagnerian strains could be heard occasionally on Israeli radio and television, but the concert hall remained off limits. In 1981, for example, Zubin Mehta was conducting part of Wagner's opera *Tristan and Isolde* as an encore when an Israeli concert was interrupted by a Holocaust survivor. Mehta stopped the piece. Ten years later, protests by concert subscribers halted the Israel Philharmonic Orchestra's plan to perform Wagner. When the Rishon Letzion protest failed to silence the "Siegfried Idyll," it was the first time that a piece by Wagner had been performed in an Israeli concert hall.

Shlomo's concert hall protest was not the first regarding the Rishon Letzion performance. In the previous April, the orchestra announced that Wagner would be on an upcoming program, along with music by Richard Strauss, who had composed during the Nazi period and whose music had been played at the 1936 Olympic Games, which were held in Hitler's Berlin. One result was that Holocaust survivors took legal action by filing a petition in a Tel Aviv district court to prohibit the Wagner performance. On the Tuesday before the Friday concert took place in Rishon Letzion, the district court judge found that freedom of expression, plus a lack of convincing evidence that Holocaust survivors would be directly harmed by the playing of Wagner, argued against banning the performance. Two days later, Israel's Supreme Court heard an appeal and upheld the district court's decision not to ban the performance. With extra security in place, the stage was set for Shlomo and his grogger. His protest did not prevail, but the world of music, like so many other areas of human expression, proved not to be free of Holocaust politics.

Few expressions stir human feeling more than music. Its presence and power in ceremonial occasions, political and religious ones especially, testify to that. So as one thinks further about the links between music and Holocaust politics, it is worthwhile to consider a Lutheran pastor's son named Horst Wessel. Like many other young men in the Germany of his day, Wessel rebelled against his bourgeois upbringing and joined the *Sturmabteilung,* or Stormtroopers, of the Nazi Party. His political activities included participation in bloody street battles with Communists. Eventually they gunned him down, and Wessel died on February 23, 1930.

As Wessel's demise reveals, history frequently pivots around small events. His death would have been inconsequential had he not written a poem sometime before. Entitled "Raise High the Flag," it had been set to a melody from an old army song. As Wessel was dying, Joseph Goebbels, the mastermind behind Nazi propaganda, saw an opportunity. Wessel's lyric immortalized those who had given their lives for the Nazi cause. Arranging to have the "Horst Wessel

Song" sung at the conclusion of a Nazi meeting, Goebbels envisioned that it would become "the hymn of the German revolution." He was correct.

Music played key parts in the Holocaust.[4] They were not restricted to the influence of Wagner's operas on Hitler. Many classical works, such as those by Mendelssohn and Mahler, were suppressed by the Nazis because of their composers' Jewish origins. Shortly after the Nazis took power in 1933, the Reich Music Office dismissed Jewish professional musicians. In Nazi culture, moreover, jazz was labeled degenerate. As illustrated in Fania Fenelon's *Playing for Time*, orchestras composed of Jewish prisoners were formed in some concentration and death camps by Nazi decree. Meanwhile, in Theresiendstadt and several other ghettos, concerts were given, operas staged, and musical works were written by Jewish composers such as Viktor Ullman, Gideon Klein, and Pavel Haas. As the "Partisans' Song" illustrates, music was important in Jewish resistance as well.

In the Holocaust's aftermath, music continues to have an important role. Using film as just one source, the musical scores for Steven Spielberg's *Schindler's List* and Deborah Oppenheimer's *Into the Arms of Strangers*, a moving documentary about the *Kindertransport* program that helped to save about 10,000 Jewish children, provide two notable examples. Claude Lanzmann's epic, *Shoah*, begins with Simon Srebnik, one of the very few survivors of Chelmno, who years later sings again the songs he sang for the Germans as a boy in the *Sonderkommando* of that death camp. Music also can be heard in the many Holocaust commemorations that now take place. It is music of that kind that evokes the theme and variations of this chapter on Holocaust politics and post-Holocaust Christianity.

A Night of "Firsts"

As one of the world's largest distributors of recorded music, Tower Records does booming business in stores that are open around the clock, 365 days a year. My eclectic musical tastes, which run from country to classical with blues and jazz between, sometimes take me on short freeway trips to browse and buy at the outlet closest to my California home. During the summer of 1994, a new CD in the classical music section caught my eye, partly because its Houston, Texas, producer—Justice Records—had a name as intriguing as it was unknown to me. The CD contains "The Papal Concert to Commemorate the Holocaust." It often accompanies my writing.

On the evening of April 7, 1994, with Pope John Paul II as their host, 7,500 people came to the huge Sala Nervi (the Paul VI Hall), which is located next to St. Peter's Basilica in the Vatican, to hear the Papal Concert to Commemorate the Holocaust. Television broadcasts in fifty countries enabled millions more to witness the event. In Rome, the impressive interfaith assembly contained numerous cardinals and rabbis—among them Rav Elio Toaff, the chief rabbi of Rome—as well as the Italian president, ambassadors, and more than two hundred Holocaust survivors from twelve different countries. In a preconcert meeting with the survivors, Pope John Paul II expressed the hope that serves as this chapter's epigraph: "The music which we shall listen to together shall reconfirm our resolve to consolidate the good relations between Christians and Jews so that with the help of almighty God, we can work together to prevent the repetition of such heinous evil."

Preparations for the concert had been under way since 1991, when the idea for it was conceived by Gilbert Levine. An American Jew, Levine had met Pope John Paul II three years earlier after being appointed music director for the orchestra of Krakow, the Polish city not far from Auschwitz that is the pope's hometown. In addition to conducting the Royal Philharmonic Orchestra, which flew from London for the concert, Levine wrote the program notes for the CD. They state that John Paul II's leadership—which included selecting the concert venue, organizing the seating, and helping to select the music—did much to make the concert moving and historic.

Levine's program notes celebrate the results, but they do so with unintended irony that reveals how truly historic the concert was, and thus how moving—in disturbing and disquieting senses—it remains. Levine emphasizes, for example, how the concert contained signs of change and hope. At the same time, his notes deserve to be heard as lamentations in a minor key, especially when he calls the concert "a night of firsts." Those "firsts," not unlike the first concert performance of Wagner in Israel, reflect the discord of Holocaust politics and suggest at least some of what is needed to reduce, if not harmonize, the dissonance.

April 7, 1994: Consider how long and late the firsts were in coming. According to Levine, the chief rabbi of Rome was invited for the first time to co-officiate at a public function in the Vatican. For the first time, Jews and Catholics prayed together, each in their own way, in such a setting. For the first time, a Jewish cantor, Howard Nevison, sang in the Vatican. For the first time, the 500-year-old Vatican Capella Giulia Choir sang a Hebrew text in performance. For the first time, the Vatican officially commemorated the Holocaust. Levine also cites the report of a Vatican official who said that the concert revealed "the best relations between Catholics and Jews in 2000 years." Glad occasions though such firsts may be, they nevertheless deepen sadness and regret as well. The same can be said about other Holocaust-related events that have taken place in the Christian world since the Papal Concert in 1994.

In March 1998, for instance, the Holy See's Commission for Religious Relations with the Jews released *We Remember: A Reflection on the Shoah*, a document that was widely expected to be the Roman Catholic Church's long-awaited statement about the Vatican's posture during the Holocaust.[5] Especially in Jewish circles, its reception was lukewarm. Two points made the document particularly vulnerable: (1) It unconvincingly separated Nazi antisemitism from Christian anti-Judaism. Differences exist between the two, but *We Remember* stressed them too much while emphasizing their connections too little. (2) *We Remember* acknowledged that Christian conduct during the Holocaust "was not that which might have been expected from Christ's followers" and went on to say that "for Christians, this heavy burden of conscience of their brothers and sisters during the Second World War must be a call to penitence."

Many Jews and Christians felt that such language misplaced responsibility for Christian failure, for *We Remember* had little, if anything, to say—implicitly or explicitly—about the shortcomings of Roman Catholic leadership during the Holocaust. It created the dubious impression that the rank and file, more than its Catholic leaders, were responsible for Christian failings. The Commission for Religious Relations did not improve its credibility by emphasizing that Pope Pius XII, whose controversial reign (1939–1958) covered the crucial Holocaust years, had been thanked by Jewish communities and leaders during and after the war for all that he and his representatives had done to "save hundred of thousands of Jewish lives."

Fairly or unfairly, Pius XII has become a lightning rod in church-related Holocaust politics.[6] He has been sharply and persistently criticized for failing to do what he should and could have done to intervene on behalf of Jews during the Holocaust. As *We Remember* indicates, his reputation has also been defended—so much so, in fact, that he may be canonized as a saint in the twenty-first century. That step, however, will probably be taken later rather than sooner, and one reason is that improved but still problematic Jewish-Roman Catholic relations are likely to be worsened if sainthood for Pius XII comes quickly. Whether those tensions can be relaxed depends in part on another vexing issue, which focuses on the Vatican's archives and especially its holdings from the reign of Pius XII.

In late October 2000, the International Catholic-Jewish Historical Commission, a distinguished panel of three Catholic scholars (Eva Fleischner, Gerald Fogarty, and John Morley) and three Jewish scholars (Michael Marrus, Bernard Suchecky, and Robert Wistrich) appointed, respectively, by the Holy See's Commission for Religious Relations with the Jews and the International Jewish Committee for Interreligious Consultations, released its preliminary report on "The Vatican and the Holocaust." The Historical Commission's detailed study focused on twelve volumes of material edited and published by the Vatican about the Vatican's activity during World War II. It was another first, for never before had a team of Jewish and Catholic scholars worked together on a project of this sort. Far from exonerating Pius XII from the criticisms that have been brought against him, let alone concurring with those who have defended the pontiff most vigorously, the panel agreed that the documents raise, rather than resolve, serious questions about the facts and the proper evaluation of Pius XII and the Vatican during the Holocaust years. While it is not certain that the Vatican's archives hold the answers to such questions, these scholars urged that the many questions they raised—forty-seven are enumerated in their report—could not be adequately addressed without full access to the Vatican's archives.

The Historical Commission's report appeared in a religious context that was already politically charged by other Holocaust-related events in the immediately preceding weeks. On September 5, 2000, the Roman Catholic Church's Congregation for the Doctrine of the Faith issued *Dominus Jesus*, a declaration "On the Unicity and Salvific Universality of Jesus Christ and the Church." Despite claims from the Vatican and Pope John Paul II that the declaration had been misinterpreted and misunderstood, controversy about the document remained widespread as the year 2000 drew to a close.

Urging repeatedly that the Church's teachings in this declaration must be "firmly believed," *Dominus Jesus* contained at least two claims that stood at the controversy's core. One was that "the salvation of all" comes uniquely, singularly, exclusively, universally, and absolutely through Jesus Christ. The other asserted that the Church is intended by God to be "the instrument for the salvation of *all* humanity," a condition entailing that "the followers of other religions," even if they may receive a kind of divine grace, remain "in a gravely deficient situation" compared to those who are fully within the Church.

Dominus Jesus claimed that its absolutist teachings about Jesus Christ and the Church (in this regard the document affirms what has long been standard teaching) express no disrespect for "the religions of the world." Subsequent Vatican commentary urged that the declaration was intended primarily to guide Catholic theologians and the Catholic faithful. Nevertheless, *Dominus Jesus* affirmed that the Vatican's version of Christianity should and does supersede every other religious tradition. In an increasingly pluralistic religious world, that stance is problematic to say the least. Adding fuel to fire, the Vatican issued its declaration only two days after Pope John Paul II had beatified Pope Pius IX, the first step on that nineteenth-century pontiff's path to canonization as a saint.[7] In ways that the Vatican seems not to have anticipated, however, this step provoked still more Holocaust politics. Not only did Pius IX reign longer than any other pope to date, but his pronouncements and policies were frequently antisemitic. His condoning of what has come to be known as the kidnapping of Edgardo Mortara, a six-year-old Jewish boy who was taken from his home by the Church after being baptized without the knowledge of his family, is only the most notorious example.[8]

Meanwhile, I hear sadness and regret in the voice of Pope John Paul II whenever I listen to the Papal Concert's ending. The pope asks listeners to observe silence and to "hear once more the plea, 'Do not forget us.' " That plea, which the pope rightly describes as "powerful, agonizing, heartrending," rises from the

Holocaust's victims, the dead and the living. As John Paul II's post-Holocaust concert remarks also underscore, there can be no memory worthy of that plea unless remembering leads people to check what he calls "the specter of racism, exclusion, alienation, slavery and xenophobia" and to act so that "evil does not prevail over good" as it did for millions of Jews during the Holocaust.

To his credit, Pope John Paul II has often acted in ways that are consistent with those views. He did so, for example, in March 2000 during a visit to Israel that also contained numerous firsts. At Yad Vashem, Israel's memorial to the Holocaust, the pope's humble silence conveyed heartfelt grief and repentance for Christianity's anti-Jewish traditions, which assisted the persecution and murder of Europe's Jews during the Holocaust. Hours before he departed Jerusalem for Rome, the pope's silence again spoke volumes when he went to Judaism's most holy site, the sacred Western Wall, which is all that remains of the Second Temple, destroyed by the Romans in the year 70. There the pope followed ancient tradition by quietly placing a written prayer in one of the Wall's cracked stones. Importantly, the pope's prayer asked God's "forgiveness for Jewish suffering caused by Christians." Perhaps even more than those words, the pope's silent presence spoke powerfully as he stood at that place and reached out to touch the Wall with humility.

One event leads to another. I suspect that Pope John Paul II's 2000 visit to Israel was inspired partly by the 1994 concert. Returning to that event, conductor Gilbert Levine made an accurate statement when he said that "the Pope himself, the leader of 900 million Catholics worldwide, spoke out clearly" on that occasion. Fortunately, the pope's doing so was not a first for him, but sadness and regret remain because his papal predecessors before and during the Holocaust typically and tragically lacked such clarity. So did most Christians, Protestant as well as Catholic, American as well as European. If the concert in the Vatican reflects and bolsters changed Christian dispositions, then well and good. But it remains dishearteningly sad that history, and particularly Christianity's role in it, resulted in the need for a Papal Concert to Commemorate the Holocaust.

Given that the Holocaust happened, I am glad to have the CD of the concert, but I cannot listen to it without feeling profoundly sad. How that sadness (which contains a sense of shame) works on me, and how I think it should continue to do so within Holocaust politics, can be seen in more detail by turning next to some of the places where memory takes me when I hear the specific pieces of music that Pope John Paul II and Gilbert Levine chose for Christians and Jews together.

Church Roads

The Papal Concert began with cello soloist Lynn Harrell and the Royal Philharmonic Orchestra playing *Kol Nidre*, Max Bruch's haunting interpretation of the moving Jewish prayer that opens the evening service on Yom Kippur, the awesome Day of Atonement, which culminates the Jewish High Holy Days with expressions of cleansing and renewal. When I hear this solemn invocation, memory often takes me to Kirkeveien 23, a place not far from the apartment in Oslo, Norway, that I once occupied. As noted earlier, hundreds of Norwegian Jews were held there when Holocaust roundups took place around the country in late October 1942.

An address on Kirkeveien, which in English means "church road," was the first place that Oslo's Jews were sent on a journey that would end in the gas chambers at Auschwitz. The sad symbolism of that configuration speaks volumes, while Bruch's setting of a penitential Jewish prayer calls me to reflect on my Christian identity.

Christianity and, more specifically, what could aptly be called "church roads" were a necessary condition for the Holocaust. Once made, however, that statement requires some careful unpacking, for identifying incrementally what it does *not* mean highlights the dreadful truth that it does contain. First, neither Christianity nor any other *single* person, institution, or motivation—from the power of Adolf Hitler and the SS, for example, to the widespread racist antisemitism embraced by millions of ordinary Germans during the Nazi period—was sufficient by itself to make the Holocaust happen. Second, the Holocaust was not inevitable. It emerged from decisions and institutions made by people who were as particular as they were ordinary. At times, however, their killing actions were also as extraordinary as they were specific. Individual people from definite times and places were responsible for murderous actions. They could have acted differently, and better, than they did.

Amplified beyond the beginning provoked by reflection on Bruch's *Kol Nidre*, those points, far from diminishing the equation's devastation, make it hold all the more: No Christianity and no "church roads" equals no Holocaust.

Common Humanity?

I have mentioned previously the Norwegian city named Tromsø. Far above the Arctic Circle, its World War II memorials include a modest stone that records the names of seventeen Jews, mostly from three families, who were deported from that town and killed during the Holocaust. I remember that Tromsø memorial when I hear the Adagio from Beethoven's Ninth Symphony, the second selection performed during the Papal Concert. I do so because two weeks before I saw it, I visited a villa at a place called Wannsee. At that beautiful spot outside of Berlin, a meeting known as the Wannsee Conference took place on January 20, 1942. Convened by SS Lieutenant General Reinhard Heydrich, the meeting coordinated plans for the Final Solution, which Heydrich had been authorized to prepare. Norway's Jews never numbered more than a few thousand, but there are connections between the Wannsee Conference and the deportation of seventeen Norwegian Jews from Tromsø. Nothing illustrates better the intended finality of the Final Solution than the simple stone that bears witness to their fate.

His magisterial music at the pinnacle of German culture, Beethoven remains one of civilization's giants. At some time in their lives, Heydrich and his followers at the Wannsee Conference probably heard the Adagio from Beethoven's Ninth. It is not unthinkable that some of them even loved it. If so, their listening still failed utterly to sense what Gilbert Levine describes as that movement's power to reveal "our common humanity." Heydrich and his followers were tone deaf when it came to respecting "our common humanity." In part, that failure happened because Christian civilization had succeeded too well for too long a time in marginalizing, if not excluding, Jews from humankind.

When I say that the devastating equation holds—no Christianity and no "church roads" equals no Holocaust—it is again important to understand what is *not* being said as well as what is. First, the relationship between Jews and Christians is asymmetrical. Although Jews and Christians are involved historically in countless ways, nothing in Jewish life logically or theologically entails Christian existence. Christian life, however, does depend essentially on Jewish life. Christianity makes no sense, it would not even exist, if the world contained no Jewish history. But Jews could certainly have existed and perhaps even flourished far more than they have without Christian existence of any kind. In theory, therefore, the world's history could have unfolded so that there were Jews but no Christians.

Second, the possibility just described could not automatically mean that Jews would forever be protected from genocide. In a world devoid of Christian identity, some human group might still have focused on Jews in such a way as to doom them. It could have been possible for the world's history to unfold so there were no Christians, but that Jewish annihilation still took place. In theory, Christianity was not necessary for genocide against the Jews.

History, however, unfolds not in theory but in practice. So while genocide against Jews did not logically necessitate the existence of Christianity as one of the conditions that had to be present to make it possible, nevertheless Christianity was, in fact, a necessary condition for the Holocaust that actually happened. The world's history consists of particularities that can be accounted for only by paying attention to relationships among the actually existing persons, communities, and powers that emerge from the realms of possibility in which men, women, and children live and move and have their being. Even with the existence of Christianity, what happened in the Holocaust was avoidable, not least because Christianity itself could have taken different historical turns than it did. But as it actually happened, the Holocaust remains unthinkable apart from the anti-Jewish practices of the Christian traditions and "church roads" that had gained so much authority and dominance in the world.

Workers of Iniquity

Listening to music in Oslo sometimes made me think of Vienna, another European capital that I know quite well from my stay in Austria on an earlier Fulbright fellowship (1973–1974). It did so because my recording of the Papal Concert includes music by Franz Schubert, a magnificent Austrian composer. The melodic beauty of his work arguably unsurpassed, Schubert, a devout Catholic, was scarcely thirty years old when he died in 1828.

According to Levine's concert notes, two years before Schubert died, he set Psalm 92's Hebrew text to music for a great cantor named Solomon Sulzer, who would sing the song with his Jewish choir to commemorate the opening of the New Synagogue in Schubert's native Vienna. Sung by Cantor Howard Nevison, a reprise of that song came third in the Papal Concert. Sadly, it recalls a tragedy that centers around the Bible.

Few things have separated Jews and Christians more than scripture, which remains a key factor in Holocaust politics. In addition, few things reveal the complexity and intensity of that separation more fully than the Bible, for the separation is not located simply in the fact that the Christian Bible contains a New Testament that Jewish Scripture does not. The separation also involves what is biblically shared, what is common to both traditions and yet interpreted so differently that destruction and death have ensued. Specifically, the interpretation has been so different historically that Christians took offense early on when Jews did not "see the light." One result was that, in Christendom, the Jews were turned into a pariah people.

Jews and Christians share the Psalms, but not nearly as well as they should have done and need to do. Psalm 92, for example, is a song of praise to God. As the text speaks of God's faithfulness and the greatness of God's works, it also affirms that "workers of iniquity . . . shall be vanquished." When Solomon Sulzer sang Franz Schubert's setting of that Hebrew text, the "workers of iniquity," far from being vanquished, had only begun to do their worst. In Schubert's Vienna, the sharing of his music at the opening of the New Synagogue was an exceptional prelude whose melody would be drowned out little more than a century later when Nazi Germany, aided and abetted by plenty of enthusiastic Austrians, crushed Vienna's Jews.

That crushing did not have to happen, but, unfortunately, a long period of preparation made it possible. Specifically, Nazi Germany's targeting of the Jews in the Holocaust cannot be explained apart from anti-Jewish images—Christ-killer, willful blasphemers, unrepentant sons and daughters of the Devil, to name only a few—that have been deeply rooted in Christian practices. Long antedating Nazism, those images and the institutions and social relationships, particularly the "church roads" that established and supported them, played key parts in bolstering the Third Reich's genocidal antisemitism.

Defined briefly and broadly, antisemitism refers to negative emotions, beliefs, and practices focused on Jews as Jews.[9] Historically, it has appeared in many forms, but here it is crucial to note that the Christian and Nazi forms have more continuity than discontinuity among them. Many Christians wanted Jews to disappear through conversion, but wanted them to disappear nonetheless. The Nazis implemented a more murderous Final Solution, but absent popular Christianity's fundamentally anti-Jewish position, it would be difficult to explain why Hitler's Germany would have targeted the Jews as it did.

It is easier to fathom, though not to accept, the anti-semitic "logic" of Nazi Germany when one takes a longer historical view. After the Roman world became Christian dominated in the fourth century, Christian images and institutions that vilified and demonized Jews stood at the foundations of an increasingly mul-tifaceted antisemitism that would become a decisively defining and governing element in many of Western civilization's most influential worldviews. Well before the Nazi Party struggled its way into existence in the aftermath of World War I, antisemitism was so axiomatic in Christian-dominated cultures that, with few exceptions, Jews could be fully included within Western civilization's Christian-defined boundaries of moral obligation only if they utterly rejected their Jewishness, which, understandably, most Jews chose not to do.

Christian antisemitism set Jews up for the kill, especially as racist forms of antisemitism took hold. Specifically, that antisemitism gained ground in Germany until its most destructive expressions appeared in the genocidal policies and practices of the Nazi state, vast numbers of its citizens, and collaborators in many other Nazi-controlled countries. Meanwhile, as Nazi Germany's threats increased the plight of the European Jews, most Christian institutions, to say nothing of nations whose cultures were decisively influenced by Christian values, did relatively little that was specifically aimed to help the endangered Jews, even when those countries were determined to defeat Nazi Germany militarily.

There can be no credible doubt about it: In the real world—not the counterfactual ones of theory—Christian antisemitism provided essential background, preparation, and motivation for the Holocaust that happened when Germans carried out the Final Solution of the so-called Jewish question. In addition, that same Christian antisemitism goes a long way to explain why overtly Christian resistance to the Holocaust was as scarce and sporadic as it turned out to be. The dominant worldview made Jews "outsiders" to such a degree that help in their times of acute need was unlikely to be much of a priority. Much more likely, Jewish misfortune would be observed indifferently, with mild regret at most, or interpreted and exacerbated as deserved. In some Christian quarters, outright elimination of the Jews may have been viewed as beneficial, even if murderous means to that end were deemed unfortunate. Resistance to those attitudes and actions could be found, but it consisted of exceptions—important exceptions, but exceptions nonetheless—that prove the rule: Owing to its deep-seated antisemitism, Christianity carries a heavy burden of responsibility for the Holocaust's destruction of the European Jews.

Confessions Must Be Made

Bruch, Beethoven, and Schubert were pre-Holocaust composers. The American composer Leonard Bernstein wrote his music after Auschwitz. When he set the Kaddish, the Jewish prayer for the dead, to music in his Third Symphony, there were six million Jews to mourn. They were murdered twice—first by starvation, shooting, or gas and then by burning, intended to make their remains disappear without even the trace that a grave could leave behind. As I hear the Academy Award–winning actor, Richard Dreyfuss, a dedicated Jewish humanitarian, recite the ancient Aramaic version that Bernstein chose, I remember that the Holocaust was intended to kill Jews a third time by wiping out Jewish tradition and, in particular, by silencing the Kaddish forever.

Fortunately, the Kaddish is still heard. Overtly saying nothing of death, it affirms life instead, magnifies the Name of the Holy One, and prays that God's kingdom will come "speedily and at a near time." Christians say a prayer—tradition holds that it was taught to them by an Aramaic-speaking Jew named Jesus—that expresses related feelings and hopes: "Our Father who art in heaven," it begins, "hallowed be thy name. Thy kingdom come, thy will be done, on earth as it is in heaven."

I learned the Lord's Prayer in the hometowns and churches of my Michigan and Indiana boyhood. Those places were a long way from Oslo and Tromsø, Berlin and Vienna. And yet, when I hear the recording of Bernstein's *Kaddish* on the Papal Concert CD,

I realize that my Christian upbringing and identity link me to those places and their Holocaust history in ways that I cannot ignore.

The Holocaust happened more than fifty years ago, but when I listen to Bernstein's *Kaddish*, reflecting on the times and places of my upbringing, I remember that the Holocaust also took place in my lifetime. Six decades is not such a long time, especially when I recall that destructive anti-Jewish attitudes have been intrinsic to Christianity, my religious tradition, for centuries. Indeed, only in the half-century of post-Holocaust history have Christians—and too few of us—made serious and sustained efforts to eradicate our tradition's anti-Jewish elements. Sadly, it took a watershed calamity to make Christianity change massively destructive ways. That work has only begun. Painful and sobering, such confessions must be made. Holocaust politics cannot be good without them.

Reforming Christianity after the Holocaust is particularly difficult because that tradition's anti-Jewish elements have not been marginal but defining features of Christian thought and action. It is no exaggeration to say that if the most typical, long-standing, and normative claims about Jesus' crucifixion, resurrection, divinity, and overall significance had never been made, then the Holocaust that in fact took place could scarcely have been imaginable let alone realized. For in one way or another, all of those claims were formed and defended in contexts that took mainstream Jewish indifference or resistance to them with deadly seriousness. If Jews were right, then Christians were wrong. Christianity dealt with that intolerable dissonance by attempts to discredit and negate its source. If those attempts did not become genocidal, they certainly left Christianity ill-prepared and unlikely to defend Jews when the genocidal onslaught came during the Nazi era.

Even if Christians were reluctant to do the Holocaust's dirty work, and by no means all of them were hesitant about it, many who identified themselves as Christians were quite willing to guard, if not to mute, their dissent against Nazi methods. Functionally, then, they looked the other way. The possibility must be faced that some of them even implicitly condoned the genocidal onslaught as a cleansing action that removed an unwanted, alien people and supported Christian hegemony.

Christianity did not have to take such turns. It contains plenty of teachings to make clear that antisemitism is arguably the most fundamental contradiction to Christian faith. I make those statements with humility and with gratitude because they are rooted in my admittedly fallible—and I hope not falsely idealized—understanding of the version of Christianity into which I was born and raised by my parents and with which I still want to identify.

Here I want to choose my words carefully and cautiously so as to make my claim as realistic as possible: No doubt my judgment about my religious upbringing has its flaws and blind spots, but I think that the version of Christianity taught to me in my parents' home and my father's church (he was a Presbyterian pastor) was probably about as free of the elements of Christian antisemitism as anything Christian was likely to be at the time. Then and now, that version of Christianity has stressed the Jewishness of Jesus in ways that make unmistakable the importance of Christian solidarity with the Jewish people as Jews. Far from emphasizing that if Jews are right, then Christians are wrong, this version of Christianity sees the two traditions as different but valid and complementary paths that search for what is good and right. Such Christianity emphatically rejects the view that Jews are threats and enemies. Instead, it underscores that Christians and Jews share a sacred trust as children of God to defend justly and to respect lovingly each other's humanity.

Tragically, however, it is only after Auschwitz—and even then only gradually, for most of us Christians have yet to confront the Holocaust's impact as much as we should—that this version of Christianity has been widely expressed and incorporated into Christian teachings worldwide. Until the Holocaust, and for too long even after it ended, those teachings were not emphasized and those interpretations too rarely made. Even when they were voiced with some authority, they lost out to arguments and policies that led Christians to see Jews primarily as benighted outsiders or worse. The price paid for those destructive historical turns remains beyond calculation.

Taking Responsibility

"Behold how good, / And how pleasant it is, / For brothers to dwell / Together in unity." With the Vatican Capella Giulia Choir singing those words from Psalm 133 in Hebrew, the second movement of Leonard Bernstein's *Chichester Psalms* drew the Papal Concert to a close. When I hear this conclusion, my thoughts often turn to Houston, Texas. One of the largest and most diverse cities in the United States, Houston is not only the home of Justice Records, the company that made it possible for me to keep listening to the Papal Concert, but it also includes Holocaust Museum Houston, an important educational center whose purposes mirror the psalmist's hope and some of its implications for Holocaust politics.

Holocaust Museum Houston opened its doors in early March 1996. Norwegian duties prevented me from attending that opening, but I was certainly there in spirit. In a gesture of trust and unity that has been deeply meaningful to me, the primarily Jewish leadership for this Houston project relied on me to write the text for the museum's permanent core. With its requirements of compactness and clarity, historical sweep, detail, and precision, this writing took well over a year, including part of my time in Norway. It proved to be among the most demanding and challenging that I have ever done. As I worked day after day to make each line of my writing count, Bernstein's *Chichester Psalms* made me listen critically to my own words. I wanted them to do their best to spread knowledge of the Holocaust in ways that make it more possible for people to see each other as brothers and sisters who do find it good and pleasant to dwell in unity.

The Papal Concert and particularly Bernstein's *Chichester Psalms* drive home an important point: The value of beliefs must be measured by the justice or injustice, the good or evil, that they produce. The Holocaust was unjust and evil, or nothing ever could be. At least in part, the value of specifically Christian beliefs needs to be tested by their contributions to the Holocaust. Such a test leaves Christianity wanting in ways that should make my religious tradition much less triumphal than it has been in the past. Far from being an occasion for regret, however, such changes ought to be welcomed because they reflect needed honesty and candor, and they could encourage atoning work that protests against injustice and that tries its best to protect those who become evil's prey.

While I am convinced that Christianity's relationship to the Jewish people could have been very different and much better than it turned out to be, my awareness of how much Christianity has contributed to the destruction of Jewish life continues to grow. That awareness complicates everything. As a Christian, for example, I am part of something far more vast and ambiguous than my particular Christian understanding alone might suggest. Thus, I cannot neatly separate and smugly compartmentalize my version of the Christian tradition from the Christian tradition as a whole.

If I strip away the positive contributions that Christianity has made to the world's goodness and to the best parts of my own nature, such as they are, very little would be recognizable to me and probably to many other people as well. But I will not see Christianity for what it has been and is, nor will I understand myself as well as I should, if I deny either that my identity as a Christian is related to that religion's long historical dominance in Western civilization or that Christianity's dominance has been rife with anti-Jewish sentiments.

I cannot account for myself apart from Christianity. So I must take my tradition's full history into consideration and not just the favorable parts that I would like most to select, emphasize, and celebrate. I have to account for how Christianity spread and developed so that it could inform my existence. When I do that, I cannot simply leave Christian antisemitism behind as though it had nothing to do with me. It defined Christianity too much for that. Such recognition should give us Christians pause before we say with too much assurance that antisemitism no longer informs our worldviews at all. If antisemitism has been Christianity's fatal flaw, then we Christians have to confront how deep-seated it has been and therefore how difficult it will be to overcome.

These circumstances leave Christianity and me in a version of what Primo Levi, an Auschwitz survivor, called "the gray zone." I would be hypocritical, my consciousness false, my self diminished, if I abandoned my Christian identity. Thus, I wish to remain what I am. That decision means, however, that I also remain identified by and with a tradition that is so much less good than it might have been because of its complicity in and inadequate opposition to the destruction of Jewish life before and during the Holocaust years.

Born in 1940, I could do nothing to respond to what happened then. Even though I did not know it for a long time, Holocaust-related failures nevertheless stained irrevocably the tradition into which I was born and raised. My Christian tradition is permanently scarred by the Holocaust, and my sadness and shame about that fact can never, indeed must not, go away. I can and must take responsibility for my Christian identity and the Christian tradition *now*. That responsibility means making my sadness not the end of my Christian life but its source of motivation for reform and renewal.

The latter statement does not limit itself to Holocaust politics that takes the form of theological revision, creedal reinterpretation, or scriptural criticism where Christian teachings about Jews are concerned. Such steps are essential for rooting out the Christian sources of antisemitism. Those sources must not only be rooted out but also they must be replaced—and to some extent, fortunately, they have been—by words and deeds that seek solidarity and continuity between the two traditions, and not separation and supersessionism. But for these developments to happen in the ways they should, something else must take place, something that is the condition for the words and deeds that are most needed. The post-Holocaust condition that is most necessary for Christians is a spiritual and ethical "turning," a soul-searching—personal and communal—that moves toward insight informed, but not consumed, by sadness and shame.[10] Such insight, I believe, should include taking responsibility in the ways that follow.

Trying to Make Things Better

When attention is paid to the Holocaust, the news about Christianity is scarcely good. So the question is: *Why be a Christian after Auschwitz?* Post-Holocaust Christians—people who identify themselves as Christians and insist that the Holocaust requires fundamental revision of Christian self-understanding—must respond credibly to that question. If we post-Holocaust Christians cannot do more than lament Christianity's sin, which has been catastrophically destructive in its anti-Jewish manifestations, the tradition will ultimately be left with little to affirm. A credible post-Holocaust Christian response to the question should go beyond confessing the tradition's faults and acknowledging shame that those faults should make us Christians feel. The importance of those acts of confession and acknowledgment cannot be underestimated, but those acts are insufficient. A credible post-Holocaust Christian response should also affirm that "this tradition is mine, and I want to make it better." Unless post-Holocaust Christians are indifferent about or despairing over the future of Christianity, we need to make our tradition better in

ways that enable us to emphasize the positive difference that post-Holocaust versions of Christianity can
make. Such steps are crucial for Holocaust politics to
be more constructive than it has often been.

To address these challenges, I want to go to the
heart of traditional Christianity. I want to reference
the Gospel of John, which is often cited as a major
source of the Christian anti-Judaism that helped to set
the stage for the Holocaust.[11] As I hope to make clear,
the move I shall make affirms Christianity in part by
using that tradition against itself, a step that must
always remain in play for post-Holocaust Christianity.
To cut to the chase, then, I want to advance the thesis
that the core of post-Holocaust Christianity is stated
in John 1:14: "And the Word became flesh, and lived
among us, . . . full of grace and truth." That New Testament claim says something fundamental about the
nature of reality, especially in the teeth of the Holocaust. Particularly by emphasizing grace and truth,
that claim announces good news.

Such an announcement should never be regarded as
compelling anyone to be a Christian, nor, in particular, should it ever be a pretext for anti-Jewish exclu-
siveness. History already contains the sorry record of
such obsessions and compulsions. Yet it is still the case
that the goodness of Christianity's message—goodness
that deserves to be expressed in spite of the Holocaust—can be a persuasive reason for being a post-
Holocaust Christian. To make that case, more needs to
be said about four topics: (1) the fundamental claim
about reality made in John 1:14, (2) the goodness of the
news that claim contains, (3) the importance of grace,
and (4) the centrality of truth. To be sure that none of
those themes loses touch with the Holocaust's deadly
particularity, including ways in which Christianity's
anti-Jewish attitudes—the Gospel of John's among

them—helped to set Jews up for the kill, I will begin my discussion of each one by recalling a moment of Holocaust history. These recollections will help to draw out key elements that post-Holocaust Christianity should proclaim self-critically for the mending of the world.

The Fundamental Claim

Theo Richmond, a Jewish journalist and scholar, spent years studying the history of Konin, the Polish town 120 miles west of Warsaw from which his parents emigrated to England just before World War I. Many of Richmond's relatives were not so lucky. Among the approximately 3,000 Jews in Konin's population of some 13,000, they witnessed the German occupation of the town on September 14, 1939. Richmond's research revealed that perhaps two hundred of Konin's Jews survived the Holocaust.

Richmond learned that a postwar trial in Konin included the deposition of a Polish Catholic who had been imprisoned by the Gestapo. Early one mid-November morning in 1941, F. Z. (as Richmond identifies him) was removed from his cell, driven to a forest clearing, and, along with about thirty other Poles, ordered to collect clothing, shoes, and valuables from Jews who were stripped before they entered the killing pits that would become their unmarked, mass graves. Specifically, F. Z. remembered the following episode: A layer of quick lime covered the larger of the two pits. Naked Jews—children, women, men—were forced into that pit until it was full.

> Two Gestapo men began to pour some liquid, like water, on the Jews. But I am not sure what that liquid was. . . . Apparently, because of the

slaking of the lime, people in the pit were boiling alive. The cries were so terrible that we who
were sitting by the piles of clothing began to tear
pieces off the stuff to stop our ears. The crying
of those boiling in the pit was joined by the wail-
ing and lamentation of the Jews waiting for their
perdition. All this lasted perhaps two hours, perhaps longer.[12]

Why were those Jews from Konin lime-boiled to a
hideous death? Good answers for that question do not
exist, but no credible response can avoid the Gospel
of John. In particular, John 8:42–45 is one of the most
virulent sources of Christianity's anti-Jewish tendencies. That text puts into Jesus' mouth damning words
about Jews who apparently challenged his authority:
"You are from your father the devil," Jesus tells them,
"and you choose to do your father's desires."

Jesus and his disciples were profoundly Jewish. The
community that produced the Gospel of John in the
80s or 90s consisted of Jewish Christians. More than
sixty times, however, far more than the first three
Gospels taken together, John uses *hoi Ioudaioi*—"the
Jews," as that Greek phrase has typically been translated—and often "the Jews" are vilified as benighted
disbelievers who are hostile to God's grace and truth.
Biblical scholars, Christians and Jews alike, have been
working diligently to produce translations that are
both more accurate and less destructive, but the
Gospel of John's negative references to "the Jews"
have by no means been removed from Christian consciousness. Much remains to be done in that regard.

Thanks to recent biblical scholarship, the context
of those polemics is better understood today than it
was for almost nineteen centuries. The Gospel of

John reflects one side—the Christian side—of a disputatious competition, a pre-Holocaust religious politics, between Jewish Christians and Jews who were reconstituting Judaism in the wake of a disastrous revolt against Roman rule (66–70 C.E.) that left Jerusalem and its sacred temple in ruins. In that situation, Jewish Christians—especially those of the Johannine community—seemed an internal threat to Jewish tradition, and they took offense when they were treated accordingly in the synagogue. The Gospel of John, including its polemics against "the Jews," reflected and emerged from this family fight. Those polemics, in short, say more about developments late in the first century than they do about the Jesus of history. Nevertheless, by the end of that century, the split between the early church and the synagogue had become wide and deep. As Christianity spread in the predominantly non-Jewish, Mediterranean world, John's Gospel was read in ways that lost sight of the details of that Jewish family fight and the divorce it produced, but that text still pitted Christians against "the Jews" in an "us" versus "them" schism. That estrangement had disastrous consequences.

Historical understanding helps to clarify that the fundamental claim of Christianity expressed in the Gospel of John is *not* about Christian-Jewish rivalry. First, the Jewishness of Jesus and his followers, the family nature of the quarrel in the Gospel of John, and John's emphasis on God's love and on Jesus' commandment to "love one another as I have loved you" (John 15:12) show that this Gospel is badly misinterpreted unless its negative rhetoric about "the Jews" is relativized by (1) an accurate understanding of that rhetoric's context and (2) an emphasis on God's love and the compassion for others that it enjoins. Second, although the Gospel of John has been disastrously misunderstood as inviting Christian hostility toward Jews, Christianity must be used against itself to change that interpretation. Especially after Auschwitz, one cannot avoid reading the Gospel of John in terms of Christian-Jewish relations, and the point of such reading must be to recognize how much harm John's anti-Jewish polemics have done to the Jewish people and to the vitality of both religious traditions. At the same time, a post-Holocaust reading of the Gospel of John should involve more than repudiation of its destructive side. As far as possible, it should also include a reclaiming of its positive themes. Such interpretation is not easy, because the two aspects mix and mingle in the text. But let us try and see what can be done.

The Gospel of John makes clear that there are differences, fundamental ones, between Christian and Jewish traditions. None is more fundamental than their disagreement about claims concerning God's incarnation in Jesus, the Jewish teacher from Nazareth. Even within that disagreement, however, there is much that Christians and Jews can mutually affirm without sacrificing their particularity or insisting that their particularity is exclusively true. Judaism never depends on Christianity as Christianity does on Judaism, but the differences between them cannot be understood without taking into account what they share—first and foremost, belief in one God and affirmation of the Hebrew Bible's authority.[13]

That said, Christian particularity resides in the fact that vast numbers of people profess that they have encountered God in life-transforming ways through the life and teachings of the Jew named Jesus. When the Gospel of John has Jesus say, "salvation is from the

Jews" (John 4:22), Christians will think of Jesus in particular and interpret his words self-referentially. But a post-Holocaust reading of that claim will be broader and more in keeping with awareness that Christian particularity makes no sense apart from Jewish particularity. The point, moreover, is not that these traditions must meet each other primarily as the disconfirming other, but that they discern related, though not identical, insights and hopes that Christians experience and express in relation to Jesus, the one through whom they have come to know the God of Abraham, Isaac, and Jacob.[14]

By professing that "the Word became flesh and lived among us," post-Holocaust Christians testify that the world is not only God's creation but also that God has neither abandoned the world nor given up on humanity in particular, even though history provides abundant reasons to do so. Furthermore, the claim is that God's embodied presence in the world constitutes light that shines in the world's darkness. Unrelenting though it may be, that darkness does not overcome the light. Even more than that, the light brings warmth that the Holocaust's ice-cold night has not destroyed. That warmth is love that will not leave us completely alone or let us go absolutely. In spite of the Holocaust, God abides.

Such claims are not made everywhere. Newscasts, philosophies, politics, the buying and selling of everyday life, let alone the Holocaust's destruction, do not contain them. They emerge, if at all, in special circumstances and traditions. Christians find these claims about reality revealed particularly in the life, death, and resurrection of Jesus. Post-Holocaust Christians share that affirmation but not in exclusivistic ways. Specifically, we see our perspective as one that depends upon a preceding and coexisting Jewish tradition, which Christianity ought to support even as it differs from Jewish ways.

The proclamation that "the Word became flesh and lived among us" is not the only way that enables people to live in the hope that darkness does not extinguish the light, but it is one of the relatively few options that keeps such hope alive. It does so, moreover, in a way that can be particularly powerful because of the claim that God's enduring Word comes to us face to face, in a personal form, in a particular life so that God does not identify with human life abstractly but in its utter particularity. God is with us.

The Goodness of the News

"It's hard to recognize," said Simon Srebnik, "but it was here. They burned people here." Srebnik, 47, had returned to Chelmno, a place he first saw in the spring of 1944 when he was sent there from the Jewish ghetto in Lodz, Poland, at the age of thirteen. The Nazi SS assigned Srebnik to a work detail. Shot and left for dead by the fleeing Nazis as Soviet troops approached in January 1945, he was one of the very few Jews who survived this killing center.

Situated in Poland, about fifty miles west of Lodz, Chelmno was the first Nazi extermination camp. Between 150,000 and 300,000 Jews and about 5,000 Gypsies were murdered there. Chelmno's victims perished in special mobile gas vans that piped deadly engine exhaust fumes into the trucks' sealed interior compartments. Chelmno operated from December 1941 to March 1943. It reopened in the spring of 1944 during the liquidation of the Lodz ghetto. That summer the Germans tried to obliterate the evidence of mass murder by exhuming the mass graves and burning the remains. "A lot of people were burned here," Srebnik recalled. "Yes, this is the place. No one ever left here again."[15]

Simon Srebnik's Holocaust recollections contain no good news. Nothing that any religious tradition can say should minimize, let alone justify or legitimate, the evil and despair evoked by memories such as his. But when Srebnik says "they burned people here," that fact raises questions that should not be minimized either, for they express heartfelt yearnings. Does evil win? Does despair prevail? Is suffering eliminated only by death? Is death the end of our personal existence and of those we love?

To such questions, the Gospel of John says *No!* Its ways of doing so involve detail about what it means to say that "the Word became flesh and lived among us." In John's narrative, that meaning is revealed in actions—things that Jesus does or that happen to him—as well as by his words, which frequently provide assurance that death is not the end. In the Gospel of John, Jesus, the Word made flesh, is active: He heals the sick, restores sight to the blind, feeds the hungry, and raises a man named Lazarus from the dead. Whether one takes those reports as factual accounts or as symbolic narratives, their message—underscored by Jesus' resurrection—is clearly that evil, despair, suffering, and death do not have the last word. That message does nothing to explain Chelmno, but nonetheless it responds powerfully to the conviction that Chelmno deserves no victory.

For post-Holocaust Christians, the goodness of the claim that "the Word became flesh and lived among us" is found in the fact that the claim persists *in spite of* the Holocaust. No doubt the Holocaust stands as a mighty objection against the claim that God's light, let alone God's love, persists in the world's darkness. And yet the promise that such claims are true has power because it protests against evil and injustice, and thus the promise corresponds to what the New Testament calls a hunger and thirst for righteousness. Such hunger yearns for Auschwitz not to be the last word in a cosmic as well as in a historical sense. The yearning and the promise are both in spite of the Holocaust—they persist even though the Holocaust took place, and, in doing so, they refuse to succumb to the despair that results.

The yearning and the promise understand, moreover, that unless there is a real, not just a symbolic, way in which darkness is subservient to light, then the darkness of death ultimately consumes the light of every human life, and the Holocaust's dead—remembered and memorialized for a time though they may be—are nevertheless dead and gone forever. The goodness of the news that Christians, perhaps especially post-Holocaust Christians, have to tell is that history, even Holocaust history, is not all there is. Light, love, life—these are not confined to history, where they so often seem to be trumped by darkness, hatred, and death. Light, love, and life abide beyond the forgetfulness of earthly memory. They outlast injustice. They survive death. They remain sources of hope that set people free to resist injustice and to show compassion. To affirm that "the Word became flesh" is a refusal to grant the Holocaust a victory it does not deserve. Post-Holocaust Christianity has news that is good because it exists in spite of Auschwitz.

The Importance of Grace

"One wants to live," wrote Salmen Lewental. Those words were found in a clandestine notebook buried near the ruins of crematorium III in Auschwitz-Birkenau, the main extermination center in the Auschwitz network of camps. "Selected" for labor when he entered Auschwitz on December 10, 1942, Lewental was put in the *Sonderkommando* a month later and condemned to work in the gas chambers.[16] He lasted long enough to join the *Sonderkommando* uprising on October 7, 1944. The date of his death is unknown.

At one point in Lewental's notebook, he imagines someone asking him, "Why do you do such ignoble work?" Beyond answering that "one wants to live," there is no good reply, for what good choices did Lewental have?

Nazi power repeatedly forced defenseless people to make "choiceless choices." Such choices, Lawrence Langer says, "do not reflect options between life and death, but between one form of 'abnormal' response and another, both imposed by a situation that was in no way of the victim's own choosing."[17] Such was Lewental's miserable situation. He did not volunteer for the *Sonderkommando* any more than he chose deportation. In Auschwitz, his "choices"—dying by suicide, dying by resisting, or dying as a *Sonderkommando*—were essentially "choiceless."

Lewental was like millions of Holocaust victims. He wanted to live, but his "choices" were "choiceless." They were devoid of grace. Death pervaded them all.

No choice that anyone makes now can undo what happened to Salmen Lewental then. Nevertheless, people today do have choices about how to respond to the fact that the Holocaust happened. Ranging far and wide, those choices are the stuff of Holocaust politics. They can reflect indifference or denial. They can also resist forgetfulness, protest against denial, encourage memory and memorialization, and insist that the Holocaust is remembered well only to the extent that such memory provokes us to relieve suffering and to combat injustice in our own times and places. In sum, post-Holocaust choices involve priorities: What most deserves to be affirmed, resisted, and encouraged?

Trusting that light, love, and life—not darkness, hate, and death—are the fundamental and ultimately lasting realities, post-Holocaust Christians should testify that Jesus embodies that message not only as a proclamation about reality but also as a call that we need to hear and heed. The Gospel of John sounds this call in variations on a central theme. The Gospel of John repeatedly has Jesus identifying himself by using the phrase "I am." That phrase recalls a crucial narrative in the Hebrew Bible (Exodus 3). Facing a burning bush that was not consumed, Moses encountered God, who commissioned Moses to deliver the people of Israel from Egyptian slavery. What should I say, Moses asked God, when the people want to know the name of the God who has sent me to them? "Thus you shall say to the Israelites," God said, "'I AM has sent me to you'" (v. 14).

In Greek, the expression "I Am" was the way that Yahweh, the sacred name of God, was translated from the Hebrew. The Gospel of John echoes that phrase in relation to Jesus, who says, for example, "I am the bread of life" (6:35, 48) or "I am the light of the world" (8:12; 9:5). The message is that Jesus embodies

God. When one discerns how John portrays this incarnation, the message gets fleshed out in greater detail, and the importance of grace is clarified.

The Word made flesh, says John, shows itself to be full of grace. As Christians understand it, grace refers to unmerited gifts from God—life itself but also time to spend, health to enjoy, strength to do what is right, courage to persevere against injustice, and love to show compassion and to heal wounds. When Jesus says "I am," the descriptions that follow indicate gifts of that kind. "I am the bread of life" identifies Jesus with the One who gives and sustains life. "I am the light of the world" identifies Jesus with the One who does not permit darkness to prevail. "I am the good shepherd" (10:11) identifies Jesus with the One who cares. "I am the resurrection and the life" (11:25) identifies Jesus with the One who will not let death win. "I am the way, and the truth, and the life" (14:6)— summed up in "I am he" (18:6)—identifies Jesus with the One who shows us how to "choose life so that you and your descendants may live" (Deut. 30:19).[18]

When the Gospel of John has Jesus say "I am," the words assert that "the Word became flesh," but the assertion is also a call to make a decision about their truth. More than one decision about their truth— including Jewish rejection of Christian claims about Jesus—can be made authentically and with integrity, and Christians should respect such differences accordingly. It is also true that both the assertion and the call have power to be heard far and wide because their appeal is so basically in tune with deeply felt human needs. Living "full of grace," Jesus helps the helpless, intercedes for those in need, feeds the hungry, defends the defenseless, heals the sick, and condemns oppression. He mends the world and calls others to follow him and to do the same by loving our neighbors as ourselves. In these acts of service and compassion, our love for God becomes incarnate as God's love for humankind enters the world visibly, though not only, through Jesus.

An essential part of the good news that post-Holocaust Christians have to tell is that Jesus, full of grace as he is, can help humankind to be more grace-full and thereby to mend the world. That task calls out to leaders and followers in the most poignant ways after Auschwitz. Acting on that call will not take the Holocaust away—nothing can—but it can make post-Holocaust life meaningful in ways that very little else is likely to do.

The Centrality of Truth

In the next chapter, I will say more about the French village of Le Chambon. Here I only want to mention that when five thousand persecuted Jews found refuge there during the Holocaust, the village's lifesaving response did not take place overnight. For years, André Trocmé, the community's Protestant minister, had preached Christianity's basic lessons—peace, understanding, love—in a church whose doorway arch was inscribed with these words from the Gospel of John: "Love one another." Trocmé's was a message of nonviolence, but a nonviolence that rejected inaction and deplored complicity with injustice.

The people of Le Chambon responded, but they were far from typical Christians during the Holocaust years. Much more typical was a pattern of betrayal, denial, and abandonment that can be found in the Gospel of John's account of the arrest, trial, and crucifixion of Jesus. In language contrasting with Jesus' "I am," his disciple, Simon Peter, three times denied knowing Jesus, saying "I am not" when asked if he was one of Jesus' followers. The difference during the Holocaust was that Christian denial was less explicit; but it was still immensely destructive in its abandonment of the Jews. Christian words still professed fidelity to Jesus during those dark times, but Christian practice typically did not do so when it came to honoring the truth that Jesus taught—namely, that the friends of Jesus are those who "do what I command you," which means to "love one another as I have loved you" (John 15:14, 12).

Post-Holocaust Christians proclaim that the Word is "full of truth." Too often, of course, the truth is not good news. The Holocaust happened; Auschwitz was real. Nonviolent resistance was not enough; it took massive bloodshed to stop Hitler. The cost of such truths is beyond calculation. They set no one free—at least not cheaply. Instead they choke us with grief, increase despair, shatter hope, mock morality, and reveal the shallowness of conventional optimism—or at least they should. Such truths also judge Christianity and find it wanting. They may even judge God and find God wanting. They leave post-Holocaust Christians with immense responsibilities.

Nevertheless, in spite of truth's all-too-frequent bad news, the Gospel of John affirms that "the truth will make you free" (8:32). If we pursue, respect, and live by what is true—confessing sin, acknowledging shame, loving one another first and foremost—then we will save life more and destroy it less. We will protest against injustice and not be indifferent to or complicit with it. In unprecedented ways, the Holocaust has much to tell us about what is evil and what is good, what is right and what is wrong. Such revelatory power does nothing to justify the Holocaust or to confer any special religious status upon it. The Holocaust ought not to have been—period. But given that the Holocaust did take place, and that life continues in its wake, those truths leave us to respond to them.

Cynicism is inviting. Despair is tempting. Resignation appeals. Gloom and discouragement await our embrace. Few are those who have encountered the Holocaust and not fallen prey—however momentarily—to any or all of those moods. But if we go deep down, the truth is that those dispositions will not strike us as the best ones for a post-Holocaust existence. If we go deep down, the truth will set us free—not to be untouched by melancholy and despair but to find strength that post-Holocaust Christianity can encourage, strength to resist despair, to refuse to allow melancholy to crush the joy that can still be found when people serve and love one another.

Post-Holocaust Christians have this good news to share: If you sincerely abhor the Holocaust, if you wholeheartedly regret it, if you refuse to let Auschwitz prevail, if you hunger and thirst for righteousness in a world scarred by the Holocaust, the good news of post-Holocaust Christianity is a good place to start and to stand. In that place, there is room to protest what humankind has done, what God has not done (and that list is long and hard), and what Christians in particular have failed to do as followers of Jesus. But at the end of the day, the claim that "the Word became flesh and lived among us, full of grace and truth" affirms good news that the world badly needs. That news will not silence every question; it will not remove Holocaust politics, for much has happened that deserves to remain unsettled and unsettling forever.

But in ways that penetrate to the very core of existence, a post-Holocaust profession that "the light shines in the darkness, and the darkness did not overcome it" still offers hope that Holocaust politics can be enlightened by grace and truth. That outcome would indeed produce music that reconfirms resolve to prevent the repetition of heinous evil.

Chapter Six

Ethics after Auschwitz

What Can Be Learned from the Holocaust?

> The plague bacillus never dies or disappears
> for good.
>
> Albert Camus, *The Plague*

W hat do students need to know? What should
people be taught? Who ought to be their
teachers? How should the answers to such questions
be determined? These issues both reflect and influence Holocaust politics. They also involve profoundly
ethical considerations, which suggest that Holocaust
politics and issues about ethics after Auschwitz are
closely intertwined. Thus, it is worth noting that by
the year 2000 there were nineteen American states
that had enacted legislation in support of Holocaust
education. According to Sarah Ogilvie, who heads the
education department at the United States Holocaust
Memorial Museum, the data about Holocaust-related
education initiatives in 2000 indicated no additional
states where such legislation was pending. Furthermore, the enacted provisions vary widely; some are
stronger, others weaker. In some states—Alabama,
Nevada, Tennessee, and West Virginia—commissions
or councils have been established to develop curricula

and classroom guidelines for instruction about the Holocaust. Other states—Connecticut, Georgia, Indiana, North Carolina, Ohio, Pennsylvania, South Carolina, Virginia, and Washington—encourage or recommend teaching about the Holocaust. In still others—California, Florida, Illinois, Massachusetts, New Jersey, and New York—the legislative verbs are stronger. In those places, some form of Holocaust education is required or mandated.

In Illinois, the first state to mandate Holocaust education, the wording of the pertinent 1990 legislation provides that

> every public elementary school and high school shall include in its curriculum a unit of instruction studying the events of the Nazi atrocities of 1933 to 1945. This period in world history is known as the Holocaust, during which 6,000,000 Jews and millions of non-Jews were exterminated. The studying of this material is a reaffirmation of the commitment of free peoples from all nations to never again permit the occurrence of another Holocaust.

The wording of this legislation is significant for ethical as well as political reasons. It underscores that the Holocaust was wrong. It was something that should not have happened, and nothing akin to it should ever happen again. Embedded in the legislation, central to the Holocaust politics that promotes education about the Holocaust, are deep-seated moral convictions about right and wrong, good and evil.

Holocaust scholar Michael Berenbaum puts the point effectively when he emphasizes that the Holocaust has become a "negative absolute." In our pluralistic world, where cultural, religious, and philosophical perspectives vary considerably, a widely held belief is that values are so relative to one's time and place that the "truth" of moral claims is much more a result of subjective preference and political power than a function of objective reality and universal reason. As Berenbaum suggests, however, that belief meets resistance in the Holocaust. Even if people remain skeptical that rational agreement can be obtained about what is right, just, and good, the Holocaust seems to reestablish conviction that what happened at Auschwitz and Treblinka was wrong, unjust, and evil—period. More than that, the scale of the wrongdoing, the magnitude of the injustice, and the devastation of the Holocaust's evil are so radical that we can ill afford not to have our ethical sensibilities informed by them. As another Holocaust scholar, Franklin Littell, has stressed, "study of the Holocaust is like pathology in medicine."[1] Pathology seeks to understand the origins and characteristics of disease and the conditions in which it thrives. If such understanding can be obtained, the prospects for resistance against disease, and perhaps even a cure, are increased. Convictions of related kinds stand at the heart of Holocaust education. Although not in ways that produce easy agreement, they govern much of Holocaust politics as well.

Unfortunately, to identify the Holocaust as a negative absolute that reinstates confidence in moral absolutes is a step that cannot easily be taken, and no one is advised to rush to judgment that study of the Holocaust can obtain the hopeful results of medical pathology at its best. The fact is that the Holocaust signifies an immense human failure. It did immense harm to ethics by showing how ethical teachings could be overridden or even subverted to serve the interests of genocide. When Berenbaum calls the Holocaust a negative absolute, the absoluteness involved means that not even ethics itself was immune from failure and, at times, complicity in the pathological conditions and characteristics that nearly destroyed Jewish life and left the world morally scarred forever. Because Holocaust politics unavoidably involves assumptions and issues about Holocaust education, and because those assumptions and issues are unavoidably matters of ethical judgment, it is crucial to think about the status of ethics after Auschwitz. One way to advance that inquiry involves a man named Calel Perechodnik.

Returning Home

On August 20, 1942, Calel Perechodnik, a Polish Jew, returned home. This fact is known because Perechodnik recorded it in writing that he began on May 7, 1943. Sheltered at the time by a Polish woman in Warsaw, the 26-year-old engineer would spend the next 105 days producing a remarkable document that is at once a diary, memoir, and confession rooted in the Holocaust.

Shortly before Perechodnik died in 1944, he entrusted his reflections to a Polish friend. The manuscript survived, but it was forgotten and virtually unknown in the United States until Frank Fox's translation appeared in 1996.[2] Charged with ethical issues, Perechodnik's testament is of special significance because he was a Jewish ghetto policeman in Otwock, a small Polish town near Warsaw. While that role was not his chosen profession, it was a part that he decided to play in February 1941—not knowing all that would soon be required of him.

Already the German occupiers of his native Poland had forced Perechodnik, his family, and millions of

other Polish Jews into wretched ghettos. "Seeing that
the war was not coming to an end and in order to be
free from the roundup for labor camps," Perechodnik
wrote, "I entered the ranks of the Ghetto Polizei."[3]

When Perechodnik returned home on August 20,
1942, he knew in ways that can scarcely be imagined
how optimistic, mistaken, fateful, and deadly even his
most realistic assumptions had been. His decision
to join what the Germans called the *Ordnungsdienst*
(Order Service) had not only required Perechodnik to
assist them in the destruction of the European Jews
but also implicated him, however unintentionally, in
the deportation of his own wife and child to the gas
chambers at Treblinka on August 19, 1942. Perechodnik's testament says that he returned home on
August 20, but his words indicate that "home" could
never be a reality for him again.

What about the century, the world, that led Perechodnik to the choices and consequences that were
his? Are such times and places ones in which we feel
casually, comfortably, confidently at home? Or does
Perechodnik's *Am I a Murderer?* make it impossible to
return home without the company of profoundly disturbing questions that rightly interrupt our comfort
and confidence?

The disturbance that Perechodnik's testament provokes can concentrate on him and his decisions. This
inquiry, however, focuses its attention differently
because it is too easy to cast blame on Perechodnik
and thereby to miss the point that most deserves consideration: A genocidal Nazi state created the circumstances in which the intention was that all Jews,
including Perechodnik, should die. By showing how
the destruction process capitalized on a cunning that
enticed and then required Jews to participate in the

annihilation of their own people, Perechodnik's case serves best as a point of departure to reveal, first, how calculated and systematic the Holocaust turned out to be and, second, how far those facts reach to question some of our fondest assumptions about moral judgments and ethical norms. Thus, with the stage set by the multifaceted tragedy of Calel Perechodnik's case, let us reflect on some of the fundamental moral dilemmas that confront humankind, and especially Americans, as we try to return home in a post-Holocaust world.

The Advance of Civilization

Nazi Germany's system of concentration camps, ghettos, murder squadrons, and killing centers destroyed millions of defenseless human lives. While not every Nazi victim was Jewish, the Nazi intent was to rid Europe, if not the world, of Jews. Hitler went far in meeting that goal. Vast numbers of the Jewish victims came from Poland—Calel Perechodnik and his family among them—where the German annihilation took about 90 percent of that country's nearly 3.5 million Jews. Located in Poland, Auschwitz-Birkenau was the largest Nazi killing center. More than one million Jews were gassed there. Although Europe's Jews resisted the onslaught as best they could, by the time Germany surrendered in early May 1945, two-thirds of the European Jews—and about one-third of the Jews worldwide—were dead.

One of the most disquieting moral issues posed by the Holocaust is summed up in *The Cunning of History*, a short book by Richard L. Rubenstein which contends that "the Holocaust bears witness to *the advance of civilization*."[4] To see how that proposition bears on

Calel Perechodnik's case and how it is charged with ominous portents for the future, consider that in 1933, the year when Hitler took power in Germany, the Chicago World's Fair celebrated what its promoters optimistically acclaimed as "A Century of Progress." As *The Cunning of History* points out, the fair's theme was expressed in a slogan: "Science Explores; Technology Executes; Mankind Conforms."[5] Cast in those terms, the Holocaust not only bears witness to the tragically cunning and ironic elements of "progress" but also delivers a warning about what could—but ought not to—lie ahead for humanity.

The Final Solution was symptomatic of the modern state's perennial temptation to destroy people who are regarded as undesirable, superfluous, or unwanted because of their religion, race, politics, ethnicity, or economic redundancy. The Nazis identified what they took to be a practical problem—the need to eliminate the Jews and other so-called racial inferiors from their midst—and they moved to solve it. The Holocaust did not result from spontaneous, irrational outbursts of random violence, nor was the Final Solution a historical anomaly. It was instead a state-sponsored program of population riddance made possible by modern planning and the best technology available at the time.

Significantly, the Holocaust did not occur until the mid-twentieth century, but conditions necessary, though not sufficient, to produce it were forming centuries before. Decisive in that process was Christian anti-Judaism and antisemitism and their demonization of the Jews. For example, Rubenstein appraises the Christian New Testament correctly in his *After Auschwitz* when he writes that "no other religion is as horribly defamed in the classic literature of a rival tradition as is Judaism."[6] The reason for that defamation

was the Christian belief that the Jews were, as Rubenstein puts it, "the God-bearing and the God-murder-
ing people *par excellence*."[7] Jesus, the incarnation of
God according to Christian tradition, was one of the
Jewish people, but the Christian telling of this story
depicted the Jews as collectively responsible for his
crucifixion and thus for rejecting God through deicide,
the most heinous crime of all. Christian contempt for
Jews was advanced further by the belief that the dis-
persion of the Jews from their traditional homeland
after the Judeo-Roman War and the fall of Jerusalem
in 70 C.E.—and perhaps all of their subsequent misfortune—was God's punishment for their failure to see
the light. The effect of this centuries-old tradition was,
as Rubenstein says, "to cast them [the Jews] out of any
common universe of moral obligation with the Christians among whom they were domiciled. In times of
acute social stress, it had the practical effect of decrim-
inalizing any assault visited upon them."[8] Building on
a long history that went beyond religious to racist antisemitism, the assaults reached their zenith as Nazi
Germany became a genocidal state.

When we think of the dilemmas that Calel Perechodnik and his family confronted in wartime Poland,
it is crucial to understand that the Nazis' racist antisemitism eventually entailed a destruction process
that required and received cooperation from every
sector of German society. On the whole, moreover,
the Nazi killers and those Germans who aided and
abetted them directly—or indirectly as bystanders—
were civilized people from a society that was scientif-
ically advanced, technologically competent, culturally
sophisticated, efficiently organized, and even religiously devout. Those people were, as Michael Berenbaum has cogently observed, "both ordinary and

extraordinary, a cross section of the men and women of Germany, its allies, and their collaborators as well as the best and the brightest."[9]

Some Germans and members of populations allied with the Nazis resisted Hitler and would not belong in the following catalog, but they were still exceptions to prove the rule that there were, for example, pastors and priests who led their churches in welcoming nazification and the segregation of Jews it entailed. In addition, teachers and writers helped to till the soil where Hitler's racist antisemitism took root. Their students and readers reaped the wasteful harvest. Lawyers drafted and judges enforced the laws that isolated Jews and set them up for the kill. Government and church personnel provided birth and baptismal records that helped to document who was Jewish and who was not. Other workers entered such information into state-of-the-art data processing machines. University administrators curtailed admissions for Jewish students and dismissed Jewish faculty members. Bureaucrats in the Finance Ministry handled confiscations of Jewish wealth and property. Postal officials delivered mail about definition and expropriation, denaturalization and deportation.

Driven by their biomedical visions, physicians were among the first to experiment with the gassing of "lives unworthy of life." Scientists performed research and tested their racial theories on those branded subhuman or nonhuman by German science. Business executives found that Nazi concentration camps could provide cheap labor; they worked people to death, turning the Nazi motto, *Arbeit macht frei* (Work makes one free), into a mocking truth. Radio performers were joined by artists such as the gifted film director, Leni Riefenstahl, to broadcast and screen the polished propaganda that made Hitler's policies persuasive to so many. Railroad personnel drove the trains that transported Jews to death, while other officials took charge of the billing arrangements for this service. Factory workers modified trucks so that they became deadly gas vans; policemen became members of squadrons that made mass murder of Jews their specialty. Meanwhile, stockholders made profits from firms that supplied Zyklon B to gas people and that built crematoriums to burn the corpses.

Engineers of Death

Richard Rubenstein argues that the Holocaust is symptomatic of an ironic advance of civilization, and his thesis gets telling support from "Engineers of Death," a 1993 *New York Times* article by Gerald Fleming. A noted historian, Fleming also wrote *Hitler and the Final Solution*, which tries to identify when the decision was made to destroy the European Jews by mass murder, a puzzle that persists because no written order by Hitler seems to exist. What occasioned Fleming's writing in the *New York Times*, however, was a Holocaust puzzle of a different kind.

Since the collapse of the Soviet Union at the end of the Cold War, scholars have had better access to historical documents in Moscow. Research about World War II and the Holocaust in particular has benefited from that accessibility. For some time, Fleming had been studying the Auschwitz Central Building Authority records that were captured by Soviet troops and stored in Soviet archives. In May 1993, his searching led him to File 17/9 of the Red Army's intelligence branch. Previously off limits to historians from the West, this file contained information about four senior engineers who had worked for a German firm named Topf und Söhne. It was known that these men had been arrested by the Soviets in 1946, but Western intelligence lost track of them after that.

Topf had been manufacturing cremation furnaces for civilian use since 1912. That fact was less than noteworthy, but the puzzle that eventually took Fleming to File 17/9 involved another piece of information that was much more significant. Nameplates on the crematorium furnaces at Nazi concentration camps in Buchenwald, Dachau, Mauthausen, Gross-Rosen, and Birkenau (the main killing center at Auschwitz) showed that they too were Topf products.

At the war's end, Kurt Prüfer, a specialist in furnace construction and one of Topf's senior engineers, had been interrogated by the American Third Army. He persuaded his interrogators that the concentration camp crematoriums had existed for health reasons only. The Americans released him. The Red Army, however, could document another story. Although German orders in late November 1944 called for the destruction of equipment and records that would implicate Auschwitz-Birkenau as a death factory, the enterprise was simply too vast to cover up. When the Red Army liberated that place two months later, the massive evidence included, in Fleming's words, details about "the construction of the technology of mass death, complete with the precise costs of crematoriums and calculations of the number of corpses each could incinerate in a day."[10] Well beyond documenting the Red Army's arrest of Prüfer and three of his colleagues in Erfurt, Germany, on March 4, 1946, File 17/9 contained transcripts of the revealing interviews that interrogators had conducted with Prüfer and his associates.

At Auschwitz-Birkenau the *Krema*, as they were sometimes called in German, became full-fledged installations of mass death.[11] Especially given the constraints on wartime building projects, the construction of the four carefully planned units at Birkenau took time. Topf was only one of eleven civilian companies needed to produce them. Utilizing prisoner labor as much as possible, the building began in the summer of 1942, but it was nearly a year before the last facility was operational. Each included an undressing room, a gas chamber, and a room containing Topf's incineration ovens. These lethal places were designed to dispatch thousands of people per day. Even so, Prüfer told his Red Army interrogators, "the [crematorium] bricks were damaged after six months because the strain on the furnaces was colossal." Periodic malfunctions notwithstanding, the gassing and burning went on and on.

"From 1940 to 1944," Prüfer went on to tell his captors, "twenty crematoriums for concentration camps were built under my direction." His work took him to Auschwitz five times; he knew that "innocent human beings were being liquidated" there. In addition to excerpts from the Red Army's interviews with Prüfer, Fleming's article contains parts of the depositions taken from one of Prüfer's superiors, Fritz Sander, a crematorium ventilation specialist whose work for Topf took him to Auschwitz three times, often in tandem with Prüfer. In late 1942, Sander submitted plans to "improve" what was happening at Auschwitz-Birkenau. He envisioned a crematorium with even higher capacity than those already planned for installation there. To Sander's dismay, his project was not accepted. It would have used "the conveyer belt principle," he explained. "That is to say, the corpses must be brought to the incineration furnaces without interruption."

Apparently without remorse or apology, Sander admitted his knowledge of the mass murder at Auschwitz. "I was a German engineer and key member of the Topf works," he reasoned on March 7, 1946. "I saw it as my duty to apply my specialist knowledge in this way in order to help Germany win the war, just as an aircraft construction engineer builds airplanes in wartime, which are also connected with the destruction of human beings." Less than three weeks later, Sander died in Red Army custody, the victim of a heart attack. Having been sentenced to "25 years deprivation of liberty," Prüfer died of a brain hemorrhage on October 24, 1952.

Right and Wrong

The Holocaust's evil appears to be so overwhelming that it forms an ultimate refutation of moral relativism. No one, it seems, could encounter Auschwitz and deny that there is a fundamental and objective difference between right and wrong. Nevertheless, as Fleming's "Engineers of Death" suggests, short of Germany's military defeat by the Allies, no other constraints—social or political, moral or religious—were sufficient to stop the Final Solution. One might argue that Nazi Germany's defeat shows that right defeated wrong and that goodness subdued evil, thus showing that reality has a fundamentally moral underpinning. The Holocaust, however, is far too awesome for such facile triumphalism.

The Nazis did not win, but they came too close for comfort. Even though the Third Reich was destroyed, it is not so easy to say that its defeat was a clear and decisive triumph for goodness, truth, and justice over evil, falsehood, and corruption. Add to those realizations the fact that the Nazis themselves were idealists. They had positive beliefs about right and wrong, good and evil, duty and irresponsibility. We can even identify something that can be called "the Nazi ethic." The Final Solution was a key part, perhaps the essence, of its practice, which took place with a zealous, even apocalyptic, vengeance.[12] It would be too convenient to assume that the Nazi ethic's characteristic blending of loyalty, faith, heroism, and even love for country and cause was simply a passive, mindless obedience. True though the judgment would be, it remains too soothing to say only that the Nazi ethic was really no ethic at all but a deadly perversion of what is truly moral. Most people are unlikely to serve a cause unless that cause makes convincing moral appeals about what is good and worthy of loyalty. Those appeals, of course, can be blind, false, even sinful, and the Nazis' were. Nevertheless, the perceived and persuasive "goodness" of the beliefs that constituted the Nazi ethic—the dedicated SS man embodied them most thoroughly—is essential to acknowledge if we are to understand why so many Germans willfully followed Hitler into genocidal warfare.

Paradoxically, the Final Solution threatens the status, practical and theoretical, of moral norms that are contrary to those that characterized the Nazi ethic, whose deadly way failed but still prevailed long enough to call into question many of Western civilization's moral assumptions and religious hopes.[13] This dilemma is underscored by statements from *The Cunning of History* that warrant repeating. As Rubenstein assesses the situation, and the case of Calel Perechodnik comes to mind again, the Holocaust suggests that "there are absolutely no limits to the degradation and assault the managers and technicians of violence can inflict upon men and women who lack the power of effective resistance."[14] A pivotal implication, adds Rubenstein, is that "until ethical theorists and theologians are prepared to face without sentimentality the kind of action it is possible freely to perpetuate under conditions of utter respectability in an advanced, contemporary society, none of their assertions about the existence of moral norms will have much credibility."[15] Rubenstein knows, of course, that there are philosophical arguments to defend "a higher moral law" and ethical principles that hold persons and even nations morally responsible for their actions. Yet the Holocaust, he contends, sadly shows that there is "little or no penalty for their violation. And norms that can be freely violated are as good as none at all."[16]

The answer to Rubenstein's dilemma, if there is one, will not be found in some clinching intellectual argument or irrefutable philosophical analysis, for the best responses to this challenge are not that easy or simple. Instead, they involve sustained reflection on the memories people should share, the emotions we should express, the beliefs we should hold, the decisions we should make about how to live after Auschwitz, and the questions that we ask about all of those aspects of our experience, individually and collectively.

The Holocaust made Perechodnik ask, "Am I a murderer?" His confession answers yes. As we hear his answer, however, it should settle nothing. Instead, it should arouse us to engage in soul searching and community building that resist as best we can every inclination and power that make the best senses of returning home impossible. Some of the steps, though by no means all, that need to be taken in that direction can be discerned by recalling some additional Holocaust encounters.

The Importance of the Purple Triangle

Conventional definitions typically state that the Holocaust was the systematic, state-organized persecution and murder of nearly six million Jews by Nazi Germany and its collaborators. Emphasizing correctly that Jews were targeted primarily and uniquely during the Holocaust, the conventional definitions go on to say that Nazi Germany's genocidal policies also destroyed millions of other defenseless people. Roma and Sinti (Gypsies) and Poles were targeted for destruction for racial, ethnic, or nationalist reasons. Soviet prisoners of war, homosexuals, and political and religious dissidents were oppressed and put to death under Nazi tyranny as well.

Usually singled out for special mention in the categories of non-Jewish or "other" victims are the Jehovah's Witnesses, the ones the Nazis called *Bibelforscher.* Sometimes the Nazis identified them as Communists, sometimes as Zionists, sometimes as having threatening American or international links, and always as religious people who had an outlook that the Nazis perceived as dangerous to their interests. As a result, no Christian denomination was persecuted by the Nazis to the same degree as the Jehovah's Witnesses, but then no Christian group resisted the Nazis so intensely either.

Although they are mentioned in Holocaust definitions, the Jehovah's Witnesses are usually not discussed at much length in Holocaust histories, which understandably focus largely on the destruction of the European Jews. Hence, most people (including most people who know something about the Holocaust) lack a very thorough understanding of the Jehovah's Witnesses, who have often been regarded as "odd" folks with religious convictions and practices that put them out of the mainstream of the societies in which they live. This pattern fits the United States, a point to which I will return.

Meanwhile, lack of attention to the Jehovah's Witnesses in Holocaust studies, and particularly in discussions about post-Holocaust ethics, is unfortunate. That lack of attention permits ignorance to persist; that ignorance, in turn, leaves in the shadows a very important moral example that ought to be highlighted. The reason why the moral example set by the Jehovah's Witnesses ought to be highlighted is not merely because it is worthy of celebration but also because it presents a crucial challenge. Although that challenge may make us uncomfortable, it can be encouraging in vital ways. To be more specific, as a Holocaust scholar who is not a Jehovah's Witness, I have come to understand that the moral example of the Jehovah's Witnesses contains elements that are essential to check the *arrogance* that led to the Holocaust. Consider the following proposition: If more people practiced versions of what the Jehovah's Witnesses preach and practice, the Holocaust could have been prevented and genocide would scourge the world no more.

Two preliminary points help to advance the exploration of that proposition. First, conventional scholarly categories that are used to classify people during the Holocaust years often refer to perpetrators, victims, and bystanders. Sometimes those three categories are supplemented by three more: neighbors, rescuers, and resisters. Another category might be witnesses. Witnesses are those who have seen or heard something. They are people who are called upon to testify. They furnish evidence. Often they sign their names to documents to certify an event's occurrence or a statement's truth.

Especially in Nazi Germany and in European countries that came under Nazi domination, Jehovah's Witnesses (or International Bible Students, as they were commonly known) fitted that description. In more ways than one, what they saw and heard put them at odds with that regime, even when the Statement of Principles (dated October 7, 1934) sent to the German government by the Jehovah's Witnesses in Germany contended that "we have no interest in political affairs."[17] Bearing witness to their opposition to Nazism, the Witnesses suffered persecution. Their examples furnish telling evidence; they certify basic moral tenets that we ignore at our peril.

The second preliminary point has to do with the prescribed markings that prisoners in Nazi Germany's concentration camps wore on their makeshift uniforms. Those markings included a serial number and colored triangles. Jews wore two of these triangles, both yellow, which formed the six-pointed Star of David. Political prisoners wore red triangles, criminals green, Roma and Sinti brown, homosexuals pink. Jehovah's Witnesses were marked by purple triangles.

The purple triangle's moral significance is that it symbolizes a specific kind of resistance that would have been sufficient to prevent the Holocaust *if it had been widely practiced in time.* These qualifying words are important. One reason is that it took massive military force to bring the Third Reich to its knees and to bring the Holocaust to an end. The resistance of the Jehovah's Witnesses did not take that form. Indeed, as

World War II wore on, the Nazis gradually understood that the Witnesses' religious beliefs would lead
neither to escape attempts nor to violent resistance in
the concentration camps or elsewhere. At least to
some extent, Nazi cunning eventually learned how to
exploit the Witnesses' trustworthy behavior for its
own purposes.

Nevertheless, the early Nazi perception that Jehovah's Witnesses threatened Nazi ideology and the
emergence of the Third Reich's power was not misplaced. The purple triangle signified a particular kind
of moral threat to the Third Reich, one so potentially
devastating to Nazi interests that it might have
stopped Hitler and their followers before the Nazi
regime became entrenched. Let us try to identify and
understand it better.

One way to illustrate the distinctively moral threat
that the Jehovah's Witnesses posed for Nazi Germany
involves the different ways in which the Nazis treated
Jews and Jehovah's Witnesses. Nazi intentions
required the annihilation of Jewish life, root and
branch. The racial nature of the Nazis' antisemitism
meant that it did not matter what Jews believed or
even what they did. True, the Nazis did all they could
to caricature Jews, to portray Jewish beliefs and practices in the most degrading ways possible, but, according to Nazi ideology, Jews were so racially inferior that
they simply had to be destroyed. Jews were targeted
simply because they were Jews. The Nazis defined the
category "Jew," and where Nazi authority prevailed,
those definitions were unrelenting and deadly.

Nazi intentions toward the Jehovah's Witnesses
were different. Some 25,000 Witnesses lived in Nazi
Germany. Although about 10,000 of them were
imprisoned in concentration camps, where up to

5,000 of them died, the Witnesses were not a racial threat, and the Nazis did not think of them in that way, partly because many Jehovah's Witnesses were of German nationality. For the Nazis, it was precisely the beliefs and practices of the Witnesses that were correctly perceived as ultimately threatening to Nazi interests. Thus, from a Nazi perspective, it could be argued that it was less important to kill Jehovah's Witnesses than to neutralize or negate their beliefs. Unlike Jews in the Nazi scheme, Witnesses who were Witnesses no longer were worth much more alive than dead.

The "victory" the Nazis needed against the Witnesses was not a "final solution" consisting of killing centers, gas chambers, and crematoriums. It was instead the "victory" that would come if Jehovah's Witnesses themselves gave up their beliefs and practices, started saluting Hitler, joined the German military, pledged their fidelity to the German state and not to God, and gave their lives not as religious martyrs but as obedient soldiers in the *Wehrmacht*.

Two strategies toward Jehovah's Witnesses indicate that the breaking of belief and practice was crucial from the Nazi point of view. Children of Jehovah's Witnesses, for example, were taken from their parents. They were sent to institutions or placed with families where a "proper Nazi upbringing" awaited them. Another illustration can be seen in the statement that imprisoned Jehovah's Witnesses could sign, often after being tortured, to renounce their beliefs. This "Declaration Renouncing Beliefs" proclaimed that its signer acknowledged that the Jehovah's Witnesses advocated "erroneous teachings" and did so with "hostile purposes against the State." By signing this document, one promised to disavow any association with

Jehovah's Witnesses, denounce others who were so associated, and turn in literature published by Jehovah's Witnesses. Furthermore, by signing this declaration, one also promised to serve and defend "the fatherland, . . . with weapon in hand . . . in the event of war." Violation of this declaration meant being "taken again into protective custody," the Nazi euphemism for a concentration camp sentence or worse. Breaking the belief and practice of Jehovah's Witnesses was the Nazi goal. The hoped-for victory, however, did not take place. With very few exceptions, the Jehovah's Witnesses stood firm.

It was not just belief in general that jeopardized the Jehovah's Witnesses and made them threatening to the Nazi regime. The particularity of that belief mattered greatly. As students of the Hebrew Bible and the Christian New Testament, the Jehovah's Witnesses fervently believed in the sovereignty of God. Human allegiance belonged not to a nation or state but to the Lord of creation. They trusted what they took to be God's promise, namely, that life in this world is not all there is, that death's sting is not ultimate for the faithful, that resurrection awaits them, that risks can be taken for what is right and good even if doing so puts one's earthly life at risk. Taking to heart the New Testament's pronouncement that "From one ancestor [God] made all nations to inhabit the whole earth" (Acts 17:26), the Witnesses' reading of scripture, moreover, left no room for racial nationalism. To the contrary, it emphasized that Jehovah's kingdom was coming.

The Witnesses would bear witness to these beliefs by publishing and distributing testimony about them, going door to door, person to person (clandestinely and even in concentration camps, if need be) to advance their understanding of the coming of Jehovah's kingdom and also, when possible, to reveal the Nazi regime's oppressive nature. Some of those reports to the world explicitly deplored the persecution of Jews.

Doing these things was of ultimate importance because nothing less was at stake than the triumph of good over evil, of right over wrong, and nothing else mattered more than to be on God's side in that struggle. In this way, the Jehovah's Witnesses were far from pacifistic, although their ways of bearing witness precluded bearing arms. Of course, it is common for groups to claim that "God is on our side," and even the Nazis used such rhetoric when it suited their purposes. Jehovah's Witnesses, however, denied that "being on God's side" could ever be equated with the political interests of a nation-state, most especially if the nation-state attempted to control and limit what one's understanding of God's will entailed. Officially, then, they were politically neutral, but far from their neutrality's aiding and abetting oppressors, the Jehovah's Witnesses "took sides" and protested in their own ways by refusing to let human prerogatives eclipse what they understood to be God's.

The Nazis surely understood, perhaps even better than the Jehovah's Witnesses themselves, how threatening the belief and practice of this group could be. When the Witnesses' 1934 Statement of Principles attempted to reassure the Nazi state that the Witnesses were not, in principle, political subversives or revolutionaries, the Nazi leadership was more enraged than reassured by Witness words stating "we have no interest in political affairs, but are wholly devoted to God's Kingdom under Christ His King." For in addition to the content of those words, they were preceded by others that judged the Nazi state and found it wanting in the most profound ways: "If your government or officers do violence to us because we are obeying God," the 1934 Statement said, "then our blood will be upon you and you will answer to Almighty God." The Nazis knew that these words were backed up by deeds; the Jehovah's Witnesses practiced what they preached.

The moral significance of the purple triangle is that it symbolizes the proposition that the highest human allegiance, our deepest loyalty, does not belong to the nation-state or to anything of merely human devising but to God, the One who tells us that it is wrong to steal and murder and that it is right and good to care for those in need and to love our neighbors as ourselves. To elaborate on those points, the purple triangle symbolizes a judgment against, and an antidote for, human arrogance, which was so destructively present in the Third Reich. Hitler and his followers put the Third Reich above everything else. That arrogance led to the antisemitic, racist catastrophe that we call the Holocaust.

The moral significance of the purple triangle is that it symbolizes a resounding No to human arrogance and a life-respecting Yes to the conviction that all human thought and action should be subservient to and judged by principles of justice, peace, love, and understanding that come to mind when we reflect sensitively on the idea of the kingdom of God. The moral significance of the purple triangle is that it should make us remember that there would have been no Third Reich, no Holocaust, if that No and Yes had been normative in human affairs. Even now, genocide would scourge the earth no longer if that No and Yes became the center of human belief and practice.

Eventually a forceful No was said to Nazi Germany, but it came only after disaster struck so hard that the world can never fully recover from it. That disaster was as unnecessary as it was destructive. It could have been prevented, especially by action taken in the early 1930s, and the testimony of the Jehovah's Witnesses gives us important clues about how. My point is not to say that more and more people should have become Jehovah's Witnesses, although that idea has more than a little to commend it, but rather to suggest that a commitment to the principles that Jehovah's Witnesses embody in their distinctive ways could have checked the worst before it happened.

Jehovah's Witnesses worried the Nazis. Ironically, however, maybe the Nazis did not need to worry so much. After all, human history shows that people easily overlook the dangers of human arrogance and forget to defend the goodness underscored by concepts like the kingdom of God. In fact, bearing witness to truths like that can be a dangerous thing to do even here in the United States. This part of the Jehovah's Witnesses' story is not well known, but historian Gerald Sittser devotes attention to it in his 1997 book, *A Cautious Patriotism*.[18]

In the United States during World War II, more than two thousand Witnesses were imprisoned because draft boards were not sympathetic to their conscientious objection against war. They were also suspect because they would not salute the American flag. More than three hundred episodes of mob violence against Witnesses were reported during the period, usually because Witnesses were accused of being unpatriotic. Even the U.S. Supreme Court ruled against them. The ruling was overturned in 1942, but in a 1939 case, *Minersville School District v.*

Gobitis, the Court decided 8–1 in favor of the school district, which had prevented children of Jehovah's Witnesses from attending school because they would not salute the American flag. In the 1939 case, the famous Jewish-American jurist Felix Frankfurter wrote the majority opinion. There were many who supported the Witnesses, but the record shows that, even in the United States, Jehovah's Witnesses have been regarded, especially in times of stress, as a social nuisance or worse. The moral significance of the purple triangle is not a warning that applies only to societies that are oceans away. Its message is for Americans too.

On March 22, 1942, the Nazis executed Wolfgang Kusserow, a twenty-year-old Witness who had refused military service. The day before his execution, he was permitted to write a final letter to his family. The ending of Kusserow's letter contains these words: "Well Satan knows that his time is short. Therefore, he tries with all his power to lead astray from God men of good will, but he will have no success. We know that our faith will be victorious. In this faith and this conviction I leave you." Such words may make some of us uncomfortable. Certainly not all of us could say them, nor do we have the confident faith that inspired Wolfgang Kusserow to write them. Nevertheless, Jehovah's Witnesses who have become Holocaust witnesses help us, I believe, to understand in our heart of hearts that we must find our own versions of related convictions if we are to mend the world and forestall disasters that are waiting to happen unless we are awake and alert.

Those who wore the purple triangle could not prevent or stop the Holocaust after things had gone too far, but if its moral significance is widely remembered in time, the purple triangle can yet be a shield against disaster, a shield whose triangular points direct our attention and commitment toward the good that most deserves human respect.

Returning to Home

About the time that Wolfgang Kusserow was executed and Calel Perechodnik was writing his testament in hiding, existentialist philosopher Albert Camus, a member of the French Resistance against Nazi Germany, was working on *The Plague*, which would become his most important novel. Set in the Algerian city of Oran in the 1940s, the story chronicles Dr. Bernard Rieux's battle against a deadly pestilence. As Pierre Sauvage points out in his masterful film, *Weapons of the Spirit*, Camus wrote *The Plague* while living in the vicinity of Le Chambon sur Lignon, a mountain village in south-central France. Led by André and Magda Trocmé, Le Chambon's Protestant pastor and his wife, that place became a haven in Nazi-occupied Europe. Jews—some five thousand—and other refugees found help there while the Holocaust raged around them.

Le Chambon did not become a Holocaust haven overnight. It did so over time and partly because the Chambonnais had a tradition of bringing their religion to pointed public expression. Since the sixteenth century, for example, Le Chambon has been predominantly Protestant, an anomaly in Catholic France. Even now, many of the villagers are descendants of Huguenots who fled to that high plateau so they could practice their Protestant Christianity without fear of punishment. But persecution persisted. Some people and pastors of Le Chambon were hanged or burned at the stake for fidelity to the biblical principles that gave meaning to their lives.

Far from weakening their faith, such persecution—and the memory of it—strengthened the solidarity of the hardy Chambonnais. That solidarity manifested itself distinctively soon after Nazi Germany invaded France on May 12, 1940. Even before that plague arrived, André and Magda Trocmé had been teaching and practicing an ethic that emphasized reading the signs of the times so that steps could be taken in time to get needy people out of harm's way. Those steps meant actively resisting evil when confronted by it. That meant remaining human in inhuman times. When the time came for the people of Le Chambon to resist the Nazi death machine, to act in solidarity and on behalf of others, the villagers—Protestant and Catholic alike—backed the Trocmés. Unlike so many other Christians during the Holocaust, they made their village an ark of hope in a sea of flames and ashes.

Le Chambon's resistance to the Holocaust started with small gestures—with Magda Trocmé, for example, opening her door and welcoming a German Jewish woman into her home. She and everyone else were aware of the danger, but that did not deter them. They regarded their acts of rescue as natural, as just the right thing to do. As Magda Trocmé said, "None of us thought that we were heroes. We were just people trying to do our best."[19] When Camus had Dr. Rieux conclude *The Plague* by observing that "there are more things to admire in men than to despise," the people of Le Chambon may well have been on his mind.[20]

In Camus's story, Rieux says that he compiled the chronicle "so that he should not be one of those who hold their peace but should bear witness in favor of those plague-stricken people; so that some memorial

of the injustice and outrage done them might endure."
Though the plague eventually left Oran, Dr. Rieux
believed that there was nothing final about the victory.
"The plague bacillus never dies or disappears for
good," he says at the novel's end. The fight against
"terror and its relentless onslaughts," he concludes,
must be "never ending."[21] Wolfgang Kusserow and
Calel Perechodnik would agree.

The writings Perechodnik left behind include a
poignant and disturbing document composed in Warsaw, Poland, on October 23, 1943. Almost apologeti-
cally, Perechodnik states, "I am not a lawyer by
profession, and so I cannot write a will that would be
entirely in order, and I cannot in the present circumstances ask for help from the outside."[22] Explaining
his "present circumstances," Perechodnik observes
that, "as a result of the order of German authorities, I
and my entire family, as well as all the Jews of Poland,
have been sentenced to death."[23] This death sentence,
he notes, has claimed almost all of his family, and thus
Perechodnik's formal, documentary language is also
an understated lamentation that records their fate as
best he knows it. He has no personal property, Perechodnik goes on to say, but he is the legal heir to property left by his father, Ussher, and his wife, Chana. He
makes clear what should be done with it. His last testament is a real will, prepared as carefully and executed as properly as Perechodnik knew how.

Nobody can say how much Perechodnik believed
that anybody, let alone any legal system, government,
or state, would care one whit about his will. Nevertheless—perhaps with irony and protest as much as
hope, perhaps to resist despair by asserting his human
dignity, or perhaps with none of those feelings—Perechodnik writes respectfully and specifically asks "the

Polish court to make possible the execution of this will according to both the spirit of my wishes as well as the law involved."[24]

Perechodnik lists the property to which he is heir and designates those to whom he wants to leave it. Giving addresses and exact locations, he carefully explains that the property exists in Otwock, his hometown. There is the movie house called "Oasis." There are two lots and two villas. The latter contain apartments.

The apartments were homes. Not just people but families—Jewish and Polish, members of Perechodnik's family, Perechodnik himself—returned to those family homes after work, school, or shopping, and after journeys that took them away but brought them back home again. After Perechodnik saw his wife and child deported to Treblinka in August 1942, he said that he returned home, but he did not return there—could not do so—because the Holocaust destroyed not only Perechodnik's physical home, leaving him ghettoized, but senses of *home* that are even more precious and profound than the specific places and times without which those deeper senses of *home* cannot exist.

If we think about the most fundamental human needs and about the most important human values, *home* looms large. *Home* means shelter and safety, care and love. It has much to do with the senses of identity, meaning, and purpose that govern our lives, because *home* involves our closest relationships with other people and provides key motivations and reasons for the work we do. Not all particular homes fit that description, which sometimes leads us to speak of "broken homes," a condition that no one chooses as good. Unfortunately, the Holocaust and the devastating world war that provided "cover" for it did more than break homes. It ruined them, physically and metaphysically, because the Nazi assault, driven by a debased yearning for an exclusively German homeland, was so successful in destroying the trust on which home depends.

The senses of *home* that we identify most with goodness depend on stability, fidelity, communal ties, mutual respect, law, a shared ethical responsibility, and, for some but not all persons, religious faith. Phrases about home—for example, "going home" or "being at home" or even "leaving home"—reflect those elements. The Holocaust, as the philosopher Jean Améry said, destroyed trust in the world. It showed that without sufficient defense, violent powers can leave people bereft of home, if those powers leave their victims alive at all. True, human resilience may act remarkably to rebuild senses of home in the ruins but never without a residue of distrust that is metaphysical and perhaps religious as well as political.

Post-Holocaust ethics must be concerned with outcomes. Seeking ways to "return home," it must emphasize not only good intentions that persist in spite of history but also how to achieve results that increase the trust on which our best senses of home depend. These considerations mean that the relationship between *might* and *right* is crucial. I reject the proposition that might *makes* right. In my view, what is good, just, and true is not determined by human pronouncement, let alone by the political power of a state. But if might does not make right, relationships between right and might still remain, and they are as important as they are complex.

Consider why Calel Perechodnik was unable to return home. He could not do so because Nazi power prevented him from doing so. I think that no ultimately sustainable reasons—judgments that could stand full critical scrutiny—could be found to justify that Nazi power, but nevertheless Perechodnik could not return home. Might did not make right in that case, but might had much to do with the functional status of right. The same point can be seen in relationships such as the following: A law that is not obeyed may still be a law, but its functional status depends on obedience and credible sanctions against disobedience. An injunction that is not heeded lacks credibility. When Nazi Germany unleashed the Holocaust, the force of the injunction "Thou shalt not murder" was impugned to the degree that millions of Jews were slaughtered before the violence of a world war crushed the Third Reich. Similarly, if God is not acknowledged, God's existence is not necessarily eliminated but God's authority is curtailed. And if God's authority lacks credibility, then the nature of God's existence is affected too.

Our senses of moral and religious authority have been weakened by the accumulated ruins of history and the depersonalized advances of "civilization" that are taking us from a bloody twentieth century into an even more problematic twenty-first. A moral spirit and religious commitment that have the courage to persist in spite of humankind's self-inflicted destructiveness are essential, but the question remains of how effective those dispositions can be in a world where power, and especially the power of governments, stands at the heart of that matter. As genocide scholar and statistician R. J. Rummel says, "Power kills; absolute Power kills absolutely," a statement that his chillingly titled book, *Death by Government*, supports as follows:

> In total, during the first eighty-eight years of this [twentieth] century, almost 170 million

men, women, and children have been shot, beaten, tortured, knifed, burned, starved, frozen, crushed or worked to death; buried alive, drowned, hung, bombed, or killed in any other of the myriad ways governments have inflicted death on unarmed, helpless citizens and foreigners. The dead could conceivably be nearly 360 million people. It is as though our species has been devastated by a modern Black Plague. And indeed it has, but a plague of Power, not germs.[25]

To find ways to affect "the powers that be" so that their tendencies to lay waste to human life are checked, ethics after Auschwitz will need to draw on every resource it can find: appeals to human rights, calls for "a return to God," respect and honor for people who save lives and resist tyranny, and attention to the Holocaust's warnings, to name only a few. Those efforts will need to be accompanied by efforts that build these concerns into our educational, religious, business, and political institutions. If it moves in those directions, Holocaust politics can take steps toward home.

If we consider human rights after the Holocaust, it is unlikely, for instance, that humankind will ever reach full agreement about one worldview that will ground belief in such rights. But it does not follow that appeals to human rights are dashed as well. If people feel the need to ground appeals to human rights, a variety of options—philosophical and religious—may remain credible even if they will not be universally accepted. More importantly, there may be considerable agreement—especially after the Holocaust—about what the functional interpretation of human rights ought to be. Here too there will not be universal agreement, but the Holocaust itself has had an important impact in helping to clarify what ought not to happen to human beings. If we think about what ought not to happen to human beings, moreover, we may find considerable agreement about what should happen. Calel Perechodnik ought not to have been prevented from returning home—in all the best senses of *home*—and if that is true, then what ought to have happened (again in all the best senses of that phrase) is not so far to find. Nazism and its Holocaust were an assault on the values that Americans and all people hold most dear when we are at our best. But these values are as fragile as they are precious, as precarious as they are fundamental. Each and every one of us needs home. If we think about that fact, we may find more to unite us than to divide us.

We need to draw on any and all resources that would have helped Calel Perechodnik from becoming homeless. Philosophical theories, religious convictions, educational policies, political strategies, even military force at times—all of those and more can be important in that regard. Holocaust-related stories of the kind highlighted in this chapter have their part to play as well. Through their particularity, stories communicate ethics more accessibly and persuasively than any other form of human communication. If I may close this chapter by speaking personally, Albert Camus's novel, *The Plague*, left a lasting moral mark on me when I read it as a college student. It informed my moral outlook because there were notes of universality and even transcendence in Camus's story about resistance against evil. Furthermore, hearing the story of Le Chambon did much to revitalize my Christian commitment, partly because that story helped me to rediscover how the particularity of one's commitment is essential for underscoring and acting on the universal importance of saving people from harm's way. Still further, reading Perechodnik's diary narrative, including his "Last Will and Testimony," left me with mixed feelings—sadness, anger, rage— that produce in me a version of what the Christian New Testament calls "hunger and thirst for righteousness," a disposition not restricted to one tradition but expressible in and through many traditions. These realizations and passions are not sufficient to mend the world, but unless they inform Holocaust politics and the education it should support, the chances to prevent homelessness akin to Calel Perechodnik's will be diminished.

Epilogue

Where Does Holocaust Politics Lead?

> After Treblinka . . .
> We see differently.
>   Edward Bond, "How We See"

James Besser is the Washington correspondent for the *Jewish Week*, a New York–based publication. His beat includes Holocaust politics and the United States Holocaust Memorial Museum. On April 28, 2000, he published "Notes from a Grieving Nation." Seeking insight about what he called "raging controversies over the nature and uses of remembrance," Besser turned to the reactions that museum visitors write in the comment books near its exits.[1] He also observed some of the people who took time to record their thoughts and feelings. One woman made a particularly strong impression upon him. "She wiped away tears," he recalled, "started to write, stopped, then crossed out a line. Then, she wrote a few words, turned and walked briskly away. 'I'll never be the same' is what she wrote."

More than a year before Besser's story appeared, Charles Ramsey visited the museum.[2] I do not know if he made an entry in one of the comment books, but this Washington, D.C., police chief did something else that reflected his "never being the same" after his museum encounter with the Holocaust. Disturbed by what he had seen, particularly the crucial parts played by German police in Nazi Germany's destruction of Jewish life, Chief Ramsey worked with the museum to establish training sessions for his officers and recruits. With the District of Columbia's initiative leading the way, additional Holocaust-education programs for police forces in the Washington-Baltimore area are taking place at the museum.

People who are touched by the Holocaust and by Holocaust politics may never be the same. But what follows from that statement? In Chief Ramsey's case we know, but a case such as the one Besser describes is more typical. Besser says that the museum visitor he observed wrote a few words and then walked away. How was she changed, once the emotional impact of her museum visit subsided? Did this Holocaust encounter affect her long-term destinations, purposes, actions, even her identity in a fundamental way? Clearly such changes took place in the lives of Holocaust survivors, but what about the vastly larger number of people whose Holocaust encounters take place at secondhand? If "I'll never be the same" is a response that even an indirect encounter with the Holocaust ought to provoke in ongoing ways, then how should *we* be changed? Ramsey's significant response underscores the importance of the question it answered so eloquently because Holocaust politics will not disappear, and increasingly its direction will be determined by generations far removed from the events that need to be remembered.

This book has explored many, though by no means all, aspects of what can be, in Besser's words, raging controversies about the Holocaust, its history, memorialization, and the uses to which remembrance is put. Therefore, as this inquiry draws to a close, it is worth asking: Where does Holocaust politics lead? My response is that Holocaust politics leads to hard choices. I will explain what I mean and then illustrate what the best decisions are likely to be and where they point.

Hard Choices

Holocaust politics leads to hard choices because the Holocaust and remembrance of it will continue to create disagreement and division. These differences exist in historical interpretation. That the Holocaust happened is a fact beyond rational dispute. Nevertheless, how and why it happened remain disquieting questions that can and do set people apart and put them on edge. Given the event's immense destructiveness and the limitations of our ability, individual and collective, to comprehend the past, let alone to master its trauma, one should not expect otherwise. That the Holocaust should be remembered is also beyond rational dispute. But how and why it should be remembered remain disquieting questions that can and do set people apart and put them on edge. Given the particularity of human experience, the intensity of feeling that particularity produces, and the ways in which emotion as well as reasoned judgment affect our identities, one should not expect otherwise.

Where Holocaust politics is concerned, however, the presence of difference and disagreement is not the ending but part of a post-Holocaust journey that will and must continue. That journey entails key turning points for Holocaust politics. As unavoidable as they are difficult, those decisions pivot around the following question: What shall we do with our Holocaust-related differences and disagreements? I believe there are three fundamental options. First, we can decide to let the controversies rage, hoping that enough power can be mustered to give some positions and policies victory while inflicting defeat upon others. On this basis, some accomplishments will follow, but the cost of time, energy, and resources spent—and often wasted—in "winning" will be very high. Second, we can practice a Holocaust politics that settles for deadlock, stalemate, even gridlock. Realizing they cannot "win," factions can still insist on having their partial ways by ensuring that no group alone controls the agenda of Holocaust politics. Third, we can try to move beyond differences, not by forgetting them or by setting them aside completely, but by recognizing both that the positions people take cannot rightly claim finality and that, as a result, we are engaged in a political process that implies an overarching goal.

The third perspective should govern Holocaust politics. Good examples of its work can be found when Holocaust scholarship is at its best. When Holocaust scholars do their work responsibly, they utilize different methods, represent different disciplines, draw on diverse experiences, and persistently strive for accuracy and sound judgment. Sometimes their disagreements are as deep as their arguments are impassioned. Sometimes misguided approaches must be revised, if not rejected, and mistaken claims must be corrected. But as the best work of Holocaust scholarship takes place, the commitment to studying the Holocaust brings two themes to the fore. First, there is dedication to inquiry, to trying to find out more and therefore to recognizing that finality is less important than learning, whose greatest enemy is arguably the insistence that "I am right." Second, there is dedication to what may be called "getting it right" or even "setting it straight." That is, there is an overarching goal, a basic priority, that governs the inquiry. The goal is to find out what happened—how and why—in the Holocaust and also, I would add, to discern more clearly the differences between right and wrong, good and evil.

Only to the degree that inquiry informs its policies can Holocaust politics truly respect the event it seeks to commemorate. Only to the extent that its heart pulses with the priorities of "getting it right" and "setting it straight" will Holocaust politics effectively educate current and coming generations so that the world will never be the same as it was during the darkness that engulfed it from 1933 to 1945. As one thinks further about the "getting it right" and "setting it straight" that are most needed in a post-Holocaust world, nothing may loom larger than the need that all people share—namely, the need for a home that is safe and secure, a place where individuals, families, and groups are able not only to pursue their own ways in peace but also to live in ways that permit others to do so as well. In large measure, the Holocaust was the destruction of home. By destroying Jewish homes, Nazi Germany created a world of homelessness and homesickness, a place in which trust can be too little put or found. Among the highest priorities for Holocaust politics, I believe, is a shared commitment to advance Holocaust-related education that helps to make the world a place in which children, women, and men can be at home not only in their own ways but also with each other. It is to those two themes—home building and education for it—that I want to turn in concluding this contribution to Holocaust politics.

The Arms of Strangers

Sigi Ziering, 72, succumbed to brain cancer on November 12, 2000.[3] Born in Kassel, Germany, he was eleven when his father, Isaac, who had fled to England from Nazi Germany, was unable to find refuge for the rest of this Jewish family. Trapped with his mother Cilly, and Herman, his older brother, Ziering was among the German Jews deported to the ghetto in Riga, Latvia, in 1941. Defying the lethal odds, all three survived the Holocaust. Along with their mother, Herman and Sigi were reunited with their father in London. In 1949, the Zierings immigrated to New York. Eventually, Sigi's scientific training and business ability enabled him to lead the Diagnostic Products Corporation, an international enterprise that specializes in medical tests and instruments that are increasingly important for human health.

Many people knew Ziering because of his philanthropic generosity, but he was best known to me because he wrote a play, *The Judgment of Herbert Bierhoff*. As Ziering explains in the preface to the privately published script that he completed in 1999, the play is based on Holocaust experiences, testimonies, and memories that "have stayed with me for these many years, usually buried in my subconscious, but surfacing from time to time, especially as I watched my children, and now my grandchildren, growing up."

Ziering and his play were on my mind in early September 2000 when my good friend Michael Berenbaum invited me to a film premiere in Hollywood, California. Several months earlier, Berenbaum had asked me to write an article about *The Judgment of*

Herbert Bierhoff, which he wanted to publish in a series of responses to the dilemmas and questions raised in Ziering's drama. My essay was late, but the film I was about to see made me write before it was too late. The film that Berenbaum and I saw that night was a special documentary about the *Kindertransport* (children's transport) program, an aspect of the Holocaust that has received too little attention. Thanks to the dedication of director Mark Jonathan Harris and Deborah Oppenheimer, the film's producer, that situation has changed.

Into the Arms of Strangers, which received the 2001 Academy Award for best documentary feature, draws on oral history and evocative film footage amplified by a moving soundtrack based on children's songs from the period.[4] In intensely personal ways, it focuses on the period between November 1938 and the beginning of World War II in September 1939. During that window of opportunity, 9,354 Jewish children were evacuated to Britain from areas under Nazi control. Assisted primarily by the Movement for the Care of Children from Germany (later named the Refugee Children's Committee or RCM), a private organization combining various Jewish and non-Jewish relief agencies, those unaccompanied girls and boys found a safe haven from the Holocaust that was about to sweep through Europe and scar the earth forever.

Oppenheimer's mother, Sylvia Avramovici Oppenheimer, was among the German Jewish children who found refuge in England when, shortly after Sylvia's eleventh birthday, her parents were able to send her there in August 1939, only days before the final train left Berlin on the last day of that month. At the time, the Final Solution had not yet unleashed mass murder in Nazi-occupied Europe. Forced emigration remained the official Nazi policy for Jews under the swastika. Unfortunately, antisemitism and fears about economic competition in circumstances still affected by the Great Depression meant that few places were interested in Jewish refugees, especially if the refugees were adults. For a few months in 1938–1939, however, the situation was slightly better for several thousand Jewish children between the ages of seven and sixteen.

In the United Kingdom (though not in the United States where welcoming legislation was initiated but blocked in Congress) a combination of private initiative, governmental support, and British generosity opened doors to safety for Jewish boys and girls when, less than two weeks after the November pogroms that the Germans euphemistically called *Kristallnacht*, Parliament announced its emergency policy on November 21, 1938: Britain would permit "an unspecified number of children up to age seventeen from German-occupied lands to enter the United Kingdom as 'transmigrants.'"[5] A few days later, on November 25, the BBC broadcast an appeal for foster homes. It was soon answered by five hundred offers and more followed. The first transport left from Berlin on December 1, followed on December 10 by one from Vienna. The trains headed for the Hook of Holland in the Netherlands. Ferries then took the children to British ports at Harwich or Southampton. Eventually the *Kindertransport* program would also rescue Jewish children from Czechoslovakia and Poland.

The stories about these Jewish children and their families, including the British foster families who sheltered and adopted them, are bittersweet. As the film's title suggests, the parting of parent and child in the Third Reich's railroad stations was heartbreaking. Families and their homes would never be the same.

Parents were sending their children into the arms of strangers, but Jewish families had to make that choice because the chances for a normal Jewish life in Germany had all but disappeared once *Kristallnacht* occurred. Uncertainty, anguish, and fear pervaded the partings. Parents reassured their children that the separation would not last long, and no doubt children sometimes did the same for their mothers and fathers, but on all sides those hopes and wishes disguised the fact that the future for these Jewish families was scarcely good. In one of the film's most gripping moments, a Holocaust survivor named Lory Cahn relates that she was put on a *Kindertransport* train in Breslau, Germany. As the train started to move, the fourteen-year-old girl reached through her compartment's open window to hold her father's hand one last time. Unable to stand the parting, he would not let go. As the train gained speed, Lory was pulled through the open window onto the railroad platform. She survived the Holocaust, but only after enduring numerous Nazi camps, including Auschwitz. When liberated from Bergen-Belsen, she weighed fifty-eight pounds. Lory Cahn lived to see her father after the war, but like Deborah Oppenheimer's mother, most of the Jewish children rescued by the *Kindertransport* never saw their parents again.

The *Kindertransport* program meant life for the precious few who qualified for its benefits, but no words can express the incalculably high price paid for that rescue. Nevertheless, it can be said that the price included terror and grief that can be at least partially felt by anyone who has even momentarily contemplated what it would be like to give up a dearly loved child—not knowing where or to whom the child may be going—or who might try to imagine a child's feelings when dearly loved parents are sending her or him away alone. For this reason, *Into the Arms of Strangers* is a film about the Holocaust that may presently be unrivaled in its ability to use history's particularity to communicate key aspects of the Holocaust's universal significance.

The Holocaust's core included the destruction of Jewish families and homes, which were and are essential for the vitality of Jewish life. Ironically, however, even the *Kindertransport* program was not entirely at odds with Nazi objectives, for it broke up families and removed Jewish children from the Reich. In addition, the British welcome was not entirely free of problematic compromise. It was arguably an understandable legal provision that the Jewish children were to be received in England on a temporary basis, for, among other things, it was probably assumed—disastrously mistaken though that belief turned out to be—that they would be reunited with their parents on the continent. It was honorable that British sterling in an amount exceeding 500,000 pounds was quickly raised to cover the fifty-pound bond that Britain required for each Jewish child. Yet it remained true that the children's parents were not welcomed for fear that they would become unwelcome job competitors or burdens on the state. The *Kindertransport* program was a blessing but not one that was unmixed. Thus, gratitude for the rescue of those Jewish children must combine with resistance to combat anything akin to the arrogantly antisemitic and racist forces that destroyed Jewish homes or the exclusionary, family-separating refugee policies that required the *Kindertransport*'s "choiceless choices" to be made at all. Otherwise the gratitude becomes sentimentality that does little to prevent or halt the genocidal destruction of families that remains a haunting threat after the Holocaust.

The Judgment of Herbert Bierhoff and *Into the Arms of Strangers* make strong companion pieces, for Ziering's "judgment" embraces "the arms of strangers," albeit in even more wrenching ways than Oppenheimer's documentary emphasizes. In her film, the strangers' arms were largely welcoming and friendly; they saved the lives of Jewish children. In his play, which is also based on actual events, the strangers' arms are hostile and murderous. They embody an escalation and radicalization of Nazi policy that went far beyond the *Kindertransport* program's prewar months. The escalation and radicalization extended to the Eastern European ghettos and killing centers that stood at the center of Nazi Germany's full-fledged effort to destroy European Jewry. In Riga, Latvia, for example, the Nazi-established Jewish ghetto was in more ways than one far removed from Britain and the safety that country gave to the Kindertransportees. Especially in 1943, no Jewish child was safe in Riga. There, parents faced predicaments of a kind that would scarcely have been imaginable even in August 1939 when Deborah Oppenheimer's mother said goodbye to her parents, departed Germany, and found a life very different from the one her parents had once envisioned for her.

German forces occupied the Baltic state of Latvia during the summer of 1941. With the help of local collaborators, the Germans had killed about 90 percent of the country's 95,000 Jews by the end of that year, including most of the approximately 30,000 Latvian Jews who were initially confined in the Riga ghetto. The clearing of that ghetto made its space available to concentrate Jews who were deported eastward from Germany and Austria during the winter of 1941–1942. By November 1943, the Riga ghetto had been "liquidated" as part of Nazi Germany's genocidal campaign to make Europe *judenrein*.

Ziering's narrative about the Bierhoff family, as well as his own life, reflects this history. The Bierhoffs—Herbert, Ruth, and their daughter Ellen, who was not yet six in the early autumn of 1943—were German Jews. They were deported from Kassel, their hometown, to Riga on December 9, 1941. Back in the prewar months of 1939, Ellen Bierhoff would have been much too young for the *Kindertransport* program. In 1943, however, her parents had successfully hidden her from the "selections" that were rapidly thinning the Riga ghetto's already reduced population as the Germans' collapsing eastern military front led them to kill the remaining Jews or to relocate those who could still be exploited as slave laborers. An "unproductive" Jewish child, Ellen Bierhoff was worse than useless to the Germans in Riga during the autumn of 1943. Hiding was unlikely to save her life much longer. No *Kindertransport*'s deliverance awaited her family, but agonizing alternatives did. Ziering makes his audience consider the unbearable dilemmas that Nazi domination forced on the Bierhoff family. If that responsibility gives his audience more than it can bear, one can scarcely imagine what the actual circumstances must have been for Herbert, Ruth, and Ellen, their precious child.

The cast of Ziering's play includes a survivor named David who sums up what happened. As a member of the Jewish ghetto police, Herbert Bierhoff knew that the Nazis were about to launch yet another *Aktion* to murder more of the Riga ghetto's diminished Jewish population. Ellen would surely fall into the brutal and murderous arms of Nazi strangers. Bierhoff would be unable to save her. He faced a decision that no parent should ever have to consider. Ellen's father, David tells us, "chose the only way open to him, the mercy killing of his beloved daughter, in order to avoid an infinitely more brutal killing by the SS."

Before he had given his daughter the poison that killed her, Bierhoff did what fathers often do. With reassuring words spoken to give a child comfort in her particular circumstances—"tomorrow you are going on a trip where you'll have many oranges, and all the food you can eat"—he said good night to Ellen. It was the last time he would do so. It was not even his fate to remember that night for long, because when the Germans discovered what he had done to Ellen, they shot him dead. Meanwhile, Ruth survived her daughter and husband but not the Holocaust. Her experiences in the Riga ghetto were too much to bear. As she lay dying, she charged Shimon, the Bierhoffs' friend, to find "competent judges who will declare that Herbert was merciful and right in giving Ellen the pill." Part of the Holocaust's oral testimony, this wrenching story came to Ziering, whose play and cast put Herbert Bierhoff's heartbreaking predicament before us.

Was Herbert Bierhoff merciful and right when he gave Ellen that pill? The survivor named David says yes. Kurt, another survivor, is not so sure. There was always the chance, somehow, that Ellen might survive. Stranger things happened in the Holocaust. Kurt also wonders why Ellen's father did not take his own life after he took hers. In addition, there is the question of whether Herbert Bierhoff should have consulted with Ruth, his wife, before he took the decision that he seems to have made alone. Esther, a third survivor, listens to David and Kurt. She feels the quandary's agony, but she has fewer answers than the men. Rejecting closure, she emphasizes that the survivors should simply "record and tell in a factual way, without embellishments, our personal experiences and the events which we witnessed." Sigi Ziering gives the play's last word to Shimon, the survivor who seeks to fulfill Ruth Bierhoff's last wish. Herbert Bierhoff, says Shimon, "did the right thing." But then Shimon pauses and delivers the last line to the audience: "Or did he?" *The Judgment of Herbert Bierhoff* asks us to consider the judgment that a Jewish father made and then to make a judgment about his decision. How can we accept this challenge? How can we not?

All of the main points in the paragraph above have a place in the response I want to make to Shimon's hard question. First and foremost, I think there is no closure, at least none that I can or should attempt to provide. If I jump to a conclusion, I do not allow the Bierhoffs' anguish to be fully expressed, for full expression requires not only a giving of testimony but a receiving of it as well. Ziering's play tells an unsettled story. It is not for me to settle what should remain unsettling.

That said, I acknowledge that Ellen, somehow, might have survived, but I also believe that Herbert Bierhoff acted out of love that was driven by the desperate choice he faced. I do not say that Bierhoff did the right thing, and certainly I do not say that he did a good thing. The words *right* and *good* can scarcely apply in the situation that the Bierhoff family faced, which was definitely not of their own choosing. One can say, I believe, that Ellen's father acted out of fatherly love, which was determined not to let his daughter fall into the arms of strangers who were hell-bent on her destruction. In that sense, as a Jewish father committed to the best he could do for his daughter in the Riga ghetto during the autumn of

1943, Herbert Bierhoff may have had but one loving choice—choiceless though it was—once the option of poisoning his child to death presented itself.

I wonder about Ruth. I tend to think that Herbert should have shared his intentions and obtained Ruth's consent, if not her help, in taking their daughter's life. But of that I am far less sure than of the moral fact that looms the largest in Ziering's play. That fact does not pertain primarily to the decisions Jews had to take in the Riga ghetto but to those that the Germans made in establishing that place and the murderous policies that governed it. Those decisions and policies were wrong—or nothing could be. Ziering's play focuses attention on the anguished dilemmas faced by the Bierhoffs and countless other Jewish families during the Holocaust. That focus, crucial though it is, will be misplaced unless it motivates post-Holocaust audiences to resist the ideologies and conditions, the leaders and followers, that may again bring about the home-destroying conditions that require parents and children to confront dilemmas like the Bierhoffs encountered in the Riga ghetto or the Oppenheimers faced as the last trains of the *Kindertransport* were organized in August 1939.

Among the touching children's songs that form the soundtrack for *Into the Arms of Strangers*, there is a simple prayer sung by a young boy. It is a prayer that loving parents might teach a child to say as darkness falls. It is a song that a loving mother or father might sing to a young son or a daughter before sleep overtakes them. "Give us, God, the evening," the words ask, "the evening, the good evening, [and] thus a cheerful morning." For Jewish parents and children during the Holocaust, good evenings and cheerful mornings were few and far between. In relatively small but still immensely important ways, the *Kinder-transport* and its welcoming arms made the Holocaust's devastation in the Riga ghetto and elsewhere less than complete. Nevertheless, Ziering's play rightly keeps the focus on the devastation by drawing us into the anguish of the Bierhoffs, one particular Jewish family. One result of that anguish and of *The Judgment of Herbert Bierhoff* deserves to be a deliberate rage, a determined anger that commits one to resist any conditions like those that made the *Kinder-transport* program necessary—and the life of Ellen Bierhoff impossible.

History Lessons

Two months before I saw *Into the Arms of Strangers*, I helped lead a conference called Remembering for the Future 2000. As I mentioned earlier, the conference was held in London and Oxford, and its theme was "The Holocaust in an Age of Genocide." Historical concerns dominated much of the discussion as some six hundred scholars from more than thirty countries absorbed new research findings and continued the important work of getting the history "right."

The effort to learn *about* the Holocaust and other genocides was not, indeed could not be, all that was involved in a conference called Remembering for the Future. The hope was to learn *from* the Holocaust as well. Artists and philosophers, theologians and teachers of many kinds joined with historians and social scientists to pursue those possibilities, but not everyone shared that hope in equal measure; in fact, some were very skeptical about it. Thus, Holocaust politics was no stranger to Remembering for the Future. Learning *from* the Holocaust, desirable though such learning may be, is easier said than done. Certainly it is more difficult than learning *about* the Holocaust, difficult though that work surely is. Nevertheless, the difficulty of learning *from* the Holocaust makes it more important that we try to do so.

Remembering for the Future 2000 concluded with a public meeting in London. On that occasion, it fell to me to address a fundamental question: Why should people learn about the Holocaust today? I posted that topic on a special web site set up for the conference. Here are a few of the responses I received: (1) We should learn about the Holocaust today, one respondent said, to ensure that children understand that indifference permits and encourages crimes against all our humanity. (2) From the daughter of Holocaust survivors: The Holocaust's lessons are very simple. Hate is deadly. A political party can find too many willing followers to destroy whoever they decide is undesirable. (3) If we learn about the Holocaust, another member of the "second generation" wrote, we will believe that any level of human cruelty is possible, and we will know to be forever vigilant.

Notice that these responses emphasize warnings and vigilance against forces that threaten humanity. Such responses do not take the question "Why should people learn about the Holocaust today?" to be simply about history or even about getting the history "right." These responses imply that there is something more than history to be learned from the Holocaust or that learning about the Holocaust entails history lessons that have ethical and political content. Those lessons are about how we should act now and about how we must act in the future.

Responses such as the ones my internet posting received can frequently be heard. They are as significant as they are common, but it must also be noted that there are critics, even from within the circles of those who study the Holocaust and genocide, who challenge such responses. One can say that it has even become fashionable for some intellectuals and academics to be skeptical about whether we *can* learn from the Holocaust and also to express the view that it may even be dangerous for the Holocaust to obtain a dominant place in human consciousness. If some of that skepticism has merit, it is also true that this skepticism has dangerous forms. They should be resisted lest they undermine and delegitimize the importance of Holocaust remembrance and education. Consider four of these skeptical criticisms about the idea that we can learn from the Holocaust. Some of the criticisms emerge from sound motives; others do not. Nevertheless, all of them are challenging and need to be answered thoughtfully and strongly.

First, there are those who suggest that the attempt to draw moral lessons from the Holocaust may detract from its particularity and overlook its utter devastation, which is so extreme that it has no moral "lesson" to convey. When Lawrence Langer, a Holocaust scholar I hold in the highest esteem, writes that "there is nothing to be learned from a baby torn in two or a woman buried alive," he advocates a version of this perspective.[6] Langer's motives need not be questioned; they are sound. He rightly understands that the Holocaust abounds in what survivors Primo Levi and Charlotte Delbo called "useless violence" and "useless knowledge," respectively, and what Jewish philosopher Emmanuel Levinas termed "useless suffering."[7] Learning *about* such realities, which cannot be avoided in Holocaust studies, can scarcely be morally edifying or spiritually uplifting. Universalizing interpretations that speak of the "triumph of the human spirit" or "the transcendence of good over evil" can preempt the Holocaust (to use Langer's phrase) in ways that distort its facticity and falsify its Jewish particularity. The strength of Langer's skepticism about learning *from* the Holocaust is its honest refusal to diminish the Holocaust's darkness. Nevertheless, that skepticism contains a serious weakness: If the Holocaust's darkness admits no learning *from* it, then one wonders why we should learn *about* it. Clearly, a scholar of Langer's stature believes that it is important to write, teach, and study about the Holocaust. In spite of his reluctance to say so, I believe that the reasons for that importance are fundamentally ethical, a point I have made before and to which I will return again.

A second criticism simply rejects the idea that we need the Holocaust to tell us about indifference, hate, and human cruelty. This criticism offers at least two reasons why: (1) the Holocaust is so extreme that it has little bearing on our everyday lives; (2) there are much more contemporary, immediate, and relevant experiences to which we can turn if we want to explore moral issues and convey ethical insights. Furthermore, a third criticism would add, not only are other events more than sufficient to present the moral predicaments we need to face, but attention to the Holocaust has not accomplished much in the way of effective moral action. To the contrary, attention to the Holocaust may even distract us from current crimes that destroy humanity or from history more directly connected to our own and with which we have yet to come to terms.

Versions of these criticisms can be found in Peter Novick's 1999 book, *The Holocaust in American Life*, which argues that the Holocaust has been emphasized in the United States to such an extent that its place has become problematic for Jews and non-Jews alike. Novick is "skeptical about the so-called lessons of history."[8] His skepticism is well taken if it is directed to ethical teachings that are so obvious as to be clichés, so general as to be empty, too vague to be effective, or so far removed from our current history as to be an irrelevant distraction. But the weakness in Novick's account is that it fails to emphasize enough how fundamentally ethical his own understanding of historical study turns out to be. He compares the historian's work to that of a medical researcher who studies diseases knowing that expressions of moral outrage will not be very helpful in achieving the goal of checking, if not eliminating them. Historical work on the Holocaust involves an analogous goal—namely, not to be satisfied with expressions of moral outrage but to limit, if not to cure, the genocidal ills that afflict humanity. We should study the Holocaust for the sake of future prevention and cure, a task that the right kind of moral outrage can help to inspire. To do otherwise would be tantamount to indifference toward the awe and horror that Novick finds always appropriate when one confronts the Holocaust.[9]

The fourth criticism goes further still. It contends that people who are concerned to teach the lessons of the Holocaust are probably giving aid and comfort to causes that are immoral, unjust, and extortionist. The implication of such allegations even seems to be that those who advocate learning from the Holocaust are "capitalizing" on the Holocaust, personally profiting from it. The attention that this criticism has gotten should not be taken lightly, for it casts harmful and unwarranted suspicion that makes Holocaust politics poisonous. A chief source of this criticism is Norman G. Finkelstein and his book, *The Holocaust Industry: Reflections on the Exploitation of Jewish Suffering*. Finkelstein is the son of Holocaust survivors. Sadly, that fact contributes to the book's pernicious effects, which include (however unintentionally) giving aid and comfort to antisemitism and Holocaust denial.

Distinguishing between "the Nazi holocaust" and "the Holocaust," which he regards as the "ideological representation" of the "actual historical event," Finkelstein ends his book by saying that we can learn from the Nazi holocaust, but only if that history is restored as "a rational subject of inquiry."[10] Accordingly to Finkelstein, however, such a "restoration" depends on dismantling what he calls "the Holocaust industry." In his view, this so-called industry includes at least the following characteristics: (1) an overemphasis on the Holocaust's uniqueness, which in Finkelstein's view leads to the claim that the Holocaust eludes rational comprehension and also involves unique suffering that, denials to the contrary notwithstanding, "confers unique entitlement" on Jews; (2) an ideological use of the Holocaust to deflect criticism from what Finkelstein calls the "morally indefensible policies" of Israel and "organized American Jewry"; (3) a restitution scheme (Finkelstein describes it as "a double shakedown of European countries as well as legitimate Jewish claimants") that has turned the Holocaust into what he calls "an outright extortion racket," which includes allegedly inflated figures for the number of Holocaust survivors.[11]

None of those overgeneralized indictments can completely withstand critical scrutiny, but Finkelstein's incendiary indictments continue as follows:

"Much of the literature on Hitler's Final Solution," he alleges, "is worthless as scholarship."[12] Libraries and bookstores, Finkelstein claims, are lined with books about the Holocaust that constitute "shelves upon shelves of shlock."[13] In addition, he claims, "the field of Holocaust studies is replete with nonsense, if not sheer fraud."[14] The United States Holocaust Memorial Museum is an "incongruous" presence on the Washington Mall. Finkelstein claims that its "political agenda" minimizes the Gypsy genocide, places Israel above reproach, and reveals American hypocrisy "in the absence of a museum commemorating crimes in the course of American history."[15] In his unrelenting ad hominem attacks, Finkelstein impugns Elie Wiesel as the captain of "the Holocaust industry." "Elie Wiesel," he charges, "*is* the Holocaust."[16] By no means least, Finkelstein casts suspicion on Holocaust education. His comments suggest that it too is a key part of "the Holocaust industry."

Finkelstein's book is an assault. It is an assault on the United States Holocaust Memorial Museum. It is an assault on many of the concerns that Holocaust scholars and educators share. It is an assault on the work they do with young people. Not only is it an assault on Elie Wiesel but also on anyone who has ever assigned Elie Wiesel's *Night* or invited him to speak to students. Far from being a constructive contribution to Holocaust politics, Finkelstein's book inflames disputes that distract Holocaust politics from its most important work: education.

As a Holocaust scholar and educator and as a participant in Holocaust politics, I regret that it is necessary for this particular debate to ensue, but there is no choice I can responsibly make except to reject and deplore Finkelstein's sweeping and unnuanced allegations. The teaching that Holocaust educators do and the research that Holocaust scholars pursue can always be done better, of course, but to allege that these efforts are mainly part of an "industry" of the kind that Finkelstein describes is outrageous. Indeed, far from protecting the memory of the Holocaust, which Finkelstein claims he wants to do, his so-called "anatomy and . . . indictment of the Holocaust industry" disrespect and harm the preservation of memory and the cause of learning about and from the Holocaust.[17] Finkelstein does so, among other reasons, because his book misstates and even falsifies history, fails to treat evidence fairly, refuses to recognize complexity, overgeneralizes, resorts to personal attacks, and displays other flaws that good teaching and sound inquiry about the Holocaust always guard against.

Finkelstein's book harms and makes more difficult the work that good Holocaust politics tries to do. That result angers me; it also leaves me to determine what to do with my anger. The answer for me, and I hope for Holocaust politics as well, is to try to study and teach about the Holocaust even more and better than we have done before. That commitment means taking even more seriously that there are history lessons to learn from the Holocaust. With those goals in mind, I now return to Remembering for the Future 2000. Later I will recall my own Holocaust classroom once more.

Several moments come to mind as I think about history lessons and Remembering for the Future 2000. First, toward the end of a seminar focused on the Holocaust and ethics, Franciszek Piper made remarks that I will not soon forget. For many years, Piper headed the department of historical research at the Auschwitz-Birkenau State Museum. He has worked, in particular, on the statistics about the number of Jews, Poles, and others who were murdered there. Speaking about the people who visit the Auschwitz camp complex and about Holocaust education, he said that the most important aspect of such encounters with Auschwitz is ethical. The people who visit Auschwitz, he hopes, will be morally moved by what they encounter there.

Stanislaw Krajewski, who contributed a brilliant paper on the site of the Auschwitz camp, added to Piper's perspective by noting that Auschwitz intrigues us because "it places before us the most profound dimension of human existence." Anyone who has been there or who has studied about the Holocaust deeply can scarcely deny that something happened at Auschwitz that compels attention as a warning, a source of profound sorrow, and a welling up of protest against the human forces that conspired to destroy Jewish life root and branch.

Study of the Holocaust and genocide can push us into pessimism and despair. How could it not? But another participant in Remembering for the Future, an American scholar named Stephen Haynes, made a crucial point about Holocaust education when he urged scholars and teachers not to give up the hope (yes, hope) that brought us to this field. "I don't know why others became interested in teaching the Holocaust," his conference paper said, "but for me the answer is tied up with a deep longing for a safer and more humane world, and with the hope that education is one way of insuring it." Then he went on to say,

"I suspect this hope is quite common among teachers of the Holocaust."

Longing and Remembering

I believe Stephen Haynes is right: We study the Holocaust because it happened, but not only for that reason. We study it and teach about it primarily for ethical reasons that are rooted in deep longing for a safer and more humane world. That deep longing has everything to do with remembering, just as the remembering can change lives and encourage us to make the longing good. The remembering does that by leading us to encounter the details of the Holocaust. Hilda Schiff, another writer for *Remembering for the Future*, caught these points admirably in her paper on Holocaust poetry and particularly in a poem she quoted. Entitled "I Keep Forgetting," it is by Lily Brett, the recipient of major literary prizes and the daughter of a death-camp survivor.

> I keep forgetting
> the facts and statistics
> and each time
> I need to know them
>
> I look up books
> these books line
> twelve shelves
> in my room
>
> I know where to go
> to confirm the fact
> that in the Warsaw ghetto
> there were 7.2 people per room

and in Lodz
they allocated
5.8 people
to each room

I forget
over and over again
that one third of Warsaw
was Jewish

and in the ghetto
they crammed 500,000 Jews
into 2.4 percent
of the area of the city

and how many
bodies they were burning
in Auschwitz
at the peak of their production

twelve thousand a day
I have to check
and re-check

and did I dream
that at 4pm on the 19th of January
58,000 emaciated inmates
were marched out of Auschwitz

was I right
to remember that in Bergen Belsen
from 4th–13th of April 1945
28,000 Jews arrived from other camps

I can remember
hundreds and hundreds
of phone numbers

phone numbers
I haven't phoned
for twenty years
are readily accessible

and I can remember
people's conversations
and what someone's wife
said to someone else's husband

what a good memory
you have
people tell me[18]

Holocaust education aims to give us good memories, which is a paradoxical statement that calls for explanation. Of course, I do not mean that the *content* of those memories is good. With the exception of the cases of rescue that were too few, most of the content of Holocaust-related memories is utterly bereft of goodness. In that sense, Lawrence Langer rightly reminds us that "there is nothing to be learned from a baby torn in two or a woman buried alive." I also do not mean that the good memories Holocaust education aims to create consist only or even primarily of recollections of figures, dates, and facts, important though those details surely are, because it is through such detail, especially when we focus on what happened to particular people in specific places, that we are helped to learn from the Holocaust.

What I do mean is that, as we learn about and from the Holocaust, our memories will become good in the sense that they will not let us forget what is most important. At least in part, this may have been what

Edward Bond, a British poet moved by the Holocaust, had in mind. As if he were making a counterpoint to Lawrence Langer, Bond wrote a poem called "How We See":

> After Treblinka
> And the *spezialkommando*
> Who tore a child with bare hands
> Before its mother in Warsaw
> We see differently.
>
> Men taken from workshops and farms to
>   fight for kaiser and king
> Lived in a world asleep in mist
> The *spezialkommando* lived in a world of
>   electric lights cinemas planes and radios
> We see racist slogans chalked on walls differently
> We see walls differently.[19]

The Holocaust can and should make us see differently. It is the responsibility of sound Holocaust politics to see that this happens well. It is most important to see the Holocaust's history lessons, and so it is that at the end of the courses I give on the Holocaust, courses that always emphasize the particularity of the Holocaust's history, I ask my students to remember certain things. I hope that their study has given them the good memories to do so.

I emphasize the latter point because learning from the Holocaust, really learning from it, takes time. A brief museum visit or a few classes are a start, but they are not enough to keep the simple statement of the lessons of the Holocaust from seeming too common-place and not particularly insightful. And yet, when those simple statements are saturated in and thoughtfully drawn from the detail of sound study of the Holocaust, then what might seem in another context to be clichéd takes on instead a depth and intensity that make a history lesson indeed.

So, believing as I do that good memories are crucial, here, very briefly stated, are ten good-memory lessons that Holocaust education should teach and that Holocaust politics ought to encourage, for the world can ill afford to forget them.

- Remember that the Holocaust targeted a particular people, the Jews, first and foremost. Consequently, the preciousness of all human life and the homes it requires, the highest qualities of goodness, and even God were assaulted as well.
- Remember the Holocaust as a warning. Do not overestimate the degree to which the Holocaust gave antisemitism and racism a bad name. Do not forget where prejudice, hate, antisemitism, and racism can lead.
- Remember that there were people who risked everything to perpetrate genocide.
- Remember not to be a perpetrator, a victim, or a bystander.
- Remember to give Hitler no posthumous victories.
- Remember that there were people who risked everything to help others. Do not allow indifference to forget or abandon them; instead, try to follow their example.
- Remember the fatal interdependence of all human actions; take responsibility for one another.

- Remember that the devil is in the details, but also that commitment, force of will, sensitivity, and healing are in the details as well. Do not overlook the fact that even small deeds and modest actions can be life-saving.
- Remember in spite of despair to build within the ruins of memory in ways that can mend the world.
- Remember to take nothing good for granted.

The last point especially deepens, intensifies, and grips me more and more as I continue my own Holocaust education and the responsible participation in Holocaust politics that it requires. So quickly, and in such devastating ways, the Holocaust swept away good things—basic ones that every person needs, such as a home, safe and secure—that too often are taken for granted. Holocaust education and the Holocaust politics needed to support it take place at memory's edge.[20] That edge is at the border between honest loss of memory and forgetting, on the one hand, and the distortion, falsification, and even denial of memory, on the other. Memory's edge must be kept sharp, clear, keen, alert, and true. To teach about the Holocaust and to learn from it—this is the ethical calling of Holocaust education and the responsibility of Holocaust politics.

Notes

Preface and Acknowledgments

1 I shall use the terms *antisemitism* and *antisemitic* instead of *anti-Semitism* and *anti-Semitic*. Particularly in the later decades of nineteenth-century European politics, the term *Semite* was exploited to set Jews apart from non-Jews, including even from other so-called Semitic peoples—Arabs, for example—and particularly to reinforce a negative, race-based perception of Jews and Judaism. The hyphenated and capitalized form *anti-Semitism* and its variations honor, however inadvertently, distinctions that are erroneous and misleading. Jews are not a race, nor is the category "Semite" a clear one. The forms *antisemitism* and *antisemitic* retain the prejudicial, anti-Jewish meaning, but they also protest the harmful confusions that attend the hyphenated and capitalized forms of those terms.

2. Peter Novick, *The Holocaust in American Life* (Boston: Houghton Mifflin Company, 1999), 15. At Northwestern University on November 18, 2000, Novick expressed regret for using the phrase "a few cheap tears." He did so during a panel discussion focused on "The Presence of the Holocaust in North America." This panel was part of Lessons and Legacies VI, which was one in a series of biennial conferences on the Holocaust sponsored by the Holocaust Educational Foundation. Led by a remarkable Auschwitz survivor, Zev Weiss, this foundation supports Holocaust education in colleges and universities.

3. Philip Hallie, *Tales of Good and Evil, Help and Harm* (New York: HarperCollins, 1997), 22.

4. Philip Paul Hallie, "Cruelty: The Empirical Evil," in *Facing*

285

Evil: Light at the Core of Darkness, ed. Paul Woodruff and Harry A. Wilmer (LaSalle, Ill: Open Court, 1988), 120. The contributions to this book are from an important 1987 Symposium on Understanding Evil, which took place at the Institute for the Humanities at Salado, Texas. The participants included the eminent Holocaust historian Raul Hilberg.

5. Hallie, *Tales of Good and Evil*, 54.
6. Hallie, "Cruelty," 120.
7. See Hallie, *Tales of Good and Evil*, 47–55, and Hallie, "Cruelty," 128–30.
8. Hallie, "Cruelty," 128.
9. Ibid., 129.

Prologue: What Is Holocaust Politics?

1. The brief quotations that follow are from Jean Améry, *At the Mind's Limits: Contemplations by a Survivor on Auschwitz and Its Realities*, trans. Sidney Rosenfeld and Stella P. Rosenfeld (New York: Schocken Books, 1986), ix, xi.
2. For a key study of Holocaust denial, see Deborah E. Lipstadt, *Denying the Holocaust: The Growing Assault on Truth and Memory* (New York: Free Press, 1993). Further light on Holocaust denial is shed by Michael Shermer, Alex Grobman, and Arthur Hertzburg, *Denying the Holocaust: Who Says the Holocaust Never Happened and Why Do They Say It?* (Berkeley, Calif.: University of California Press, 2000).
3. Mr. Justice Gray's discerning opinion in this case can be found in *The Irving Judgment: David Irving v. Penguin Books and Professor Deborah Lipstadt* (London: Penguin Books, 2000). For further reflections on this important trial, see Richard J. Evans, *Lying about Hitler: History, Holocaust, and the David Irving Trial* (New York: Basic Books, 2001), and D. D. Guttenplan, *The Holocaust on Trial* (New York: W. W. Norton & Co., 2001).
4. In late March 2001, a lawsuit against IBM was dropped. It contended that the executives who led International Business Machines helped to equip Nazi Germany to persecute Jews and other minorities. The lawsuit was not pursued because the litigations might further delay payments from a $4.5 billion German fund established to compensate former slave laborers, an aging group whose numbers dwindle daily. As this part of Holocaust politics played out, *IBM and the Holocaust: The Strategic Alliance between Nazi Germany and America's Most Powerful*

Corporation (New York: Crown Publishers, 2001), Edwin Black's controversial study, achieved best-seller status.

5. Norman G. Finkelstein's *The Holocaust Industry: Reflections on the Exploitation of Jewish Suffering* (London: Verso, 2000) is an extreme example of such criticism. More responsible, though not unflawed, versions of this critical perspective can be found in Tim Cole, *Selling the Holocaust: From Auschwitz to Schindler—How History Is Bought, Packaged, and Sold* (New York: Routledge, 1999), and Peter Novick, *The Holocaust in American Life* (Boston: Houghton Mifflin Company, 1999).

6. In April 2001, the Polish government took steps to close the discotheque that was housed in the former Auschwitz tannery. Meanwhile, James E. Young's work is especially important for its insights about the development of Holocaust memorials and the contentious dilemmas that have surrounded them. See *The Texture of Memory: Holocaust Memorials and Meaning* (New Haven, Conn.: Yale University Press, 1993) and *At Memory's Edge: After-Images of the Holocaust in Contemporary Art and Architecture* (New Haven, Conn.: Yale University Press, 2000).

7. Yom Hashoah takes place in the spring. It is also observed in Europe, but since 2000, most European countries commemorate the Holocaust on January 27, the anniversary of the liberation of the Nazi death camp at Auschwitz.

8. The literature on the Americanization of the Holocaust, which reflects important aspects of Holocaust politics and is itself part of the process of the Holocaust's Americanization, continues to grow. A range of views on the subject can be found in works such as the following: Michael Berenbaum, *After Tragedy and Triumph: Modern Jewish Thought and the American Experience* (Cambridge: Cambridge University Press, 1990); Hilene Flanzbaum, ed., *The Americanization of the Holocaust* (Baltimore: Johns Hopkins University Press, 1999); Alvin Rosenfeld, "The Americanization of the Holocaust," *Commentary*, June 1995; and Jeffrey Shandler, *While America Watches: Televising the Holocaust* (New York: Oxford University Press, 1998). See also Cole, *Selling the Holocaust*, and Novick, *Holocaust in American Life*.

9. For more on the history of New York's Museum of Jewish Heritage, see Rochelle G. Saidel, *Never Too Late to Remember: The Politics behind New York City's Holocaust Museum* (New York: Holmes & Meier, 1996).

10. Further detail about the history of the United States Holocaust

Memorial Museum can be found in Edward T. Linenthal, *Preserving Memory: The Struggle to Create America's Holocaust Museum* (New York: Viking, 1995) and Jeshajahu Weinberg and Rina Elieli, *The Holocaust Museum in Washington* (New York: Rizzoli, 1995). Jeshajahu "Shaike" Weinberg, who died on January 1, 2000, at the age of 81, was USHMM's founding director. A distinguished Israeli theater and museum director, he came out of retirement to be a senior consultant at the museum in 1988. The following year he became the museum's first director. Taking USHMM from the drawing boards to reality, he held that position until 1995. Weinberg's book with Rina Elieli portrays the development and construction of the museum. Probing deeper, Linenthal's book details and analyzes many of the crucial debates about the museum's content and perspective. A crucial example pivoted around the following question, which, in one way or another, continues to reverberate in the museum's Holocaust politics: To what extent should the museum focus on the particularity and uniqueness of the Jewish experience during the Holocaust, and to what extent should "the boundaries of inclusion," to use Linenthal's phrase, be expanded so that greater attention might be drawn, for instance, to the Armenian genocide as a precursor of the Holocaust, or to the plight of Roma and Sinti (Gypsies), who were arguably targeted for genocide by the Nazis' racial policies, or to the disheartening continuation of ethnic cleansing and genocide that has followed the Holocaust with few signs of relenting?

11. This language is drawn from *Remembrance*, a book prepared for the museum's Fifth Anniversary Commemorative Dinner, which was held on April 23, 1998, at the J. W. Marriott Hotel in Washington, D.C.

12. See Barton Gellman, "Holocaust Museum Denies Arafat an Official Welcome," *Washington Post*, January 17, 1998, A13.

13. See Marc Fisher, "Holocaust Museum to Welcome Arafat," *Washington Post*, January 22, 1998, C1.

14. See Marc Fisher, "Holocaust Museum Ousts Director," *Washington Post*, February 19, 1998, A1.

15. Greenberg's long and distinguished guidance at the museum dates to the earliest planning stages in the late 1970s. In April 2000, President Bill Clinton appointed him to head the United States Holocaust Memorial Council. Apart from resignation, only the president can remove the person who holds that posi-

tion. Greenberg had been in office less than a year before he became the target of the misguided factionalism that often makes Holocaust politics malicious, vengeful, and destructive. This episode began with an attack launched by a journalist named Ira Stoll (for more on him, see note 17 below) who savaged Greenberg for a speech he had given to the United Jewish Communities General Assembly in November 2000. Stoll's irresponsible article created the false impression that Greenberg blamed "Arab casualties in Israel, the West Bank and Gaza over the past few months on 'overreaction' by 'gun-happy' Israeli soldiers and police." (See "Enemies: A Museum Story," *Wall Street Journal*, December 29, 2000, W11.) Stoll further claimed that the U.S. Holocaust Memorial Council "has become, in recent years, something of a playpen for Clinton loyalists. They've ventured far beyond Holocaust remembrance, preferring to dabble in left-wing politics of the anti-Israel and anti-American kind. Perhaps," Stoll added, "George W. Bush will set things right." Greenberg and his many supporters responded strongly, accurately, and effectively to counter Stoll's attack, which made clear that the journalist represents a faction that seeks to use Holocaust politics to gain greater control over USHMM.

Unfortunately, different but related forms of factionalism intensified a short time later when news broke that Greenberg was among several important American Jews (including another museum council member, Abraham Foxman, national director of the Anti-Defamation League) who had written to Clinton to support a pardon for financier Marc Rich, the wealthy American who fled to Europe in 1983 instead of facing charges that he conspired to defraud the U.S. government of $48 million in taxes. While in exile, Rich has contributed to various Jewish causes, and his philanthropy included a $5 million contribution to Birthright Israel, a foundation that Greenberg helped to found and supports. A firestorm of controversy broke when Clinton pardoned Rich under dubious circumstances only a few days before the president's second term ended in January 2001. Meanwhile, Greenberg's December 11, 2000, letter supporting the pardon was written on USHMM stationery, and his action in this matter inflamed criticism. A *Wall Street Journal* editorial on February 5, 2001, for example, called for President Bush to "depoliticize" USHMM and by implication to dump

Greenberg. How such political action would "depoliticize" the museum, the editorial did not say.

In late January 2001, Greenberg apologized to the U.S. Holocaust Memorial Council for the letter he had written to Clinton on Rich's behalf. If his apology was accepted, that appearance did not fully fit reality, for as Greenberg caught a flight from Detroit on April 4, Harvey Meyerhoff, a current council member and its former chairman (he served from 1987 to 1993 when Clinton appointed Miles Lerman to replace him) met Greenberg at the airport and handed him a letter. Signed by seventeen present and former members of the museum's council, including Deborah Lipstadt and Kitty Dukakis, the former Massachusetts first lady, the letter urged Greenberg's resignation, contending, among other things, that Greenberg's action in the Rich affair had damaged the museum's nonpolitical reputation. Greenberg responded by saying that he would not resign, but at the time of this writing in the spring of 2001, another unfortunate episode in Holocaust politics remained unresolved, not least because the museum's executive director, Sara Bloomfield, and its senior staff find themselves caught in the middle of this struggle. It is unclear how they will be affected.

Backing for Greenberg runs strong. A few days after receiving the April 4 letter, which was delivered just before the Jewish Passover holiday began, Greenberg got a letter of support from thirty-five of the more than fifty noncongressional council members. Its signers included Elie Wiesel and Stuart Eizenstat, who played a key role in the recent Holocaust reparation negotiations with several European countries. Subsequently, President Bush toured the museum before speaking on April 19 at the annual Yom Hashoah observance in the Capitol Rotunda. He stressed that "we are bound by conscience to remember what happened and to whom it happened." The U.S. Holocaust Memorial Council met that same day. Without dissent, the council passed a resolution that dissociated itself from Greenberg's pardon appeal, which it called a mistake, but also formally accepted a second apology from Greenberg and commended him for leadership in Holocaust education. Within the council, but perhaps not in every quarter, these actions ended calls for Greenberg to resign as the council's leader.

Commenting on these events, Michael Berenbaum, a vigorous

Greenberg supporter, made an apt observation: "The periodical struggles and bloodletting in the museum may be a result of the fact that it's dealing with such a horrific event—the horror of the event and the evil of the event spill back on the people that work with it." As the council confirmed, Greenberg's outstanding long-term contributions to Holocaust remembrance and education outweigh his admitted errors of judgment in the Rich case. He deserves to prevail, but the future of his leadership and even Bloomfield's administration at USHMM may depend on the decisions that President Bush takes later on. For more detail, see two articles by Jacqueline Trescott, "Holocaust Council Head Urged to Resign," *Washington Post*, April 5, 2001, C9, and "35 Council Members Back Chairman," *Washington Post*, April 13, 2001, C3. See also "Board Backs Museum Head," *Washington Post*, April 20, 2001, C2, and Jim Abrams, "Museum Council Criticizes Chairman," *New York Times*, April 19, 2001.

16. For the article in question, see John K. Roth, "Genocide as Political Science," *Los Angeles Times*, November 12, 1988, sec. 2, p. 8.

17. Less than two years later, a shakeup at the *Forward* led to the departure of Stoll and his mentor, Seth Lipsky, who resigned as editor and president of that publication in May 2000. Lipsky has long-standing ties to the *Wall Street Journal*, where he serves as a contributing editor. Stoll edits www.Smartertimes.com, an electronic op-ed publication that describes itself as "dedicated to assembling a community of readers to support a new newspaper that would offer an alternative" to the *New York Times*. Stoll also contributes to www.OpinionJournal.com, a *Wall Street Journal* outlet, and to the print pages of the *Journal* itself. As in the case of Stoll's attack on Irving Greenberg (see note 15 above), it is no accident that the *Wall Street Journal's* recent opinion pieces about USHMM have done little to improve the integrity of Holocaust politics because they tend to attack unfairly not only the museum's leadership and policies but also the quality of Holocaust scholarship that is currently being done in the United States.

18. R. G. Collingwood, *An Autobiography* (Oxford: Oxford University Press, 1939), 79.

19. Emil Fackenheim, "The Holocaust and Philosophy," *Journal of Philosophy* 82 (October 1985): 505. Among American philosophers, Berel Lang has been an especially important contributor to reflection about the Holocaust. His major books in this area

include *Act and Idea in the Nazi Genocide* (Chicago: University of Chicago Press, 1990), *The Future of the Holocaust: Between History and Memory* (Ithaca, N.Y.: Cornell University Press, 1999), *Heidegger's Silence* (Ithaca, N.Y.: Cornell University Press, 1996), and *Holocaust Representation: Art within the Limits of History and Ethics* (Baltimore: Johns Hopkins University Press, 2000).

As of June 30, 2000, the regular and international associate members of the American Philosophical Association, which is the main professional organization for professors and scholars of philosophy in the United States, numbered about 7,650. A very small percentage of the APA's membership, about sixty in number, belongs to the Society for the Philosophic Study of Genocide and the Holocaust.

20. Fackenheim is known best for urging that post-Holocaust Jews must do nothing that would give Hitler posthumous victories. He takes this imperative to be a 614th commandment that should be added to the 613 commandments that define traditional Judaism. The 614th commandment, he argues, requires Jews "to survive as Jews, lest the Jewish people perish. We are commanded, second, to remember in our very guts and bones the martyrs of the Holocaust, lest their memory perish. We are forbidden, thirdly, to deny or despair of God, however much we may have to contend with Him or with belief in Him, lest Judaism perish. We are forbidden, finally, to despair of the world as the place which is to become the kingdom of God, lest we help make it a meaningless place in which God is dead or irrelevant and everything is permitted." (See Fackenheim's contribution to "Jewish Values in the Post-Holocaust Future: A Symposium," *Judaism* 16 [Summer 1967].) Fackenheim's most important books on the Holocaust include *God's Presence in History: Jewish Affirmations and Philosophical Reflections* (New York: New York University Press, 1970), *The Jewish Bible after the Holocaust: A Re-reading* (Bloomington, Ind.: Indiana University Press, 1990), *The Jewish Return into History: Reflections in the Age of Auschwitz and a New Jerusalem* (New York: Schocken Books, 1978), and *To Mend the World: Foundations of Future Jewish Thought* (New York: Schocken Books, 1982).

21. Fackenheim, "Holocaust and Philosophy," 505.

22. Ibid., 507.

23. Ibid., 509. Barbara Forrest also cites Fackenheim's point in her instructive article, "The Philosopher's Role in Holocaust Studies," *Teaching Philosophy* 22 (December 1999): 327–59, esp. 328.

ment: *David Irving v. Penguin Books and Professor Deborah Lipstadt* (London: Penguin Books, 2000), 195–206; Peter Hayes, *Industry and Ideology: I. G. Farben in the Nazi Era* (Cambridge: Cambridge University Press, 1993); and Raul Hilberg, *The Destruction of the European Jews*, 3 vols., rev. and definitive ed. (New York: Holmes & Meier, 1985), 3:885–92.

11. Jane R. Eisner, "A Smear Campaign Shames the Lessons of the Holocaust," *Philadelphia Inquirer,* June 21, 1998. Eisner, whom I have never met, was one of many persons who came to my defense. Including in her criticism not only Zionist Organization of America president Morton Klein and syndicated columnist George F. Will but also the two congressmen—Jon Fox (R., Pa.) and Michael Forbes (then R., N.Y.)—who had joined them in attacking me, Eisner lamented that "a scholar's writings are picked apart, lifted out of context, and, without regard for a lifetime of work and study, turned into the kind of smear that once was the sole province of politicians." Although Holocaust politics has never been the province of politicians, its viciousness can remind one of that domain.

12. Lawrence L. Langer, *Admitting the Holocaust: Collected Essays* (New York: Oxford University Press, 1995), 3.

13. Ibid.

14. Schoenfeld, "Auschwitz and the Professors," 44, 46.

15. Sara R. Horowitz, a distinguished scholar who writes about Holocaust literature and issues about women in the Holocaust, is one who has done so with vigor and lucidity. During the year 2000, she carried on an instructive debate with Gabriel Schoenfeld in the pages of *Prooftexts*, a journal of Jewish literary history published at Brandeis University.

16. See Myrna Goldenberg, "Different Horrors, Same Hell: Women Remembering the Holocaust," in *Thinking the Unthinkable: Meanings of the Holocaust*, ed. Roger S. Gottlieb (New York: Paulist Press, 1991), 150–66.

17. Cohen's web site can be found at http://www.interlog.com/~mighty. For another example of this kind, see http://www.rememberwomen.org, the web site for the Remember the Women Institute, founded by Holocaust scholar Rochelle Saidel. Its special emphasis on women in the Holocaust features extensive information about Ravensbrück, a concentration camp situated not far from Berlin that the Nazis established for women. Thousands of women, Jews and non-Jews, were

enslaved, subjected to brutal medical experiments, and murdered there.

18. As illustrated by Bernhard Schlink, *The Reader*, trans. Carol Brown Janeway (New York: Pantheon, 1997), even Holocaust-related fiction can become involved in Holocaust politics. Schlink's widely read and controversial novel focuses on Hanna Schmitz, who is tried and convicted of wartime crimes against Jews. Partly because Schlink portrayed this fictional SS guard as illiterate, in fact an unlikely scenario, his novel created sympathy for Hanna but also provoked dissent about the legitimacy and authenticity of Schlink's interpretation of the Holocaust and the part of ordinary Germans in it.

19. Holocaust memoirs by women are more numerous than ever. Arguably none is more important than Charlotte Delbo's. As a non-Jew and a member of the French resistance, she survived both Auschwitz and Ravensbrück. See the trilogy contained in her *Auschwitz and After*, trans. Rosette C. Lamont (New Haven, Conn: Yale University Press, 1995). Among the most important scholarly books about women in the Holocaust, the following are representative: Judith Tydor Baumel, *Double Jeopardy: Gender and the Holocaust* (London: Vallentine Mitchell, 1998); Brana Gurewitsch, ed., *Mothers, Sisters, Resisters: Oral Histories of Women Who Survived the Holocaust* (Tuscaloosa, Ala.: University of Alabama Press, 1998); Marion A. Kaplan, *Between Dignity and Despair: Jewish Life in Nazi Germany* (New York: Oxford University Press, 1998); S. Lillian Kremer, *Women's Holocaust Writing: Memory and Imagination* (Lincoln, Nebr.: University of Nebraska Press, 1999; Mary Lagerwey, *Reading Auschwitz* (Walnut Creek, Calif.: AltaMira Press, 1998); Dalia Ofer and Lenore Weitzman, eds., *Women in the Holocaust* (New Haven, Conn: Yale University Press, 1998); Michael Phayer and Eva Fleischner, *Cries in the Night: Women Who Challenged the Holocaust* (Kansas City, Mo.: Sheed & Ward, 1997); and Roger A. Ritvo and Diane M. Plotkin, *Sisters in Sorrow: Voices of Care in the Holocaust* (College Station, Tex.: Texas A&M University Press, 1998). As illustrated by these writings, major areas of research interest about women in the Holocaust currently include the roles that women—Jews and non-Jews—played in resistance against the Holocaust, the responsibilities that Jewish women had for maintaining families and households that were increasingly savaged by Nazi policy, the distinctive ways

in which women in the Nazi camps established and sustained relationships of caring with one another, and women's activities—both among the perpetrators and the victims—as nurses, physicians, and other health professionals.

20. My source is "Cohesion and Rupture: The Jewish Family in the East European Ghettos during the Holocaust," a paper presented by Dalia Ofer at the 1998 Association for Jewish Studies conference in Boston, Massachusetts. Her paper was part of a session on "Women in the Holocaust: New Research."

21. See Gisela Bock, "Ordinary Women in Nazi Germany: Perpetrators, Victims, Followers, Bystanders," in *Women in the Holocaust*, ed. Dalia Ofer and Lenore Weitzman (New Haven, Conn.: Yale University Press, 1998), 85–100, esp. 95–97.

22. Lawrence L. Langer, "Gendered Suffering? Women in Holocaust Testimonies," in *Women in the Holocaust*, ed., Ofer and Weitzman, 362. An insightful and highly respected Holocaust scholar, who concentrates on Holocaust literature and oral history in ways that emphasize the contributions of women and men alike, Langer certainly finds study of women in the Holocaust to be important, but he is also among the critics who question the amount and kind of emphasis that this area of Holocaust studies has been receiving.

23. The quotation is from a speech that Himmler gave to SS leaders in October 1943. See Paul Mendes-Flohr and Yehuda Reinharz, eds., *The Jew in the Modern World: A Documentary History*, 2d ed. (New York: Oxford University Press, 1995), 685.

24. Raul Hilberg, *Perpetrators Victims Bystanders: The Jewish Catastrophe 1933–1945* (New York: HarperCollins, 1992), 126. Every scholar and student of the Holocaust is indebted to Raul Hilberg and his magisterial three-volume work, *The Destruction of the European Jews*, the revised and definitive edition of which was published in 1985. Hilberg, however, has been no stranger to Holocaust politics either. In his memoir, *The Politics of Memory: The Journey of a Holocaust Historian* (Chicago: Ivan R. Dee, 1996), he recalls how difficult it was to find a publisher for his landmark study and then how much hostility the work received when it questioned deep-seated beliefs about Jewish resistance and martyrdom. In 2000, Hilberg entered the frays of Holocaust politics in another way when he defended aspects of Norman G. Finkelstein's assault on what the latter calls "the Holocaust industry." Finkelstein's controversial views, about

which there will be more to say later, are contained in *The Holocaust Industry: Reflections on the Exploitation of Jewish Suffering* (London: Verso, 2000).

25. See Gertrud Kolmar, *Dark Soliloquy: The Selected Poems of Gertrud Kolmar*, trans. Henry A. Smith (New York: Seabury Press, 1975), 55–57.

26. Danuta Czech, *The Auschwitz Chronicle 1939–1945*, trans. Barbara Harshav, Martha Humphreys, and Stephen Shearier (New York: Henry Holt, 1990), 652.

27. Ibid., 608. Often Czech's data about the arriving transports at Auschwitz-Birkenau make clear that more women than men were immediately dispatched to the gas chambers and that fewer women than men were spared for slave labor and the survival chances, however remote, that such a fate might offer.

28. Giuliana Tedeschi, *There Is a Place on Earth: A Woman in Birkenau*, trans. Tim Parks (New York: Pantheon Books, 1992), 9–10.

29. Some scholarship about women in the Nazi camps emphasizes the distinctive qualities of sisterly relationships—rooted in friendship as well as in family connections—that could be found in those places. Examples appear in Gurewitsch, *Mothers, Sisters, Resisters*.

30. Tedeschi, *There Is a Place on Earth*, 10.

31. Ibid., 90.

32. Ibid., 89.

33. Ibid., 94.

34. Ibid., 95.

35. See Peter Hellman, *The Auschwitz Album: A Book Based upon an Album Discovered by a Concentration Camp Survivor, Lili Meier* (New York: Random House, 1981), 38. Although *The Auschwitz Album* identifies her only as S. Szmaglewska, it is likely that this woman is the Polish author of early memoirs about Birkenau, which, unfortunately, have long been out of print. See Seweryna Szmaglewska, *Smoke over Birkenau*, trans. Jadwiga Rynas (New York: Henry Holt, 1947), and *United in Wrath* (Warsaw: "Polonia" Foreign Languages Publishing House, 1955). Szmaglewska's testimony at the Nuremberg Trials can be found in *Trial of the Major War Criminals before the International Military Tribunal* (Nuremberg: 1947), 8:317–23. In this testimony, Szmaglewska, who says she was in Birkenau from October 7, 1942, until January 1945, is identified as Severina Shmag-

levskaya. For another reference to the baby strollers in Auschwitz, see Rudolf Vrba and Alan Bestic, *I Cannot Forgive* (New York: Grove Press, 1964). With help from the camp resistance, Vrba, a Slovakian Jew, escaped from Auschwitz in the spring of 1944 and reported what was happening there. Before his escape, he worked in "Canada," the storehouse area in Auschwitz-Birkenau.

36. Tedeschi, *There Is a Place on Earth*, 1.

37. Ibid., 94.

2. What Can and Cannot Be Said about the Holocaust?

1. See, for example, Elie Wiesel, *Against Silence: The Voice and Vision of Elie Wiesel*, ed. Irving Abrahamson, 3 vols. (New York: Holocaust Library, 1985), 1:158, 211, 272.

2. The term *moral equivalence*, one that contentious critics such as Morton Klein, Gabriel Schoenfeld, and Ira Stoll are likely to employ against Holocaust interpretations and interpreters they dislike, enters Holocaust politics at this point. When one does not like an interpretation that relates the Holocaust to other events in the world, it is convenient but frequently inaccurate to accuse the interpreter of making some other event "morally equivalent" to the Holocaust or to some aspect of that disaster. In the views of those who typically play the "moral equivalence" card, there can be nothing equivalent to the Holocaust, morally or otherwise. So their accusation carries the implication that the accused has disrespected, if not trivialized or blasphemed, the Holocaust. Usually the "moral equivalence" accusation creates more heat than light because it is often used as a rhetorical weapon that overlooks differences specified or entailed by comparative analysis.

3. A resolution condemning as genocide the forced relocation and mass killing of Armenians—as many as 1.5 million of them—carried out by the Ottoman Empire in Turkey from 1915 to 1923 was scuttled in the United States House of Representatives in late October 2000. Partly because there are 1 to 1.5 million Americans of Armenian descent, the resolution will be reintroduced in later sessions of Congress, but Turkey's insistent denial of the Armenian genocide includes intense pressure against such official acknowledgments of the genocide. Turkey's status as a NATO ally, and also as a power that influences stability in the volatile Middle East, has thus far led the

United States government to bow to Turkey's wishes in this matter, which corroborates the unsurprising but unfortunate conclusion that historical truth often takes second place to political expediency. More forthcoming, if belatedly, was the New York Life Insurance Company. On April 11, 2001, in response to a federal class-action lawsuit brought in Los Angeles, the insurer agreed to pay up to $10 million to heirs of Armenian genocide victims. An additional $3 million will go to Armenian charities, mostly church groups.

Earlier, as Bill Clinton's second term drew to a close, American policy left another genocide-related matter unresolved. In June 1998, international deliberations in Rome proposed the formation of a permanent International Criminal Court whose mandate would be to try persons indicted for genocide, war crimes, and other crimes against humanity. By December 2000, more than one hundred nations had signed—including all of America's NATO allies—and twenty-five had ratified the treaty that would establish the court, but the United States had done neither. The court cannot begin trying cases until sixty treaty ratifications are obtained.

Meanwhile, in other quarters, stronger stands about the Armenian genocide have been taken. In mid-November 2000, the European Parliament, which at the time was assessing Turkey's status for European Union membership, passed a resolution (according to the *New York Times* [November 15, 2000] the vote was 234 to 213) stating that the Armenians had suffered genocide eighty-five years ago, before the modern state of Turkey was established. Formal acknowledgment of the Armenian genocide was also announced in late 2000 by the French and Italian parliaments and also by the Vatican. For a historical study of the varied stances toward the Armenian genocide taken by the Jewish community in Palestine (the Yishuv) and the State of Israel, see Yair Auron, *The Banality of Indifference: Zionism and the Armenian Genocide* (New Brunswick, N.J.: Transaction Books, 2000).

4.   Fueled by recent Holocaust restitution settlements, the debate about reparations for the descendants of American slaves has heated up. The neoconservative David Horowitz, for example, inflamed the issue in March 2001 when he submitted advertisements to about fifty college newspapers. This advertising, which drew national attention, opposed reparations for slavery,

and the advocates for reparations were duly provoked. A helpful Holocaust-related overview of developments in the slavery reparations debate is provided by Marc Perelman's "Blacks Eye Shoah Model in Slave Reparations Bid," *Forward*, March 30, 2001, which can be accessed online at www.forward.com. In "Jewish and Japanese-American Reparations: Political Lessons for the Africana Community," a paper that sociologist Ricardo René Laremont presented at a conference on "Confronting the Past: Memory, Identity, and Society" at UCLA on February 5, 2001, the author estimated that if reparations to the twenty million descendants of Africans enslaved in the United States were paid at the same rate received by the Japanese-American community in the aftermath of World War II internment, the amount would be $400 billion. For a selection of opinion about issues concerning reparations for American slavery, see Diane Cardwell, "Seeking Out a Just Way to Make Amends for Slavery," *New York Times*, August 12, 2000; Glenn C. Loury, "It's Futile to Put a Price on Slavery," *New York Times*, May 29, 2000; and Brent Staples, "How Slavery Fueled Business in the North," *New York Times*, July 24, 2000. Also relevant is an Associated Press story, "Report Recounts Tulsa Race Riots," *New York Times*, December 6, 2000, which discusses reparations efforts on the behalf of the living survivors and descendants of the primarily African-American neighborhood in Tulsa, Oklahoma, that was attacked by whites on May 31 and June 1, 1921. For a historical overview of issues pertaining to dilemmas about reparations and restitution, see Elazar Barkan, *The Guilt of Nations: Restitution and Negotiating Historical Injustices* (New York: W. W. Norton & Co., 2000).

5. Jonathan Glover, *Humanity: A Moral History of the Twentieth Century* (London: Jonathan Cape, 1999), 396. Glover's impressive book devotes several chapters to Nazi Germany and the Holocaust. His discussion of what he calls "the distinctive Nazi darkness" is brief but pointed. He defends the view that the Holocaust has "a terrible darkness all its own," which he defines by citing Eberhard Jäckel's statement that "the National-Socialist murder of the Jews was unique because never before had a nation with the authority of its leader decided and announced that it would kill off as completely as possible a particular group of humans, including old people, women, and children, and infants, and actually put

this decision into practice, using all the means of governmental power at its disposal" (396). Significantly, Glover points out this "terrible darkness" not simply to defend its distinctiveness but for the ethical lessons that he believes the darkness suggests.

6. Gavriel D. Rosenfeld, "The Politics of Uniqueness: Reflections on the Recent Polemical Turns in Holocaust and Genocide Scholarship," *Holocaust and Genocide Studies* 13 (Spring 1999): 47. Rosenfeld's article provides an excellent overview and critique of the positions held by major proponents and opponents of the Holocaust's uniqueness. Significant discussion about Holocaust uniqueness is also concentrated in Alan S. Rosenbaum, ed., *Is the Holocaust Unique? Perspectives on Comparative Genocide*, 2d ed. (Boulder, Colo.: Westview Press, 2001). This chapter incorporates much of "The Ethics of Uniqueness," my essay from Rosenbaum's volume.

7. In the following preliminary statements, which define my understanding of the Holocaust and briefly outline the underpinning argument concerning the Holocaust's distinctiveness, I draw on material I prepared for John K. Roth et al., *The Holocaust Chronicle: A History in Words and Pictures* (Lincolnwood, Ill.: Publications International, 2000).

8. The word *Holocaust* itself exacerbates Holocaust politics, for there are disputes about its origins and meanings as well as how it came to be the name for the event it designates. The German historian Eberhard Jäckel notes how he once thought that *Holocaust's* biblical connections made it an "utterly inappropriate" name for the genocide that Nazi Germany directed against the Jews. More recently, after consulting the *Oxford English Dictionary* and other sources, he saw that *holocaust*—in ancient, nonbiblical Greek as well as in English and other modern languages—also had a nonreligious history and meaning. Especially in usages from the seventeenth century onward, the term's typically secular meaning referred to "a complete destruction, especially of a large number of persons; a great slaughter or massacre." At the very least, the word was not explicitly invented to designate Nazi Germany's mass murder of the Jews, nor was it necessarily drawn from biblical sources by all those who used it to name that particular genocide. It was, however, a word that was sparsely used; it tended to be reserved for particularly catastrophic events. Summing up his current position

on the issue in his plenary address at the Remembering for the Future 2000 conference in Oxford, England, on July 17 of that year, Jäckel stated that, insofar as *Holocaust* refers to a complete destruction, a massacre of people, "the word is not inappropriate, as I once said, but perfectly appropriate to designate what the Nazis called the Final Solution. The term conveys very precisely the totality of the Nazi attempt to destroy Jewry completely, and it also conveys the idea of the uniqueness of this action." The full text of Jäckel's remarks appears in John K. Roth and Elisabeth Maxwell, eds., *Remembering for the Future: The Holocaust in an Age of Genocide*, 3 vols. (New York: Palgrave, 2001), 1:12–14. For more on issues related to the term *Holocaust*, see Jon Petrie, "The Secular Word HOLOCAUST: Scholarly Myths, History, and 20th Century Meanings," *Journal of Genocide Research* 2 (2000): 31–63.

9. R. J. Rummel, *Death by Government* (New Brunswick, N.J.: Transaction Publishers, 1997), 31. Issues about how genocide should be defined and understood are part of the Holocaust's legacy and Holocaust politics. Raphael Lemkin, a Jewish lawyer who fled from Poland during the Holocaust, coined the term in 1944. With Nazi Germany's annihilation of the Jews in mind, he defined genocide as "the destruction of a nation or of an ethnic group." Lemkin's influence was crucial in 1948, when the United Nations adopted the Convention on the Prevention and Punishment of the Crime of Genocide. This document defined genocide as "any of the following acts committed with intent to destroy, in whole or in part, a national, ethnical, racial or religious group, as such: a. Killing members of the group; b. Causing serious bodily or mental harm to members of the group; c. Deliberately inflicting on the group conditions of life calculated to bring about its physical destruction in whole or in part; d. Imposing measures intended to prevent births within the group; e. Forcibly transferring children of the group to another group." In addition, the UN Convention provided that punishable acts should include not only genocide itself but also "conspiracy to commit genocide; direct and public incitement to genocide; attempt to commit genocide; complicity in genocide."

Neither Lemkin's nor the UN's definitions, however, make the identification of genocide an easy matter. The reasons include the following: First, the definitions depend on determining intent, which can be difficult to do. Second, they acknowledge that the methods of genocide can be diverse. Those methods are not restricted to outright killing and mass murder, and they may take a long time to do their work. Such factors complicate the problem of stating when genocide is under way. Third, the definitions allow for more or less extreme cases of depopulation, and it can be complicated to determine when a group is being functionally, if not totally, destroyed. Fourth, the definitions fail to state explicitly that genocide can extend to groups—political ones, for example—targeted for destruction by their own government.

The standard definitions are inadequate. One challenge is to find definitions that are not, on the one hand, so broad as to trivialize genocide and to render uses of the term frivolous or, on the other hand, so narrow that cases of mass death are unreasonably excluded from the category of genocide. Another challenge is to establish credible international law based on sound definitions of genocide. Still other challenges include the establishment of potent sanctions and persuasive early warning systems against genocide.

Meanwhile, no plausible definition will exclude the Holocaust as a case of genocide. But the matter does not end there, because the advocates of Holocaust uniqueness will want to reserve a special place for the Holocaust in genocide's spectrum of disasters. That result fuels rivalries between two schools of thought. One believes that attention should fall primarily on genocide, with the Holocaust as one example. The other believes that attention should fall primarily on the Holocaust, not to the exclusion of other genocides but precisely because the Holocaust is the most extreme instance of genocide to date. These rivalries find expression in debates about education, the organization of scholarly conferences, and institutions of various kinds, including museums and their personnel appointments.

For more on the topics discussed in this note, see Israel W. Charny, ed., *Encyclopedia of Genocide*, 2 vols. (Santa Barbara, Calif: ABC-CLIO, 1999), esp. 1:3–40.

10. Steven T. Katz, "The Uniqueness of the Holocaust: The Historical Dimension," in Rosenbaum, ed., *Is the Holocaust Unique?* 49–50.

11. In ways never seen before or since, says Bauer, Nazi ideology, a "pure fantasy" that combined racial antisemitism with belief in

a global Jewish conspiracy to control the world, condemned Jews "anywhere in the world" to death "just for being born" and murdered them in killing centers that were brought "to a totally new stage of development." Although Bauer currently prefers *unprecedented* to *unique*, "contrary to [his] usage in previous publications," this change reaffirms the Holocaust's uniqueness. "The Holocaust," he writes, "has no precedent," but, he adds, "it could become one." See Yehuda Bauer, *Rethinking the Holocaust* (New Haven, Conn.: Yale University Press, 2001), esp. 20–21, 74, 265–67, and 278n.6.

12. Yehuda Bauer, *The Holocaust in Historical Perspective* (Seattle: University of Washington Press, 1978), 37.

13. Charlotte Delbo, *Auschwitz and After*, trans. Rosette C. Lamont (New Haven, Conn.: Yale University Press, 1995), 352.

14. Ibid., 351.

15. Controversy about Pope Pius XII has been especially keen. Key work about this Roman Catholic leader during the Holocaust years can be found in Pierre Blet, *Pius XII and the Second World War: According to the Archives of the Vatican*, trans. Lawrence J. Johnson (New York: Paulist Press, 1999); James Carroll, *Constantine's Sword: The Church and the Jews* (Boston: Houghton Mifflin Company, 2001); John Cornwell, *Hitler's Pope: The Secret History of Pius XII* (New York: Viking, 1999); Michael Phayer, *The Catholic Church and the Holocaust, 1930–1965* (Bloomington, Ind.: Indiana University Press, 2000); Carol Rittner and John K. Roth, eds., *Pope Pius XII and the Holocaust* (London: Continuum, 2001); and Susan Zuccotti, *Under His Very Windows: The Vatican and the Holocaust in Italy* (New Haven, Conn.: Yale University Press, 2001).

16. See Bauer, *Rethinking the Holocaust*, 273.

17. Delbo, *Auschwitz and After*, 230.

18. Patton's military leadership helped to crush the Third Reich and bring the Holocaust to an end. His attitudes toward Jews, however, were problematic. When the war ended, Patton commanded the U.S. Third Army. Upper Bavaria, the area where most of the Jewish "displaced persons" (DPs) lived after liberation, was under his administration. According to Michael Brenner, Patton's diary entries "leave no doubt about his feelings toward those survivors. After a visit to a DP camp in September 1945, he noted: 'We entered the synagogue which was packed by the greatest stinking bunch of humanity I have ever

seen. . . . Either the Displaced Persons never had any sense of decency or else they lost it all during their period of internment by the Germans. My personal opinion is that no people could have sunk to the level of degradation these have reached in the short space of four years.'" Michael Brenner, "Displaced Persons," in *The Holocaust Encyclopedia*, ed. Walter Laqueur and Judith Tydor Baumel (New Haven, Conn.: Yale University Press, 2001), 157.

19. *Time*'s Person of the Century web site can be accessed through http://www.yahoo.com. Enter "Person of the Century" in the search engine. Then click on TIME.com: Person of the Century—January 3, 2000.

   Time named Franklin D. Roosevelt, the American president during World War II, and the Indian civil rights leader Mohandas Gandhi as runners-up to Albert Einstein. In what the magazine described as "an unscientific, informal survey for the interest and enjoyment of TIME.com users," the final tally put rock musician Elvis Presley and Israeli leader Yitzhak Rabin first and second, respectively. Albert Einstein finished fifth. Between Rabin and the evangelist Billy Graham, third place went to Adolf Hitler. He received more than half a million votes—about 11 percent of all that were cast. *Time* hastened to add that its unscientific, informal survey "may not be indicative of popular opinion."

20. Ron Rosenbaum, *Explaining Hitler: The Search for the Origins of His Evil* (New York: Random House, 1998), xii.

21. Ibid., 427.

22. Ibid., xxv.

23. Ibid., 212, 215.

24. Ibid., xliv.

25. Unfortunately, this position is more problematic than it seems. If no one, in fact, can explain Hitler, then how does it make sense to say that, in principle, Hitler is explainable? At best, we seem to be left with hypotheses that are "likely stories"—some far better documented and more accurate than others—but probably not more. For more on Bauer's position, see *Rethinking the Holocaust*, esp. 14–38.

26. Rosenbaum, *Explaining Hitler*, 393.

27. Fritz Redlich, *Hitler: Diagnosis of a Destructive Prophet* (New York: Oxford University Press, 1998), 253.

28. Ibid., 294.

29. Ibid., 340.

30. Ibid., 341.

31. Brigitte Hamann, *Hitler's Vienna: A Dictator's Apprenticeship*, trans. Thomas Thornton (New York: Oxford University Press, 1999), 406.

32. Ibid., 356.

33. Ibid., 405.

34. Ian Kershaw, *Hitler 1889–1936: Hubris* (New York: W. W. Norton & Co., 1999), 591.

35. Ian Kershaw, *Hitler 1936–1945: Nemesis* (New York: W. W. Norton & Co., 2000), 841.

36. Ibid., 839–40.

37. Kershaw, *Hitler 1889–1936*, xii.

38. Ibid., xiv; and Kershaw, *Hitler 1936–1945*, xviii.

3. How Is the Holocaust Best Remembered?

1. Elie Wiesel, "Let Him Remember," in *Against Silence: The Voice and Vision of Elie Wiesel*, 3 vols., ed. Irving Abrahamson (New York: Holocaust Library, 1985), 1:368.

2. Raul Hilberg, *The Destruction of the European Jews*, rev. and definitive ed. (New York: Holmes & Meier, 1985), 3:1220.

3. My discussion of Mengele is indebted to Robert Jay Lifton, *The Nazi Doctors: Medical Killing and the Psychology of Genocide* (New York: Basic Books, 1986), 338–44. In addition, both my narrative about Mengele and Pope Pius XI and the following account regarding Gerda Weissmann Klein and Telford Taylor draw on my contributions to John K. Roth et al., *The Holocaust Chronicle: A History in Words and Pictures* (Lincolnwood, Ill.: Publications International, 2000). See also Michael Berenbaum, ed., *Witness to the Holocaust* (New York: HarperCollins, 1997), 135, 345; Hilberg, *Destruction of the European Jews*, 1:287–88, 3:1074–80; Saul Friedländer, *Nazi Germany and the Jews: The Years of Persecution, 1933–1939* (New York: HarperCollins, 1997), 46–49, 250–52; Martin Gilbert, *The Holocaust: A History of the Jews of Europe during the Second World War* (New York: Henry Holt, 1985), 53–56; *In Pursuit of Justice* (Washington, D.C.: United States Holocaust Memorial Museum, 1996), 231–42; Gerda Weissmann Klein, *All but My Life*, expanded ed. (New York: Hill & Wang, 1995), 247–61; Georges Passelecq and Bernard Suchecky, *The Hidden Encyclical of Pius XI*, trans. Steven Rendall (New York: Harcourt Brace Jovanovich, 1997);

Joseph E. Persico, *Nuremberg: Infamy on Trial* (New York: Penguin Books, 1994), 204–7.

4. Gilbert, *Holocaust*, 54.

5. My discussion of the "hidden encyclical" is indebted to Passelecq and Suchecky, *Hidden Encyclical of Pius XI*. See also Friedländer, *Nazi Germany and the Jews*, 250–52.

6. A long-standing international dimension of Holocaust politics involves issues about the extent of Polish antisemitism and complicity in the destruction of Polish Jewry during the Nazi occupation of Poland. In 2001, that debate intensified when Jan T. Gross, a Polish-born New York University political scientist published *Neighbors: The Destruction of the Jewish Community in Jedwabne, Poland* (Princeton, N.J.: Princeton University Press, 2001). Gross documents what happened in Jedwabne, a village about eighty-five miles northeast of Warsaw, on July 10, 1941, a few weeks after the Nazi invasion of Soviet-held territory put the town under German occupation. On that day, 1,600 of Jedwabne's Jews were beaten and brutally murdered by their non-Jewish neighbors. A postwar monument falsely attributed the slaughter to the Germans. They undoubtedly approved it, but Poles did the killing. In March 2001, Polish authorities removed the old monument. A more appropriate one will take its place, but that will not quiet controversy about the complex relations between Jews and Poles in a country where Nazi Germany's Final Solution annihilated about ninety percent of Poland's nearly 3.5 million Jews.

7. Klein, *All but My Life*, 249–50.

8. Ibid., 252–53.

9. Berenbaum, ed., *Witness to the Holocaust*, 135.

10. Shmuel Spector, "Otto Ohlendorf," in *Encyclopedia of the Holocaust*, ed. Israel Gutman et al. (New York: Macmillan, 1990), 3:1085.

11. Berenbaum, ed., *Witness to the Holocaust*, 345–46.

12. Klein, *All but My Life*, 261.

13. See Joseph Freeman, *Job: The Story of a Holocaust Survivor* (Westport, Conn.: Praeger Publishers, 1996).

14. See Joseph Freeman, *The Road to Hell: Recollections of the Nazi Death March* (St. Paul: Paragon House, 1998).

15. Young uses the concept of memory-work in his insightful book *The Texture of Memory: Holocaust Memorials and Meaning* (New Haven, Conn.: Yale University Press, 1993). Two more excel-

lent works on Holocaust memories and memorializations are Lawrence L. Langer, *Holocaust Testimonies: The Ruins of Memory* (New Haven, Conn.: Yale University Press, 1991), and Edward T. Linenthal, *Preserving Memory: The Struggle to Create America's Holocaust Museum* (New York: Viking, 1995).

16. Primo Levi, *The Drowned and the Saved*, trans. Raymond Rosenthal (New York: Summit Books, 1988), 23.

17. Ibid., 24.

18. In the late 1990s, three other Holocaust-related films won Academy Awards in the documentary category. In 1996, the award for best documentary feature film went to *Anne Frank Remembered*, while *One Survivor Remembers* received an Oscar for best documentary short subject. The 1998 award for best documentary feature film went to *The Long Way Home*. Academy Awards for Holocaust-related films continued in the twenty-first century. The 2001 Oscar for best documentary feature went to *Into the Arms of Strangers*, which is discussed in this book's epilogue.

19. Roger Rosenblatt, "Paying for Auschwitz," *Time*, April 12, 1999, 108.

20. In late October 2000, during an interview with CBS's *60 Minutes II* program, Yugoslavia's newly elected president, Vojislav Kostunica, seemed to acknowledge that the Yugoslav army and police, under the leadership of Kostunica's predecessor, Milosevic, had committed genocide in Kosovo. Confusion followed, however, when Kostunica disputed that interpretation, calling the network's journalism "unprofessional and unethical" and criticizing, in particular, its handling of excerpts from the discussion. See "Yugoslav Leader Acknowledges Genocide in Kosovo," *Los Angeles Times*, October 24, 2000, and "Kostunica Disputes CBS Broadcast," *New York Times*, October 26, 2000. Meanwhile, news reports on December 12, 2000, quoted Milosevic as saying that his "conscience is clear," while he described the United Nations tribunal that indicted him for war crimes as "a political institution which is part of the mechanism of genocide against the Serbian nation." See "Milosevic Says Conscience Is Clear," *New York Times*, December 12, 2000.

Despite Milosevic's "clear conscience," Serbian police arrested him on April 1, 2001, on charges of embezzlement and abuse of power. At the time of this writing, it remained unclear whether Milosevic would stand trial before the United Nations war crimes tribunal in The Hague. That court, one of the positive legacies of the Holocaust and the Nuremberg Trials, has indicted Milosevic for crimes against humanity and violation of the laws and customs of war. Evidence is being gathered for a possible charge of genocide. See "Charges Against Milosevic by U.N. Tribunal," *New York Times*, April 3, 2001.

21. In addition to Deborah E. Lipstadt, *Denying the Holocaust: The Growing Assault on Truth and Memory* (New York: Free Press, 1993), an intriguing account of Holocaust denial can also be found in Michael Shermer, Alex Grobman, and Arthur Hertzberg, *Denying the Holocaust: Who Says the Holocaust Never Happened and Why Do They Say It?* (Berkeley, Calif.: University of California Press, 2000).

22. See Oskar Mendelsohn, *The Persecution of the Norwegian Jews in WW II* (Oslo: Norges Hjemmefrontmuseum, 1991), 5. For further information about the Holocaust in Norway, see Per Ole Johansen, "Norway," in *The Holocaust Encyclopedia*, ed. Walter Laqueur and Judith Tydor Baumel (New Haven, Conn.: Yale University Press, 2001), 446–51.

23. Lawrence L. Langer, ed., *Art from the Ashes: A Holocaust Anthology* (New York: Oxford University Press, 1995), 6.

24. See Ida Fink, *A Scrap of Time and Other Stories*, trans. Madeline Levine and Francine Prose (New York: Schocken Books, 1987), 3.

4. How Is the Holocaust a Warning?

1. My citations from Elie Wiesel's speech are taken from an electronic version of his text, which was sent to me by Professor Zev Garber on October 23, 2000.

2. Colum Lynch, "Anti-Israeli Resolution Passed," *Washington Post*, October 21, 2000, A19. Austria, Belgium, France, the Russian Federation, and Turkey were among the countries voting for the resolution. Germany, the Netherlands, Norway, Poland, and the United Kingdom were among those abstaining.

3. Deborah Sontag, "Two Die in Gaza Bombing of Israelis' School Bus," *New York Times*, November 21, 2000.

4. Jane Perlez, "After Gaza Rocket Attack, State Dept. Gives Israel Stern Warning," *New York Times*, November 21, 2000.

5. Deborah Sontag, "Car Bomb Kills 2 in Central Israeli Town, *New York Times*, November 22, 2000, A3.

6. Israel's population includes about 5.2 million Jews and more

than a million Arab citizens. Some three million Palestinians inhabit the West Bank and the Gaza Strip. A public opinion poll taken in late April 2001, when Israel observed the fifty-third anniversary of its independence, found that 75 percent of the Israelis expected continued violence. See "Israel Somber as It Turns 53," *New York Times*, April 25, 2001.

7. John J. Goldman, "Holocaust Settlement Approved," *Los Angeles Times*, November 23, 2000, A41. According to Goldman's account, $800 million will go to the owners or heirs of about 26,000 bank accounts from the World War II period that are linked to victims of the Holocaust. The remaining $450 million is designated for "refugees who were refused entry to Switzerland, people who were forced into slave labor for companies with Swiss accounts and Holocaust victims whose possessions were stolen by the Nazis and ended up in Switzerland."

8. The text of Lieberman's acceptance speech was published in the *New York Times*, August 17, 2000. On December 14, 2000, the day after Al Gore and Joseph Lieberman conceded the election to George W. Bush and Dick Cheney, their Republican opponents, Lieberman expressed related sentiments in his speech on the floor of the United States Senate. Referring to the unprecedented selection of a Jewish American to be a presidential candidate's running mate, Lieberman stated that every American parent should feel encouraged "to dream the biggest dreams for each and every one of their children. Anything is possible for anyone in America."

9. Theodor Herzl, "A Solution of the Jewish Question," in *The Jew in the Modern World: A Documentary History*, 2d ed., ed. Paul Mendes-Flohr and Jehuda Reinharz (New York: Oxford University Press, 1995), 533–35.

10. My discussion of Jewish DPs is indebted to Leonard Dinnerstein's introduction to *Liberation 1945* (Washington, D.C.: United States Holocaust Memorial Museum, 1995) and to Abraham J. Peck's essay, "A Continent in Chaos: Europe and the Displaced Persons," which appears in the same volume. See especially 11–22 and 101–16, respectively. See also Henry Friedlander, "Darkness and Dawn in 1945: The Nazis, the Allies, and the Survivors," *1945: The Year of Liberation* (Washington, D.C.: United States Holocaust Memorial Museum, 1995), 11–35. Such statistics are necessarily imprecise, but historian Yehuda Bauer estimates that about 200,000 Jews

"emerged alive from the Nazi concentration and labor camp system." See Yehuda Bauer, "The DP Legacy," in *Life Reborn: Jewish Displaced Persons 1945–1951*, ed. Menachem Z. Rosensaft (Washington, D.C.: United States Holocaust Memorial Museum, 2001), 25.

11. My immigration statistics are from Raul Hilberg, *The Destruction of the European Jews*, rev. and definitive ed. (New York: Holmes & Meier, 1985), 3:1150–51. Figures from other sources vary but remain similar. For example, Michael Brenner's article on DPs in *The Holocaust Encyclopedia*, ed. Walter Laqueur and Judith Tydor Baumel (New Haven, Conn.: Yale University Press, 2001), indicates that between 1947 and 1950 about 120,000 Jewish DPs immigrated to Israel, about 80,000 to 90,000 went to the United States, and about 20,000 found homes in Canada. See 150–59, esp. 157.

12. On the fiftieth anniversary of Israeli independence in 1998, it was estimated that about 360,000 Holocaust survivors lived in Israel, where, along with their children and grandchildren, they comprised about 20 percent of the population. See "Israel at 50," a special report in the *Los Angeles Times*, April 12, 1998, S8.

13. There is ongoing scholarly debate about the extent and adequacy of American responses to the Holocaust. Among the significant studies that have appeared most recently, the following works are noteworthy: Robert H. Abzug, *America Views the Holocaust: A Brief Documentary History* (Boston: Bedford/St. Martin's, 1999); Henry L. Feingold, *Bearing Witness: How America and Its Jews Responded to the Holocaust* (Syracuse, N.Y.: Syracuse University Press, 1995); Michael J. Neufeld and Michael Berenbaum, eds., *The Bombing of Auschwitz: Should the Allies Have Attempted It?* (New York: St. Martin's Press, 2000); William D. Rubinstein, *The Myth of Rescue: Why the Democracies Could Not Have Saved More Jews from the Nazis* (New York: Routledge, 1997); David S. Wyman and Charles H. Rosenzveig, eds., *The World Reacts to the Holocaust* (Baltimore: Johns Hopkins University Press, 1996).

14. See, for example, Aaron Hass, *The Aftermath: Living with the Holocaust* (Cambridge: Cambridge University Press, 1995), and William B. Helmreich, *Against All Odds: Holocaust Survivors and the Successful Lives They Made in America* (New Brunswick, N.J.: Transaction Books, 1999). For two important studies that emphasize how the Holocaust has left its survivors to live with

immensely difficult, even devastating, memories, see Henry Greenspan, *On Listening to Holocaust Survivors: Recounting and Life History* (Westport, Conn.: Praeger Publishers, 1998), and Lawrence L. Langer, *Holocaust Testimonies: The Ruins of Memory* (New Haven, Conn.: Yale University Press, 1991).

15. The quotations from President Clinton's 1998 Labor Day message are taken from the United States Information Service's Daily Foreign Policy Summary for September 7, 1998.

16. Arthur Miller, *Death of a Salesman* (New York: Penguin Books, 1983), 138.

17. James Truslow Adams, *The Epic of America* (Boston: Little, Brown & Co., 1934), viii.

18. Ibid., 415.

19. My reconstructions of dialogue from the film have relied on Max Allan Collins, *Saving Private Ryan* (New York: Signet, 1998), 311, 316–17. This book is a novel based on Robert Rodat's screenplay for the Spielberg production.

20. Gitta Sereny, *Into That Darkness: An Examination of Conscience* (New York: Vintage Books, 1983), 15. Sereny sheds additional light on the Holocaust in *Albert Speer: His Battle with Truth* (New York: Vintage Books, 1996).

21. Sereny, *Into That Darkness*, 23.

22. Ibid., 15.

23. William Styron, *Sophie's Choice* (New York: Modern Library, 1999), 29. The novel was originally published by Random House in 1979. My citations are to the twentieth-anniversary edition, which contains useful biographical information about Styron as well as his instructive afterword.

24. Ibid., 248.

25. Ibid., 572.

26. This statement is from Elie Wiesel's foreword to Harry James Cargas, *Shadows of Auschwitz: A Christian Response to the Holocaust* (New York: Crossroad, 1990), ix.

27. *Los Angeles Times*, October 7, 1990, A4. On November 9, 2000, President Bill Clinton announced a plan to preserve the sites of camps where the Japanese Americans were interned. In addition to the California sites, land will be acquired for preservation of sites in the states of Wyoming, Utah, Idaho, and Arkansas. The occasion for this announcement was the dedication of a memorial in Washington, D.C. Situated near the Capitol, it commemorates the interned Japanese American

citizens and also the 33,000 Japanese Americans who fought for the United States in World War II. With its stone panels identifying each of the ten internment camps, the memorial was scheduled for completion in 2001. President Clinton's announcement letter stated that Americans must "never forget this sad chapter in our history." He went on to say that "we are diminished when any American is targeted unfairly because of his or her heritage. . . . This memorial and the internment sites are powerful reminders that stereotyping, discrimination, hatred and racism have no place in this country." See "Internment Sites to Be Preserved," *Los Angeles Times*, November 10, 2000, A19.

28. For elaboration on these points, see two books by David S. Wyman, *Paper Walls: America and the Refugee Crisis, 1938–1941* (Amherst, Mass.: University of Massachusetts Press, 1968) and *The Abandonment of the Jews: America and the Holocaust, 1941–1945* (New York: Pantheon Books, 1984).

29. Wyman, *Abandonment of the Jews*, 12.

30. Ibid., 15.

31. Allan A. Ryan, Jr., *Quiet Neighbors: Prosecuting Nazi War Criminals in America* (San Diego: Harcourt Brace Jovanovich, 1984), 344. For an insightful account of another dimension of Holocaust politics—the use of Nazi scientists in the postwar development of the American space program—see Guy B. Adams and Danny L. Balfour, *Unmasking Administrative Evil* (Thousand Oaks, Calif.: Sage Publications, 1998). Adams and Balfour concentrate on institutions and procedures that compartmentalize tasks and diffuse responsibilities in ways that can produce immense harm and yet leave administrators and bureaucrats convinced that they are doing what is right and good. The authors show how this administrative evil helped to make the Holocaust happen and also how contemporary versions of administrative evil continue to inflict pain and suffering.

32. Ralph Ellison, *Invisible Man* (New York: Vintage Books, 1982), xv. These comments are taken from Ellison's introduction to the thirtieth-anniversary edition of *Invisible Man*. All subsequent references are to this edition of his novel.

33. Ibid., x.

34. Langston Hughes, "Let America Be America Again," as reprinted in *American Ground: Vistas, Visions, and Revisions*, ed. Robert H. Fossum and John K. Roth (St. Paul: Paragon House,

1988), 350.

35. Ellison, *Invisible Man*, 566–67.

36. Elie Wiesel, "Telling the Tale," in *Against Silence: The Voice and Vision of Elie Wiesel*, 3 vols., ed. Irving Abrahamson (New York: Holocaust Library, 1985), 1:234.

37. Ellison, *Invisible Man*, 7–8. The lyrics to this 1929 Fats Waller song are by Andy Razaf.

38. See Lawrence L. Langer, "The Dilemma of Choice in the Deathcamps," in *Holocaust: Religious and Philosophical Implications*, ed. John K. Roth and Michael Berenbaum (St. Paul: Paragon House, 1989), 221–32.

39. Styron, *Sophie's Choice*, 562. In his afterword to the novel, Styron explains that one inspiration for *Sophie's Choice* came from Olga Lengyel's Holocaust memoir, *Five Chimneys*. First published in 1946 in France and then in the United States in 1947, Lengyel's book is one of the earliest testimonies authored by an Auschwitz survivor. Clearly written from a woman's perspective, it emphasizes the especially painful way in which she lost Arvad, her older, adopted son, when Lengyel and her family were deported from Hungary to Auschwitz in May 1944. The Nazi doctor conducting the "selection" asked Lengyel about her son's age. Unable to know what was coming but hoping that she was making a lifesaving choice, Lengyel truthfully told the doctor that Arvad was not more than twelve. Very well, said the doctor, and the boy was sent to the left, the same direction that Lengyel had persuaded her mother to take so that she could look after Thomas, Lengyel's younger son. Off the three went with the other children and the elderly. Lengyel never saw them again, because left was the way to the gas chambers. (See Olga Lengyel, *Five Chimneys* [Chicago: Academy Chicago Publishers, 1995], 21–24.) Styron misidentifies Lengyel as a Gentile. The account she gave for the Shoah Visual History Foundation in August 1998 indicates that she came from a highly assimilated Jewish family.

40. Richard L. Rubenstein, *The Cunning of History: The Holocaust and the American Future* (New York: Harper Torchbooks, 1987), 90. Rubenstein's best-known book is *After Auschwitz: History, Theology, and Contemporary Judaism*, 2d ed. (Baltimore: Johns Hopkins University Press, 1992). Originally published in 1966, it was among the earliest and remains among the most profound books to explore the Holocaust's devastating theological

and religious implications. Increasingly, Rubenstein's thought has found its place in the mainstream of post-Holocaust Jewish reflection, but when his questioning of traditional ideas about the "God of history" and the Jewish people's special covenantal relationship with God first appeared, Rubenstein experienced versions of religiously related Holocaust politics that sought to marginalize him and his unorthodox views. Nevertheless, his work consistently receives attention, and its hard-earned respect shows that Rubenstein's detractors not only failed to prevail but to a large extent have disappeared. See also Rubenstein's *The Age of Triage: Fear and Hope in an Overcrowded World* (Boston: Beacon Press, 1983).

41. Rubenstein, *Cunning of History*, 89.
42. Jean Améry, *At the Mind's Limits: Contemplations by a Survivor on Auschwitz and Its Realities*, trans. Sidney Rosenfeld and Stella P. Rosenfeld (New York: Schocken Books, 1986), 86. The book was originally published in 1966.
43. Ibid., 28.
44. Ibid., 94–95.
45. Ibid., 89.

5. Holocaust Politics and Post-Holocaust Christianity

1. "Holocaust Survivor Protests Concert," *New York Times*, October 27, 2000. For an earlier report about the Wagner performance, see "Holocaust Survivors Oppose Concert," *New York Times*, October 23, 2000.
2. Grounded in the biblical book of Esther, Purim celebrates the ancient rescue of exiled Jews from annihilation that Haman, a Persian leader, threatened to unleash before Esther intervened to stop him. Traditional observances include the use of noise-makers to drown out Haman's name during the reading of the biblical story. Although the celebration is joyous, Irving Greenberg observes that Purim "may well be the darkest, most depressing holiday of the Jewish calendar," for it commemorates a narrowly averted genocide. See Irving Greenberg, *The Jewish Way: Living the Holidays* (New York: Summit Books, 1988), 224. Greenberg's book is important because it interprets the Jewish calendar's special days in relation to the Holocaust's implications for those traditions.
3. For more detail on the connections between the Wagner family and Nazi Germany, including Adolf Hitler in particular, see

Gottfried Wagner, *Twilight of the Wagners: The Unveiling of a Family's Legacy* (New York: St. Martin's Press, 1999). Richard Wagner was Gottfried Wagner's great-grandfather.

4. A growing literature displays the variations on this theme. In the year 2000 alone, several books focused on music-related testimonies by Jewish survivors and their families. See, for example, Martin Goldsmith, *The Inextinguishable Symphony: A True Story of Music and Love in Nazi Germany* (New York: John Wiley & Sons, 2000); Szymon Laks, *Music of Another World* (Evanston, Ill: Northwestern University Press, 2000); Anita Lasker-Wallfisch, *Inherit the Truth: A Memoir of Survival and the Holocaust* (New York: St. Martin's Press, 2000); and Richard Newman, *Alma Rosé: Vienna to Auschwitz* (New York: Amadeus, 2000). The works by Laks, Lasker-Wallfisch, and Newman show how the Germans exploited the musical talents of camp inmates and also how that same talent may have helped a few Jews to survive. For accounts that analyze how the Third Reich both encouraged and suppressed musical expression, see the trilogy by Michael H. Kater: *Composers of the Nazi Era: Eight Portraits* (New York: Oxford University Press, 2000), *Different Drummers: Jazz in the Culture of Nazi Germany* (New York: Oxford University Press, 1992), and *The Twisted Muse: Musicians and Their Music in the Third Reich* (New York: Oxford University Press, 1997). Another helpful study is provided by Alan E. Steinweis, *Art, Ideology, and Economics in Nazi Germany: The Reich Chambers of Music, Theater, and the Visual Arts* (Chapel Hill, N.C.: University of North Carolina Press, 1996).

5. My discussion of *We Remember* draws on material I prepared for John K. Roth et al., *The Holocaust Chronicle: A History in Words and Pictures* (Lincolnwood, Ill.: Publications International, 2000).

6. Scholarly studies that confirm this judgment about Holocaust politics are numerous and significant. Among the more recent examples, see Pierre Blet, *Pius XII and the Second World War: According to the Archives of the Vatican*, trans. Lawrence J. Johnson (New York: Paulist Press, 1999); James Carroll, *Constantine's Sword: The Church and the Jews* (Boston: Houghton Mifflin Co., 2001); John Cornwell, *Hitler's Pope: The Secret History of Pius XII* (New York: Viking, 1999); Michael Phayer, *The Catholic Church and the Holocaust, 1930–1965* (Bloomington, Ind.: Indiana University Press, 2000); Carol Rittner and John

K. Roth, eds., *Pope Pius XII and the Holocaust* (London: Continuum Books, 2001); Garry Wills, *Papal Sin: Structures of Deceit* (New York: Doubleday, 2000); and Susan Zuccotti, *Under His Very Windows: The Vatican and the Holocaust in Italy* (New Haven, Conn.: Yale University Press, 2001). Blet defends Pius XII's record during World War II. The other scholars, especially Cornwell, are more critical. Phayer's book has much to commend it, partly because his explorations include the postwar years up to 1965.

7. It has been argued that Pope Pius IX has temporarily overtaken, if not replaced, Pope Pius XII on the way to sainthood. Holocaust politics, this view suggests, has made Pius XII too hot to handle where early twenty-first century sainthood is concerned. Yet a canonization from conservative Catholic ranks is needed to balance the official saintly status that the much more liberal Pope John XXIII is expected to receive without much difficulty.

8. For a detailed account of the Mortara episode and its historical and religious contexts, see David I. Kertzer, *The Kidnapping of Edgardo Mortara* (New York: Alfred A. Knopf, 1997).

9. The term *antisemitism* and its variations are relatively recent, having appeared in the second half of the nineteenth century. That fact helps to substantiate the distinction sometimes made between *antisemitism* and Christian *anti-Judaism*, which might be regarded as earlier and different from *antisemitism*. I believe, however, that common usage now follows the broad definition of antisemitism I have offered. Christian anti-Judaism, then, becomes a foundational form, but not the entirety, of Christian antisemitism. The former is chiefly characterized by supersessionism, which, James Carroll notes, derives from the Latin *supersedere* (to sit on). Citing theologian Mary Boys as his source, Padraic O'Hare identifies supersessionism's defining features: "(1) revelation in Jesus Christ supersedes the revelation to Israel; (2) the New Testament fulfills the Old Testament; (3) the church replaces the Jews as God's people; (4) Judaism is obsolete, its covenant abrogated; (5) post-exilic Judaism was legalistic; (6) the Jews did not heed the warning of the prophets; (7) the Jews did not understand the prophecies about Jesus; (8) the Jews were Christ killers." In a word, supersessionism means that Christianity, with a vengeance, allegedly trumps Judaism. Understood in this way, Christian anti-Judaism is highly theological, and the concept does not capture as well as *antisemitism* the fact that Christian animosity has been directed at Jews as Jews, not just at Judaism or at Jews as religious prac-

titioners. More than that, Christian animosity toward Jews is not restricted to religious considerations alone. The religious aspects mix and mingle with a wide variety of other prejudicial ingredients that are social, political, and economic. While recognizing the particular and foundational reality of Christian anti-Judaism, I refer to Christian antisemitism because, in addition to fitting better with common usage, the concept's scope reaches further and deeper than that of Christian anti-Judaism alone. In making these points, I am indebted to Carroll, *Constantine's Sword*, 58, 633n.1 and to Padraic O'Hare, *The Enduring Covenant: The Education of Christians and the End of Antisemitism* (Valley Forge, Pa.: Trinity Press International, 1997), 7. As illustrated by the vigorous and at times acrimonious debate provoked by Daniel Goldhagen's *Hitler's Willing Executioners: Ordinary Germans and the Holocaust* (New York: Alfred A. Knopf, 1996), a controversial study in which the author claimed that leading Holocaust scholars such as Yehuda Bauer, Christopher Browning, and Raul Hilberg had obscured the importance of German antisemitism, issues about how to interpret antisemitism's role in causing the Holocaust have often agitated scholarly versions of Holocaust politics.

10. Signs of such turning can be found, for example, in acknowledgments of Holocaust-related guilt such as those expressed by the leaders of Poland's Roman Catholic Church in August 2000 and by Germany's Lutheran Church in November 2000.

11. For an excellent and succinct overview of scholarship about the anti-Jewish polemics in the Gospel of John, see Norman A. Beck, *Mature Christianity in the 21st Century: The Recognition and Repudiation of the Anti-Jewish Polemic in the New Testament*, rev. ed. (New York: Crossroad, 1994), 285–312. In the remaining pages of this chapter, my interpretation of the Gospel of John and post-Holocaust Christianity draws on my essay, "Good News after Auschwitz: Does Christianity Have Any?" in *"Good News" after Auschwitz? Christian Faith within a Post-Holocaust World*, ed. Carol Rittner and John K. Roth (Macon, Ga.: Mercer University Press, 2001).

12. Theo Richmond, *Konin: A Quest* (New York: Vintage Books, 1996), 480.

13. Here it is important to note *Dabru Emet* (Hebrew for "speak truth"), a statement initiated by the Jewish scholars Tikva Frymer-Kensky, David Novak, Peter Ochs, and Michael Signer and endorsed by nearly 170 Jewish scholars and rabbis on September

10, 2000, just five days after the release of *Dominus Jesus*, the previously discussed Roman Catholic document about the singular truth of Christianity. *Dabru Emet* certainly did not have *Dominus Jesus* in mind, but the Jewish statement warmly acknowledged that post-Holocaust Christianity embodies many changes for the good. While urging full and respectful recognition of the fact that there is a "human irreconcilable difference between Jews and Christians," *Dabru Emet* also emphasized that Jews and Christians share a great deal, including belief in the same God and normative texts from the Hebrew Bible. The statement also points out that Christianity has expressed remorse for "Christian mistreatment of Jews and Judaism" and has considerably reformed its characterization and understanding of Jewish life and tradition. Correctly asserting that Christianity's anti-Jewish teachings and policies helped to make the Holocaust possible and that many Christians were implicated in the Holocaust, *Dabru Emet* also declares unequivocally that "Nazism was not a Christian phenomenon," and it expresses profound gratitude for Christians who rescued Jews during those dark times.

14. When I write "come to know," I mean to take at least two factors into account. First, I regard Christian faith in God as a kind of grafting on to Jewish faith. Not only do Christians properly affirm that the God they worship is the same God whom Jews worship, but also Christian understanding of that point is correct just to the extent that it grasps Christian dependence on Jewish understandings of God and respects those Jewish understandings accordingly. Second, to a large degree, Jewish understandings of God were both spread and modified in the Western world by missionizing Christians. Absent Christianity, faith in God might have spread far and wide through Jewish practice and commitment, but there is no question that the spread of Christianity became the primary historical path through which the God of Israel became known to vast numbers of people.

15. My account of Chelmno is drawn from material I prepared for Roth et al., *Holocaust Chronicle*. See also Claude Lanzmann, *Shoah: An Oral History of the Holocaust* (New York: Pantheon Books, 1985), 5.

16. See Jadwiga Bezwinska and Danuta Czech, eds., *Amidst a Nightmare of Crime: Manuscripts of Members of the Sonderkommando* (Oswiecim: Publications of State Museum at Oswiecim, 1973), 125–78, esp. 139. The following account of "choiceless choices" draws on material I prepared for Roth et al., *Holocaust Chronicle*. As a member of the *Sonderkommando*, Lewental was

required to herd Auschwitz prisoners into the gas chambers and then to dispose of their bodies (by burning in crematoria or pits) but not before every useful body part, including hair and gold teeth, was salvaged. Typically, although members of the *Sonderkommando* temporarily received somewhat better treatment than other Auschwitz prisoners, they lived only a few months before being killed to remove any chance that they would survive as witnesses.

17. Lawrence L. Langer, "The Dilemma of Choice in the Death-camps," in *Holocaust: Religious and Philosophical Implications*, ed. John K. Roth and Michael Berenbaum (St. Paul: Paragon House, 1989), 224.

18. Reflecting the Gospel of John's contentious origins, John 14:6 also attributes to Jesus the claim, "No one comes to the Father except through me." The Holocaust shows how harmful such exclusive, supersessionist language has been. Post-Holocaust Christianity should reject it.

6. Ethics after Auschwitz

1. I quote from Littell's concluding plenary speech at Remembering for the Future 2000, a major international conference on the Holocaust held in Oxford, England, July 16–23, 2000. See John K. Roth and Elisabeth Maxwell, eds., *Remembering for the Future: The Holocaust in an Age of Genocide*, 3 vols. (New York: Palgrave, 2001), 3:8–9.

2. Calel Perechodnik, *Am I a Murderer? Testament of a Jewish Ghetto Policeman*, ed. and trans. Frank Fox (Boulder, Colo.: Westview Press, 1996).

3. Ibid., 9.

4. Richard L. Rubenstein, *The Cunning of History: The Holocaust and the American Future* (New York: Harper Torchbooks, 1987), 91. The italics are Rubenstein's.

5. Ibid., 78.

6. Richard L. Rubenstein, *After Auschwitz: History, Theology, and Contemporary Judaism*, 2d ed. (Baltimore: Johns Hopkins University Press, 1992), 131.

7. Ibid.

8. Ibid., 132.

9. Michael Berenbaum, *The World Must Know: The History of the Holocaust as Told in the United States Holocaust Memorial Museum* (Boston: Little, Brown & Co., 1993), 220.

10. Gerald Fleming, "Engineers of Death," *New York Times*, July

18, 1993, E19. In my discussion of Fleming's findings, all the quotations are from this same source and page.

11. Two especially significant works on Auschwitz are Yisrael Gutman and Michael Berenbaum, eds., *Anatomy of the Auschwitz Death Camp* (Washington, D.C.: United States Holocaust Memorial Museum; Bloomington, Ind.: Indiana University Press, 1994); and Debórah Dwork and Robert Jan van Pelt, *Auschwitz: 1270 to the Present* (New York: W. W. Norton & Co., 1996). In the context of this discussion, the following essays in *Anatomy of the Auschwitz Death Camp* are particularly relevant: Francisek Piper, "Gas Chambers and Crematoria," 157–82; and Jean-Claude Pressac with Robert Jan Van Pelt, "The Machinery of Mass Murder at Auschwitz," 183–245. For further information about Kurt Prüfer, see *Auschwitz: 1270 to the Present*, esp. 269–71.

12. For an important discussion of these themes, see Peter J. Haas, *Morality after Auschwitz: The Radical Challenge of the Nazi Ethic* (Philadelphia: Fortress Press, 1988). Related topics are discussed in John K. Roth, ed., *Ethics after the Holocaust: Perspectives, Critiques, and Responses* (St. Paul: Paragon House, 1999).

13. Even with respect to Berenbaum's appealing idea that the Holocaust is a negative absolute, I believe this judgment remains valid. There is no guarantee that universal moral reason or intuition exists or that, if they do, they will automatically conclude without disagreement that the Holocaust is a negative absolute. In ethics, the human will is decisive in determining how good and evil, right and wrong are understood. Reason and intuition inform our willing and choosing, but without the latter, our senses of good and evil, right and wrong, lack the force that gives them full reality and makes them effective. Willing and choosing alone do not determine what is ethical, but in the fullest sense no determination of right and wrong takes place without them.

14. Rubenstein, *Cunning of History*, 90.

15. Ibid., 67.

16. Ibid., 88.

17. The text of this document is reprinted in *Jehovah's Witnesses*, a pamphlet from the United States Holocaust Memorial Museum, Washington, D.C. See also Christine King, "Jehovah's Witnesses under Nazism," in *A Mosaic of Victims: Non-Jews Persecuted and Murdered by the Nazis*, ed. Michael Berenbaum

(New York: New York University Press, 1990), 188–93. The Watchtower Bible and Tract Society of New York has produced an informative film, *Stand Firm*, which, along with the other sources mentioned here, informs my account of the Jehovah's Witnesses. For a moving memoir about the struggles a young Jehovah's Witness endured under Nazi rule, see Simone Arnold Liebster, *Facing the Lion: Memoirs of a Young Girl in Nazi Europe* (New Orleans: Grammaton Press, 2000). The Germans sent Jehovah's Witnesses to many concentration camps. The Witnesses were well situated to see the effects of the Third Reich's anti-Jewish policies and, later, to testify about them.

18. See Gerald L. Sittser, *A Cautious Patriotism: The American Churches and the Second World War* (Chapel Hill, N.C.: University of North Carolina Press, 1997), 186–88.

19. This account of Le Chambon draws on Carol Rittner and John K. Roth, eds., *Different Voices: Women and the Holocaust* (St. Paul: Paragon House, 1993), 309–16.

20. Albert Camus, *The Plague*, trans. Gilbert Stuart (New York: Vintage Books, 1991), 308.

21. Ibid.

22. Perechodnik, *Am I a Murderer?* 211.

23. Ibid., 209.

24. Ibid., 211.

25. R. J. Rummel, *Death by Government* (New Brunswick, N.J.: Transaction Publishers, 1997), 1, 9. *Democide* is the term Rummel coined to refer to genocide and government mass murder. If one adds together the human cost of democide and war, he concludes, "Power has killed over 203 million people in this [twentieth] century" (13).

Epilogue: Where Does Holocaust Politics Lead?

1. See James D. Besser, "Notes from a Grieving Nation," *Jewish Week*, April 20, 2000, 1, 30–31. As Besser notes, the museum's comment books serve two purposes. The books give museum officials a glimpse of visitor reaction, and they also offer an opportunity for visitors to express the feelings evoked by the overwhelming history they have encountered. The museum preserves the comment books, and it will be both interesting and important to see how the comments compare and contrast as time passes.

2. See Peter Slevin, "A Lesson from Nazi History," *Washington*

Post, October 7, 1999, District Weekly Section, 1–2. See also a related story by Erin Texeira, "Police Trainees Get Lesson in Sensitivity at Museum," *Baltimore Sun*, November 4, 1999, B1, B5.

3. For Ziering's obituary, see Myrna Oliver, "Sigi Ziering: Tycoon Survived Nazi Camps," *Los Angeles Times*, November 14, 2000, B6.

4. For a companion book to the film, see Mark Jonathan Harris and Deborah Oppenheimer, *Into the Arms of Strangers: Stories of the Kindertransport* (London: Bloomsbury, 2000).

5. Eve Nussbaum Soumerai and Carol D. Schulz, *Daily Life during the Holocaust* (Westport, Conn.: Greenwood Press, 1998), 64. Soumerai was one of those rescued by the *Kindertransport*. On June 30, 1939, she boarded a train in Berlin and became a refugee in England the next day, leaving behind forever her father, mother, and brother Bibi.

6. Lawrence L. Langer, *Preempting the Holocaust* (New Haven, Conn.: Yale University Press, 1998), 10. For further debate about the Holocaust's lessons, see *Dimensions*, vol. 12, no. 1, 1998. With articles by Langer, Omer Bartov, and other important thinkers, this issue focuses on "Holocaust Education: Traditions, Touchstones and Taboos."

7. See Primo Levi, *The Drowned and the Saved*, trans. Raymond Rosenthal (New York: Summit Books, 1988), 105–26; Charlotte Delbo, *Auschwitz and After*, trans. Rosette C. Lamont (New Haven, Conn.: Yale University Press, 1995), 115–231; Emmanuel Levinas, *Entre Nous: On Thinking-of-the-Other*, trans. Michael B. Smith and Barbara Harshav (New York: Columbia University Press, 1998), 91–101.

8. Peter Novick, *The Holocaust in American Life* (Boston: Houghton Mifflin Company, 1999), 261.

9. Ibid., 262.

10. Norman G. Finkelstein, *The Holocaust Industry: Reflections on the Exploitation of Jewish Suffering* (London: Verso, 2000), 3, 150.

11. Ibid., 47, 149, 89, 83.

12. Ibid., 55.

13. Ibid., 7.

14. Ibid., 55.

15. Ibid., 72.

16. Ibid., 55.

17. Ibid., 3.
18. Brett's poem can be found in *Holocaust Poetry*, ed. Hilda Schiff (New York: St. Martin's Press, 1995), 138–39.
19. Bond's poem can be found in ibid., 156.
20. See James E. Young, *At Memory's Edge: After-Images of the Holocaust in Contemporary Art and Architecture* (New Haven, Conn.: Yale University Press, 2000).

Select Bibliography

Abzug, Robert H. *America Views the Holocaust: A Brief Documentary History*. Boston: Bedford/St. Martin's Press, 1999.

Adams, Guy B., and Danny L. Balfour. *Unmasking Administrative Evil*. Thousand Oaks, Calif.: Sage Publications, 1998.

Adams, James Truslow. *The Epic of America*. Boston: Little, Brown & Co., 1934.

Aly, Götz. *"Final Solution": Nazi Population Policy and the Murder of the European Jews*. Translated by Belinda Cooper and Allison Brown. London: Arnold, 1999.

Améry, Jean. *At the Mind's Limits: Contemplations by a Survivor on Auschwitz and Its Realities*. Translated by Sidney Rosenfeld and Stella P. Rosenfeld. New York: Schocken Books, 1986.

Auron, Yair. *The Banality of Indifference: Zionism and the Armenian Genocide*. New Brunswick, N.J.: Transaction Books, 2000.

Ayçoberry, Pierre. *The Social History of the Third Reich 1933–1945*. Translated by Janet Lloyd. New York: New Press, 1999.

Barkan, Elazar. *The Guilt of Nations: Restitution and Negotiating Historical Injustices*. New York: W. W. Norton & Co., 2000.

Barnett, Victoria J. *Bystanders: Conscience and Complicity during the Holocaust*. Westport, Conn.: Praeger Publishers, 1999.

Bartov, Omer. *Mirrors of Destruction: War, Genocide, and Modern Identity*. New York: Oxford University Press, 2000.

Bauer, Yehuda. *The Holocaust in Historical Perspective*. Seattle: University of Washington Press, 1978.

———. *Rethinking the Holocaust*. New Haven, Conn.: Yale University Press, 2001.

Baumel, Judith Tydor. *Double Jeopardy: Gender and the Holocaust*. London: Vallentine Mitchell, 1998.

Beck, Norman A. *Mature Christianity in the 21st Century: The Recognition and Repudiation of the Anti-Jewish Polemic in the New Testament*. Revised edition. New York: Crossroad, 1994.

Benz, Wolfgang. *The Holocaust: A German Historian Examines the Genocide*. Translated by Jane Sydenham-Kwiet. London: Profile Books, 2000.

Berenbaum, Michael. *After Tragedy and Triumph: Modern Jewish Thought and the American Experience*. Cambridge: Cambridge University Press, 1990.

————. *The World Must Know: The History of the Holocaust as Told in the United States Holocaust Memorial Museum*. Boston: Little, Brown & Co., 1993.

————, ed. *A Mosaic of Victims: Non-Jews Persecuted and Murdered by the Nazis*. New York: New York University Press, 1990.

————, *Witness to the Holocaust*. New York: HarperCollins, 1997.

Bezwinska, Jadwiga, and Danuta Czech, eds. *Amidst a Nightmare of Crime: Manuscripts of Members of the Sonderkommando*. Oswiecim: Publications of the State Museum at Oswiecim, 1973.

Black, Edwin. *IBM and the Holocaust: The Strategic Alliance between Nazi Germany and America's Most Powerful Corporation*. New York: Crown Publishers, 2001.

Blet, Pierre. *Pius XII and the Second World War: According to the Archives of the Vatican*. Translated by Lawrence J. Johnson. New York: Paulist Press, 1999.

Browning, Christopher R. *Nazi Policy, Jewish Workers, German Killers*. Cambridge: Cambridge University Press, 2000.

————. *Ordinary Men: Reserve Police Battalion 101 and the Final Solution in Poland*. New York: HarperCollins, 1992.

Burleigh, Michael. *The Third Reich: A New History*. New York: Hill and Wang, 2000.

Camus, Albert. *The Plague*. Translated by Gilbert Stuart. New York: Vintage Books, 1991.

Cargas, Harry James. *Shadows of Auschwitz: A Christian Response to the Holocaust*. New York: Crossroad, 1990.

Carroll, James. *Constantine's Sword: The Church and the Jews*. Boston: Houghton Mifflin Company, 2001.

Charny, Israel W., ed. *Encyclopedia of Genocide*. 2 vols. Santa Barbara, Calif.: ABC-CLIO, 1999.

Clendinnen, Inga. *Reading the Holocaust*. Cambridge: Cambridge University Press, 1999.

Cole, Tim. *Selling the Holocaust: From Auschwitz to Schindler How History Is Bought, Packaged, and Sold.* New York: Routledge, 1999.

Collingwood, R. G. *An Autobiography.* Oxford: Oxford University Press, 1939.

Collins, Max Allan. *Saving Private Ryan.* New York: Signet, 1998.

Cornwell, John. *Hitler's Pope: The Secret History of Pius XII.* New York: Viking, 1999.

Czech, Danuta. *The Auschwitz Chronicle 1939–1945.* Translated by Barbara Harshav, Martha Humphreys, and Stephen Shearier. New York: Henry Holt, 1990.

Davies, Ian, ed. *Teaching the Holocaust: Educational Dimensions, Principles and Practice.* New York: Continuum, 2000.

Delbo, Charlotte. *Auschwitz and After.* Translated by Rosette C. Lamont. New Haven, Conn.: Yale University Press, 1995.

Dwork, Debórah, and Robert Jan van Pelt. *Auschwitz: 1270 to the Present.* New York: W. W. Norton & Co., 1996.

Ellison, Ralph. *Invisible Man.* New York: Vintage Books, 1982.

Evans, Richard J. *Lying about Hitler: History, Holocaust, and the David Irving Trial.* New York: Basic Books, 2001.

Fackenheim, Emil. *God's Presence in History: Jewish Affirmations and Philosophical Reflections.* New York: New York University Press, 1970.

———. *The Jewish Bible after the Holocaust: A Re-reading.* Bloomington, Ind.: Indiana University Press, 1990.

———. *The Jewish Return into History: Reflections in the Age of Auschwitz and a New Jerusalem.* New York: Schocken Books, 1978.

———. *To Mend the World: Foundations of Future Jewish Thought.* New York: Schocken Books, 1982.

Feingold, Henry L. *Bearing Witness: How America and Its Jews Responded to the Holocaust.* Syracuse, N.Y.: Syracuse University Press, 1995.

Fink, Ida. *A Scrap of Time and Other Stories.* Translated by Madeline Levine and Francine Prose. New York: Schocken Books, 1987.

Finkelstein, Norman G. *The Holocaust Industry: Reflections on the Exploitation of Jewish Suffering.* London: Verso, 2000.

Flanzbaum, Hilene, ed. *The Americanization of the Holocaust.* Baltimore: Johns Hopkins University Press, 1999.

Fossum, Robert H., and John K. Roth, eds. *American Ground: Vistas, Visions, and Revisions.* St. Paul: Paragon House, 1988.

Freeman, Joseph. *Job: The Story of a Holocaust Survivor*. Westport, Conn.: Praeger Publishers, 1996.

————. *The Road to Hell: Recollections of the Nazi Death March*. St. Paul: Paragon House, 1998.

Friedländer, Saul. *Nazi Germany and the Jews: The Years of Persecution, 1933–1939*. New York: HarperCollins, 1997.

Frymer-Kensky, Tikva, David Novak, Peter Ochs, David Sandmel, and Michael Signer. *Christianity in Jewish Terms*. Boulder, Colo.: Westview Press, 2000.

Gellately, Robert. *Backing Hitler: Consent and Coercion in Nazi Germany*. New York: Oxford University Press, 2001.

Geras, Norman. *The Contract of Mutual Indifference: Political Philosophy after the Holocaust*. London: Verso, 1999.

Gilbert, Martin. *The Holocaust: A History of the Jews of Europe during the Second World War*. New York: Henry Holt, 1985.

Glover, Jonathan. *Humanity: A Moral History of the Twentieth Century*. London: Jonathan Cape, 1999.

Goldsmith, Martin. *The Inextinguishable Symphony: A True Story of Music and Love in Nazi Germany*. New York: John Wiley & Sons, 2000.

Gottlieb, Roger S., ed. *Thinking the Unthinkable: Meanings of the Holocaust*. New York: Paulist Press, 1991.

Greenberg, Irving. *The Jewish Way: Living the Holidays*. New York: Summit Books, 1988.

Greene, Joshua M., and Shiva Kumar. *Witness: Voices from the Holocaust*. New York: Free Press, 2000.

Greenspan, Henry. *On Listening to Holocaust Survivors: Recounting and Life History*. Westport, Conn.: Praeger Publishers, 1998.

Gross, Jan T. *Neighbors: The Destruction of the Jewish Community in Jedwabne, Poland*. Princeton, N.J.: Princeton University Press, 2001.

Gurewitsch, Brana, ed. *Mothers, Sisters, Resisters: Oral Histories of Women Who Survived the Holocaust*. Tuscaloosa, Ala.: University of Alabama Press, 1998.

Gutman, Israel, et al., eds. *Encyclopedia of the Holocaust*. 4 vols. New York: Macmillan, 1990.

Gutman, Yisrael, and Michael Berenbaum, eds. *Anatomy of the Auschwitz Death Camp*. Washington, D.C.: United States Holocaust Memorial Museum; Bloomington, Ind.: Indiana University Press, 1994.

Guttenplan, D. D. *The Holocaust on Trial*. New York: W. W. Norton & Co., 2001.

Haas, Peter J. *Morality after Auschwitz: The Radical Challenge of the Nazi Ethic*. Philadelphia: Fortress Press, 1988.

Hallie, Philip. *Lest Innocent Blood Be Shed: The Story of Le Chambon and How Goodness Happened There*. New York: HarperPerennial, 1994.

———. *Tales of Good and Evil, Help and Harm*. New York: Harper-Collins, 1997.

Hamann, Brigitte. *Hitler's Vienna: A Dictator's Apprenticeship*. Translated by Thomas Thornton. New York: Oxford University Press, 1999.

Harris, Mark Jonathan, and Deborah Oppenheimer. *Into the Arms of Strangers: Stories of the Kindertransport*. London: Bloomsbury, 2000.

Hass, Aaron. *The Aftermath: Living with the Holocaust*. Cambridge: Cambridge University Press, 1995.

Hayes, Peter. *Industry and Ideology: I. G. Farben in the Nazi Era*. Cambridge: Cambridge University Press, 1993.

Haynes, Stephen R. *Reluctant Witnesses: Jews and the Christian Imagination*. Louisville, Ky.: Westminster John Knox Press, 1995.

Haynes, Stephen R., and John K. Roth, eds. *The Death of God Movement and the Holocaust: Radical Theology Encounters the Shoah*. Westport, Conn.: Greenwood Press, 1999.

Hellman, Peter. *The Auschwitz Album: A Book Based upon an Album Discovered by a Concentration Camp Survivor, Lili Meier*. New York: Random House, 1981.

Helmreich, William B. *Against All Odds: Holocaust Survivors and the Successful Lives They Made in America*. New Brunswick, N.J.: Transaction Books, 1999.

Herbert, Ulrich, ed. *National Socialist Extermination Policies: Contemporary German Perspectives and Controversies*. New York: Berghahn, 2000.

Hilberg, Raul. *The Destruction of the European Jews*. Revised and definitive edition. 3 vols. New York: Holmes & Meier, 1985.

———. *Perpetrators Victims Bystanders: The Jewish Catastrophe 1933–1945*. New York: HarperCollins, 1992.

———. *The Politics of Memory: The Journey of a Holocaust Historian*. Chicago: Ivan R. Dee, 1996.

In Pursuit of Justice. Washington, D.C.: United States Holocaust Memorial Museum, 1996.

The Irving Judgment: David Irving v. Penguin Books and Professor Deborah Lipstadt. London: Penguin Books, 2000.

Johnson, Eric A. *Nazi Terror: The Gestapo, Jews, and Ordinary Germans*. New York: Basic Books, 1999.

Jones, David H. *Moral Responsibility in the Holocaust: A Study in the Ethics of Character*. New York: Rowman & Littlefield, 1999.

Kaplan, Marion A. *Between Dignity and Despair: Jewish Life in Nazi Germany*. New York: Oxford University Press, 1998.

Kater, Michael H. *Composers of the Nazi Era: Eight Portraits*. New York: Oxford University Press, 2000.

———. *Different Drummers: Jazz in the Culture of Nazi Germany*. New York: Oxford University Press, 1992.

———. *The Twisted Muse: Musicians and Their Music in the Third Reich*. New York: Oxford University Press, 1997.

Kershaw, Ian. *Hitler 1889–1936: Hubris*. New York: W. W. Norton & Co., 1999.

———. *Hitler 1936–1945: Nemesis*. New York: W. W. Norton & Co., 2000.

Kertzer, David I. *The Kidnapping of Edgardo Mortara*. New York: Alfred A. Knopf, 1997.

Klein, Gerda Weissmann. *All but My Life*. Expanded edition. New York: Hill and Wang, 1995.

Kolmar, Gertrud. *Dark Soliloquy: The Selected Poems of Gertrud Kolmar*. Translated by Henry A. Smith. New York: Seabury Press, 1975.

Kremer, S. Lillian. *Women's Holocaust Writing: Memory and Imagination*. Lincoln, Nebr.: University of Nebraska Press, 1999.

Lagerwey, Mary. *Reading Auschwitz*. Walnut Creek, Calif.: Alta Mira Press, 1998.

Laks, Szymon. *Music of Another World*. Evanston, Ill.: Northwestern University Press, 2000.

Lang, Berel. *Act and Idea in the Nazi Genocide*. Chicago: University of Chicago Press, 1990.

———. *The Future of the Holocaust: Between History and Memory*. Ithaca, N.Y.: Cornell University Press, 1999.

———. *Heidegger's Silence*. Ithaca, N.Y.: Cornell University Press, 1996.

———. *Holocaust Representation: Art within the Limits of History and Ethics*. Baltimore: Johns Hopkins University Press, 2000.

Langer, Lawrence L. *Admitting the Holocaust: Collected Essays*. New York: Oxford University Press, 1995.

———. *Holocaust Testimonies: The Ruins of Memory*. New Haven, Conn.: Yale University Press, 1991.

———. *Preempting the Holocaust*. New Haven, Conn.: Yale University Press, 1998.

———, ed. *Art from the Ashes: A Holocaust Anthology*. New York: Oxford University Press, 1995.

Lanzmann, Claude. *Shoah: An Oral History of the Holocaust*. New York: Pantheon Books, 1985.

Laqueur, Walter, and Judith Tydor Baumel, eds. *The Holocaust Encyclopedia*. New Haven, Conn.: Yale University Press, 2001.

Lasker-Wallfisch, Anita. *Inherit the Truth: A Memoir of Survival and the Holocaust*. New York: St. Martin's Press, 2000.

Lengyel, Olga. *Five Chimneys*. Chicago: Academy Chicago Publishers, 1995.

Levi, Primo. *The Drowned and the Saved*. Translated by Raymond Rosenthal. New York: Summit Books, 1988.

Levinas, Emmanuel. *Entre Nous: On Thinking-of-the-Other*. Translated by Michael B. Smith and Barbara Harshav. New York: Columbia University Press, 1998.

Lewy, Guenter. *The Nazi Persecution of the Gypsies*. New York: Oxford University Press, 2000.

Liebster, Simone Arnold. *Facing the Lion: Memoirs of a Young Girl in Nazi Europe*. New Orleans: Grammaton Press, 2000.

Lifton, Robert Jay. *The Nazi Doctors: Medical Killing and the Psychology of Genocide*. New York: Basic Books, 1986.

Linenthal, Edward T. *Preserving Memory: The Struggle to Create America's Holocaust Museum*. New York: Viking, 1995.

Lipstadt, Deborah E. *Denying the Holocaust: The Growing Assault on Truth and Memory*. New York: Free Press, 1993.

Marrus, Michael R. *The Nuremberg War Crimes Trial 1945–46: A Documentary History*. Boston: Bedford, 1997.

Mendelsohn, Oskar. *The Persecution of the Norwegian Jews in WW II*. Oslo: Norges Hjemmefrontmuseum, 1991.

Mendes-Flohr, Paul, and Yehuda Reinharz, eds. *The Jew in the Modern World: A Documentary History*. 2d edition. New York: Oxford University Press, 1995.

Minow, Martha. *Between Vengeance and Forgiveness: Facing History after Genocide and Mass Violence*. Boston: Beacon Press, 1998.

Morrison, Jack G. *Ravensbrück: Everyday Life in a Women's Concentration Camp 1929–45*. Princeton, N.J.: Markus Wiener Publishers, 2000.

Neufeld, Michael J., and Michael Berenbaum, eds. *The Bombing of Auschwitz: Should the Allies Have Attempted It?* New York: St. Martin's Press, 2000.

Newman, Richard. *Alma Rosé: Vienna to Auschwitz*. New York: Amadeus, 2000.

1945: The Year of Liberation. Washington, D.C.: United States Holocaust Memorial Museum, 1995.

Novick, Peter. *The Holocaust in American Life.* Boston: Houghton Mifflin Company, 1999.

Nozick, Robert. *The Examined Life: Philosophical Meditations.* New York: Simon & Schuster, 1989.

Ofer, Dalia, and Lenore Weitzman, eds. *Women in the Holocaust.* New Haven, Conn.: Yale University Press, 1998.

Passelecq, Georges, and Bernard Suchecky. *The Hidden Encyclical of Pius XI.* Translated by Steven Rendall. New York: Harcourt Brace Jovanovich, 1997.

Perechodnik, Calel. *Am I a Murderer? Testament of a Jewish Ghetto Policeman.* Edited and translated by Frank Fox. Boulder, Colo.: Westview Press, 1996.

Persico, Joseph E. *Nuremberg: Infamy on Trial.* New York: Penguin Books, 1994.

Petropoulos, Jonathan. *Art as Politics in the Third Reich.* Chapel Hill, N.C.: University of North Carolina Press, 1996.

———. *The Faustian Bargain: The Art World of Nazi Germany.* New York: Oxford University Press, 2001.

Phayer, Michael. *The Catholic Church and the Holocaust, 1930–1965.* Bloomington, Ind.: Indiana University Press, 2000.

Phayer, Michael, and Eva Fleischner. *Cries in the Night: Women Who Challenged the Holocaust.* Kansas City, Mo.: Sheed & Ward, 1997.

Pogany, Eugene. *In My Brother's Image: Twin Brothers Separated by Faith after the Holocaust.* New York: Viking, 2000.

√ Redlich, Fritz. *Hitler: Diagnosis of a Destructive Prophet.* New York: Oxford University Press, 1998.

Richmond, Theo. *Konin: A Quest.* New York: Vintage Books, 1996.

Rittner, Carol, and John K. Roth, eds. *Different Voices: Women and the Holocaust.* St. Paul: Paragon House, 1993.

———. *"Good News" after Auschwitz? Christian Faith within a Post-Holocaust World.* Macon, Ga: Mercer University Press, 2001.

———. *Pope Pius XII and the Holocaust.* London: Continuum Books, 2001.

Rittner, Carol, Stephen D. Smith, and Irena Steinfeldt, eds. *The Holocaust and the Christian World.* London: Continuum Books, 2000.

Ritvo, Roger, and Diane M. Plotkin. *Sisters in Sorrow: Voices of Care in the Holocaust.* College Station, Tex.: Texas A&M University Press, 1998.

Rosenbaum, Alan S., ed. *Is the Holocaust Unique? Perspectives on Comparative Genocide*. 2d edition. Boulder, Colo.: Westview Press, 2001.

———. *Prosecuting Nazi War Criminals*. Boulder, Colo.: Westview Press, 1993.

Rosenbaum, Ron. *Explaining Hitler: The Search for the Origins of His Evil*. New York: Random House, 1998.

Rosensaft, Menachem Z., ed. *Life Reborn: Jewish Displaced Persons 1945–1951*. Washington, D.C.: United States Holocaust Memorial Museum, 2001.

Roth, John K., et al. *The Holocaust Chronicle: A History in Words and Pictures*. Lincolnwood, Ill.: Publications International, 2000.

Roth, John K., ed. *Ethics after the Holocaust: Perspectives, Critiques, and Responses*. St. Paul: Paragon House, 1999.

———. *World Philosophers and Their Works*. 3 vols. Pasadena, Calif.: Salem Press, 2000.

Roth, John K., and Michael Berenbaum, eds. *Holocaust: Religious and Philosophical Implications*. St. Paul: Paragon House, 1989.

Roth, John K., and Elisabeth Maxwell, eds. *Remembering for the Future: The Holocaust in an Age of Genocide*. 3 vols. New York: Palgrave, 2001.

Rubenstein, Richard L. *After Auschwitz: History, Theology, and Contemporary Judaism*. 2d edition. Baltimore: Johns Hopkins University Press, 1992.

———. *The Age of Triage: Fear and Hope in an Overcrowded World*. Boston: Beacon Press, 1983.

———. *The Cunning of History: The Holocaust and the American Future*. New York: Harper Torchbooks, 1987.

Rubenstein, Richard L., and John K. Roth. *Approaches to Auschwitz: The Holocaust and Its Legacy*. Atlanta: John Knox Press, 1987.

Rubinstein, William D. *The Myth of Rescue: Why the Democracies Could Not Have Saved More Jews from the Nazis*. New York: Routledge, 1997.

Rummel, R. J. *Death by Government*. New Brunswick, N.J.: Transaction Publishers, 1997.

Ryan, Allan A., Jr. *Quiet Neighbors: Prosecuting Nazi War Criminals in America*. San Diego: Harcourt Brace Jovanovich, 1984.

Saidel, Rochelle. *Never Too Late to Remember: The Politics behind New York City's Holocaust Museum*. New York: Holmes & Meier, 1996.

Schiff, Hilda, ed. *Holocaust Poetry*. New York: St. Martin's Press, 1995.

Schlink, Bernhard. *The Reader*. Translated by Carol Brown Janeway. New York: Pantheon Books, 1997.

Sereny, Gitta. *Albert Speer: His Battle with Truth*. New York: Vintage Books, 1996.

———. *Into That Darkness: An Examination of Conscience*. New York: Vintage Books, 1983.

Shandler, Jeffrey. *While America Watches: Televising the Holocaust*. New York: Oxford University Press, 1998.

Shermer, Michael, Alex Grobman, and Arthur Hertzburg. *Denying the Holocaust: Who Says the Holocaust Never Happened and Why Do They Say It?* Berkeley, Calif.: University of California Press, 2000.

Siedlecki, Janusz Nel, Krystyn Olszewski, and Tadeusz Borowski. *We Were in Auschwitz*. Translated by Alicia Nitecki. New York: Welcome Rain Publishers, 2000.

Signer, Michael A., ed. *Humanity at the Limit: The Impact of the Holocaust Experience on Jews and Christians*. Bloomington, Ind.: Indiana University Press, 2000.

Sittser, Gerald L. *A Cautious Patriotism: The American Churches and the Second World War*. Chapel Hill, N.C.: University of North Carolina Press, 1997.

Sluga, Hans. *Heidegger's Crisis: Philosophy and Politics in Nazi Germany*. Cambridge, Mass.: Harvard University Press, 1993.

Soumerai, Eve Nussbaum, and Carol D. Schulz. *Daily Life during the Holocaust*. Westport, Conn.: Greenwood Press, 1998.

Steinberg, Paul. *Speak You Also: A Survivor's Reckoning*. Translated by Linda Coverdale with Bill Ford. New York: Henry Holt, 2000.

Steinweis, Alan E. *Art, Ideology, and Economics in Nazi Germany: The Reich Chambers of Music, Theater, and the Visual Arts*. Chapel Hill, N.C.: University of North Carolina Press, 1996.

Styron, William. *Sophie's Choice*. New York: Modern Library, 1999.

Szmaglewska, Seweryna. *Smoke over Birkenau*. Translated by Jadwiga Rynas. New York: Henry Holt, 1947.

Tedeschi, Giuliana. *There Is a Place on Earth: A Woman in Birkenau*. Translated by Tim Parks. New York: Pantheon Books, 1992.

Vrba, Rudolf, and Alan Bestic. *I Cannot Forgive*. New York: Grove Press, 1964.

Wagner, Gottfried. *Twilight of the Wagners: The Unveiling of a Family Legacy*. New York: St. Martin's Press, 1999.

Weinberg, Jeshajahu, and Rina Elieli. *The Holocaust Museum in Washington*. New York: Rizzoli, 1995.

Wiesel, Elie. *Against Silence: The Voice and Vision of Elie Wiesel.* 3 vols. Edited by Irving Abrahamson. New York: Holocaust Library, 1985.

———. *Night.* Translated by Stella Rodway. New York: Bantam Books, 1986.

Wills, Garry. *Papal Sin: Structures of Deceit.* New York: Doubleday, 2000.

Woodruff, Paul, and Harry A. Wilmer, eds. *Facing Evil: Light at the Core of Darkness.* LaSalle, Ill.: Open Court, 1988.

Wyman, David S. *The Abandonment of the Jews: America and the Holocaust, 1941–1945.* New York: Pantheon Books, 1984.

———. *Paper Walls: America and the Refugee Crisis, 1938–1941.* Amherst, Mass.: University of Massachusetts Press, 1968.

Wyman, David S., and Charles H. Rosenzveig, eds. *The World Reacts to the Holocaust.* Baltimore: Johns Hopkins University Press, 1996.

Young, James E. *At Memory's Edge: After-Images of the Holocaust in Contemporary Art and Architecture.* New Haven, Conn.: Yale University Press, 2000.

———. *The Texture of Memory: Holocaust Memorials and Meaning.* New Haven, Conn.: Yale University Press, 1993.

Zuccotti, Susan. *Under His Very Windows: The Vatican and the Holocaust in Italy.* New Haven, Conn.: Yale University Press, 2001.

Index